THE WRECKAGE OF PHILOSOPHY

Carlo Michelstaedter and the Limits of Bourgeois Thought

The Wreckage of Philosophy

Carlo Michelstaedter and the Limits of Bourgeois Thought

MIMMO CANGIANO

UNIVERSITY OF TORONTO PRESS
Toronto Buffalo London

Toronto Buffalo London
utorontopress.com

ISBN 978-1-4875-0464-9

Toronto Italian Studies

Library and Archives Canada Cataloguing in Publication

Cangiano, Mimmo, author
The wreckage of philosophy : Carlo Michelstaedter and the limits of bourgeois thought / Mimmo Cangiano.

(Toronto Italian studies)
Includes bibliographical references and index.
ISBN 978-1-4875-0464-9 (cloth)

1. Michelstaedter, Carlo, 1887–1910 – Criticism and interpretation.
I. Title. II. Series: Toronto Italian studies

PQ4829.I38Z65 2019 851'.912 C2018-904203-6

This book has been published with the assistance of The Hebrew University of Jerusalem.

University of Toronto Press acknowledges the financial assistance to its publishing program of the Canada Council for the Arts and the Ontario Arts Council, an agency of the Government of Ontario.

Funded by the Government of Canada
Financé par le gouvernement du Canada
Canada

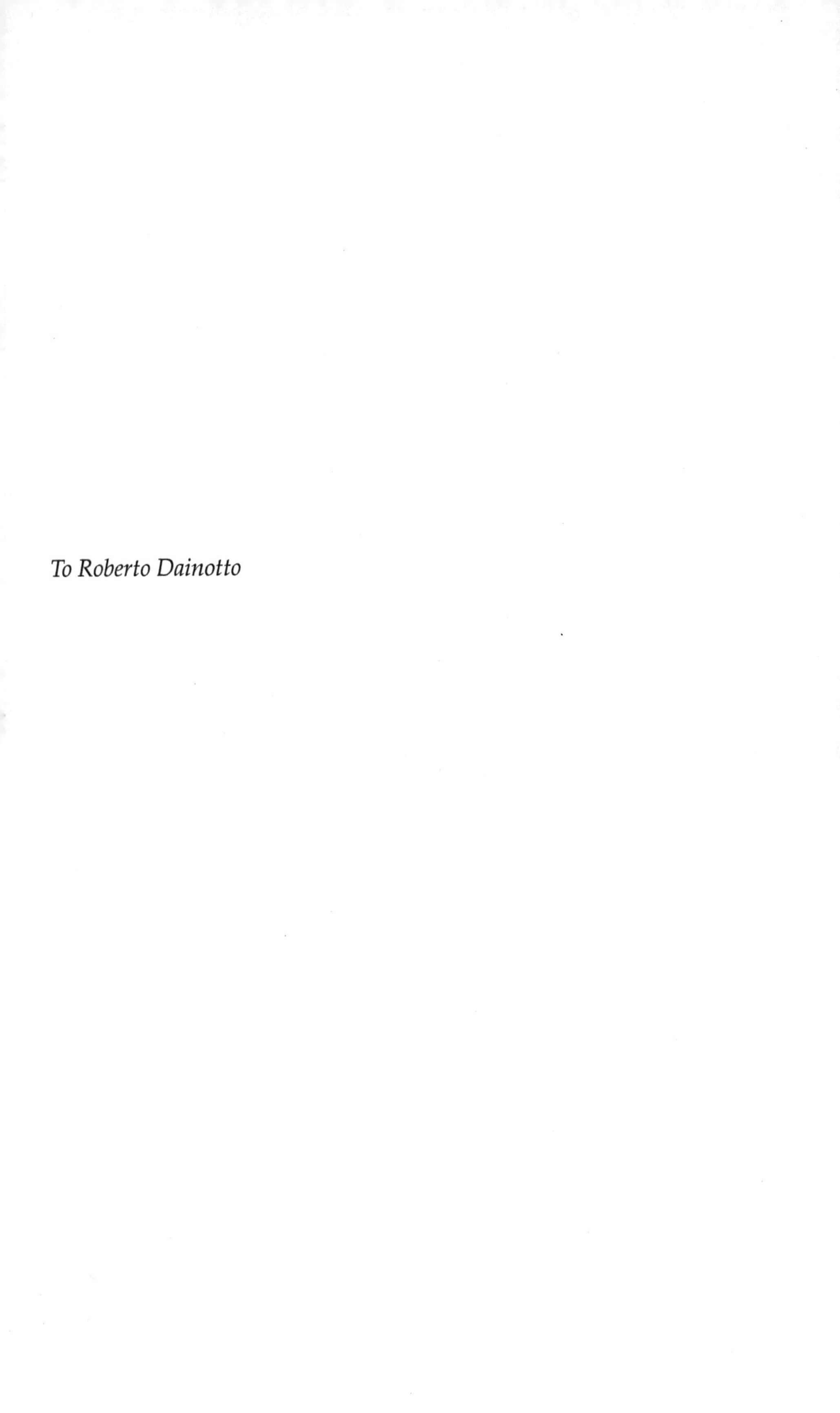

To Roberto Dainotto

Contents

Acknowledgments

Many thanks first of all to Fredric Jameson, who first had the idea for this book and who encouraged me to write it. I would like to thank Luca Somigli of the University of Toronto, Federico Luisetti of the University of North Carolina at Chapel Hill, and Michael Hardt of Duke University for guiding me through this research project. I am in great debt to Thomas Harrison of UCLA, whose passion for Michelstaedter's thought has always been a wonderful example. Several sections of this book were discussed and presented at lectures, colloquia, seminars, and sometimes courses that I gave at Duke University and at my own institution, the Hebrew University of Jerusalem. I would like to thank the colleagues and friends who offered me these opportunities for debate, as well as the researchers and students who took part in them. Though unable to mention everyone, I would particularly like to remember Saskia Ziolkowski of Duke University; Valerio Cappozzo of the University of Mississippi, Giuseppe Gazzola of Stony Brook University, and Rossella Riccobono, organizer of the conference "Science in Culture" at the University of St Andrews, Scotland. Besides seminars and conferences, this book owes much to the reflections on modernist philosophy that I have been conducting for several years now together with Achille Castaldo, Guido Mattia Gallerani, Daria Biagi, Francesco Frisari, Stefano Ercolino, Alberto Comparini, Can Evren, Bennett Carpenter, Danila Cannamela, Lorenzo Mari, Vincenzo Salvatore, and Stephen Marth. I extend to them my friendship and all my gratitude. I also owe a debt of gratitude to Mark Thompson, attentive reader of my manuscript, for having accepted it for the University of Toronto Press. Finally, I would like to thank my beloved wife, Laura Moure Cecchini, for our life between the desert, the snow, and the sea of Parmenides (and I mean literally).

Acknowledgments

THE WRECKAGE OF PHILOSOPHY

Carlo Michelstaedter and the Limits of Bourgeois Thought

Introduction

Everything is relative and confused down here.

Alberto Michelstaedter (Carlo's father)

Everything is preferable to the truth.

Franz Joseph I (Emperor of Austria)

Carlo Michelstaedter was born into a bourgeois Jewish family with pro-Italian leanings in 1887 in Gorizia, when that city was still part of the Austro-Hungarian Empire. He had an elder brother, Gino, who committed suicide in New York in 1909, and two sisters, Elda (who would be deported to Auschwitz along with their mother) and Paula (who would escape to Switzerland). As an adolescent he attended the local *liceo* (secondary school) and became friends with two other Gorizians: Nino Paternolli (who owned the garret where Michelstaedter would write his dissertation, *Persuasion and Rhetoric*) and Enrico Mreule (who would go on to live an adventurous life, first in Argentina and then in Dalmatia). Their friendship, which is narrated in the *Epistolario* (his *Tagebuch*), was used as fodder by Claudio Magris for his novel *Un altro mare*.

Michelstaedter had decided to study mathematics in Vienna. But in 1905 he changed his mind: he went to Florence instead, where he focused on the humanities at the Istituto di Studi Superiori – a common destination for many Austrian intellectuals with pro-Italian leanings (among whom could be counted Scipio Slataper as well as the Stuparich brothers, Giani and Carlo). In the early years of the twentieth century, Florence was the intellectual capital of Italy, where the foundations for modernist Italian literature and philosophy were being laid. The militant journal *Leonardo*, overseen by Giovanni Papini, though waning, was still active when Carlo moved to Florence. In the pages of *Leonardo*, Papini and his followers presented readers with articles about the most important thinkers of the time: Henri Bergson, William James, Ernst Mach, and, of course, Friedrich Nietzsche, who in Italy was by then being liberated from Gabriele D'Annunzio's decadent reading of his work. Late in 1908, Giuseppe Prezzolini founded *La Voce*, which would come to serve as a proving ground for the young Italian intelligentsia of the time. It published contributions by authors like Slataper, Stuparich, Giovanni Boine, and Piero Jahier alongside articles by Benedetto Croce and Giovanni Gentile. *La Voce* served as a forum for a variety of issues, such as theological modernism (Alfred Loisy, George Tyrrell, Édouard Le Roy), nationalism (in 1910 the Associazione Nazionalista Italiana would be founded in Florence), and the crisis of socialism. Around this time, *La Voce* published a number of influential writings, including those of Georges Sorel and Otto Weininger, as well as Gaetano Salvemini's thoughts on social reform; Ardengo Soffici's on recent artistic developments in France; and Benito Mussolini's on "*questione trentina*." *La Voce* counted Antonio Gramsci among its admiring subscribers.

Michelstaedter read *La Voce* (he brought a few issues back with him to Gorizia), and though he remained disengaged from the intellectual battles being waged by this squadron of intellectuals, philosophers, and writers, he shared their cultural coordinates – that is, his readings covered more or less the same ground as theirs. That said, his thought cannot be ascribed to any of the modernist orientations vying for ground at the time in what Martin Heidegger would later call the "crisis of the foundations." Indeed, in the last years of his life Michelstaedter would move beyond the main philosophical orientations of his era. Instead, the trajectory of his reflections pointed him towards the Frankfurt School, Ludwig Wittgenstein, and Simone Weil. He shared with the latter an interest in Greek thought, as well as a unique concept of justice and a critique of the conjoined operations of specialization and technology.

Studies of Michelstaedter have long approached his thought as a more or less unified whole, neglecting the transformations it underwent during his five years of intellectual activity. The present work posits that we can delineate three general phases in the development of his philosophy. Between 1905 and 1907 – his university years – Michelstaedter's thought was characterized by a decadent, "Dannunzian" influence, albeit with constant attention to the relationship between the individual and society, to everything social that impedes the individual's expression of singularity.

From late 1907 through 1908, Michelstaedter made a key contribution in Europe to the study of the tragic as a possible means of salvaging an immanent meaning, a resistant centre to the "crisis of the foundations" that had transformed existence – in the words of György Lukács – into an "an anarchy of chiaroscuro" (*Soul and Form*, 228). In 1908 Michelstaedter added his voice to those of Henrik Ibsen, Otto Weininger, Scipio Slataper, and Giovanni Amendola in Italy, who would turn to "tragic thought" as a response to the abyss opened by nihilism.

In 1909, catalysed by the task of writing a university thesis on the concepts of persuasion and rhetoric in the works of Plato and Aristotle, Michelstaedter's thought underwent a shift – one that would continue after he returned to Gorizia.[1] His analysis now sought to provide the possibility of resisting the abstracting force that social consensus exercised on both philosophical and quotidian forms of thought. It is clear in his later writings that he understood that all philosophical approaches must be analysed in terms of how they are abstracted (alienated) from themselves within the structures of societal consensus. Building on this foundation, he came to understand culture as societal behaviour rather than as something created by the subject; this paved the way for a series of reflections on the relationship between epistemology and ideological consensus that would have more in common with Lukács's ideas in *History and Class Consciousness* (1922) than with the Lukács of *Soul and Form* (1910), to which Michelstaedter's work has often been compared.

On 17 October 1910, after finishing his thesis and its profoundly important appendixes, Michelstaedter shot himself. Besides his thesis, he left behind thousands of pages of poetry, stories, letters, and above all notes on philosophy.

This book sets out to analyse Michelstaedter's intellectual trajectory in its entirety, moving in chronological order through the three phases of his thought (1906–7; 1908; and 1909–10). The main objective here is to demonstrate how Michelstaedter arrived at a thought that was both in dialogue with and radically antithetical to the main philosophical currents of his time. At the heart of my interpretation is Michelstaedter's unique analysis of the concept of "abstraction." For him, abstraction was the means by which society reabsorbed the various ideological and cultural perspectives and (on a material level) the needs of individuals, by adapting them so as to reintegrate them into its mode of operation. A corollary to this was his development of a cultural perspective according to which thought (his own included), rather than being autonomous, is forced to develop on the basis of directions that are ideologically and materially imposed by the social structure and therefore constantly in danger of being absorbed. At the root of this uniform social abstraction – and this is what really sets Michelstaedter apart – we do not find a societal appeal to order, to absolute values or an immutable truth, but rather the same contrasting ideological positions that form the social whole. For Michelstaedter, the uniformity of the social structure (and of thought) was not the result of underlying principles of an essentialistic nature; it stemmed, rather, from the need to manage and rationalize – without ever definitively arriving at a resolution – the relativity of ideologies, wills, needs, and ways of living. The abstraction of this underlying relativity was what Michelstaedter called rhetoric: reproposing the untouched contrast of ideas and existences with the appearance of being. The goal of rhetoric is to present the contrast of opinions and philosophical orientations in society as Being itself.

The first chapter of this book discusses the cultural context in which Michelstaedter developed his ideas. It begins with an overview of the different philosophical perspectives that were in vogue at the time and a survey of the various critical perspectives from which his work has been interpreted by scholars. It then analyses his writings from 1906 to 1907 in relation to the decadent and aesthetic tendencies of the period and notes how his particular interpretation of those poetics would impact the development of his philosophy. In analysing some of these early writings by Michelstaedter, the chapter emphasizes the emergence of a *tragical* ethical perspective, one that seeks a solution to the contrast between the individual and society – on an artistic-philosophical level – in the genre of tragedy (both classical and Ibsenian). Here I observe how his analysis of the "chorus" as the whole of society in classical tragedy foreshadowed future developments in his thought. His interpretation of the chorus as a social consortium that orders the hero to respect society's laws and shared ideas anticipates the role that society would play in shaping the ideas and actions of the individual.

The second chapter focuses on Michelstaedter's philosophy, beginning with a central element of his thought: the concept of will. His concept of will, which is clearly indebted to Schopenhauer's philosophy, extends beyond the will of the subject to include the subject's state of need. Will is the phenomenological manner in which the subject interprets the world propelled by his state of need; it is a state of dissatisfaction that leads him to situate his momentary will/need as the basis of his entire interpretation of realty. In the moment of need, the subject reads all of reality according to the characteristics of his own needs. When this mechanism is extended from the individual to the whole of society, the result is what Michelstaedter describes as "correlativity," that is, a system of contrasting wills that leads individuals to see everything contained in the real (including other subjects) in relation to their own needs, and thus as objects to be annexed for their "usefulness." Michelstaedter calls this mechanism the "direct mode." At the end of the chapter I introduce the cornerstone of Michelstaedter's philosophy: the passage from the "direct mode" to the "connective mode." I contend that the dichotomy between these two modes, which has been ignored by critics up until now, represents the core of Michelstaedter's philosophy. Passage from the "direct mode" to the "connective mode" is necessary in order to reconfigure the relativistic contrast of will/needs into a cultural and material code (rhetoric) that, while leaving the contrast untouched, is capable of stabilizing it in appearance.

The third chapter analyses the various aspects of rhetoric, beginning with the forms it assumes in the linguistic sphere. Through a comparison with Giuseppe Prezzolini and some of the principal interpreters of the *Sprachkritik* movement, I show how Michelstaedter's critique of language is different from the nihilist positions of the period that viewed *words* as inevitably separated from the reality to which they refer. Michelstaedter's critique of language focuses on its role as a medium of abstraction in society – as a means to transform words (as in the case of the will) into a code to which individuals must adapt in order to satisfy their needs. I then point out how for Michelstaedter – through his peculiar reading of the Hegelian master–slave dialectic – this code is not constructed on a set of random elements; rather, it is determined by the wills/needs of those who control the social system through property and money. The *power* these two elements give to the subject is such that these individuals dictate the rules of the code itself, ensuring that their will/needs – their interpretation of the real – prevails over those of others. In the "connective mode," the other individuals will find it easier to satisfy their own needs by adapting to interpretations of reality that do not challenge those at the top of the system of correlativity. The last section of the chapter presents Michelstaedter's idea of "consensus." I observe how this idea serves as the basis of his concept of rhetoric as an imitative principle, and show how Michelstaedter forms this idea through his interpretation of the passage from Plato's to Aristotle's philosophy.

In the final chapter I observe how rhetoric and persuasion (i.e., for Michelstaedter, the capacity to resist the consensus implemented by rhetoric) are historical rather than metaphysical–ontological forms. As the abstraction of relativity, rhetoric can only exist as an ontological form in appearance, transforming itself over time following the changing conformation of social relations within the system of correlativity. In the same way, persuasion, which can only emerge in relation to the present form of rhetoric, must also transform itself over time. As such, the form of rhetoric we find in Michelstaedter is derived from the prevailing scientific–technological perspective of his time. For Michelstaedter this perspective directly shaped modes of pedagogy on the basis of principles of (1) "utility": that which is true is that which is useful; (2) "contemplativity": the apparent inability to intervene in order to modify the system of rhetoric; and (3) "calculation": shaping one's activity, thought, and actions in relation to calculations made on how to best exploit the advantages and avoid the disadvantages of the system, and thereby reducing one's activity to mimetically adapting to the system itself.

In the conclusion, I underscore the uniqueness of Michelstaedter's philosophical findings relative to those of his time and link *Persuasion and Rhetoric* to Lukács's *History and Class Consciousness*, the work that marked the birth of twentieth-century Hegelian Marxism. At this point the Marxist structure of my approach to analysing Michelstaedter's thought, present throughout the book, emerges clearly, as it also does in my observation of the many inevitable differences between Michelstaedter and Lukács. As such, "the limits of bourgeois thought" – limits that have been the object of Michelstaedter's analysis – show themselves to be in part inherent in Michelstaedter himself. This does not of course undermine the profound originality of his thought, which stands at the point of contact between a philosophy that still believes itself to be autonomous and one that recognizes itself as dialectically conditioned by the social-historical space in which it originates. Having set out to reveal the relationships between cultural interpretations and this social space, Michelstaedter arrived at the point past which bourgeois thought was unable to proceed without negating its own modes of operation, without destroying itself.

1 The Crisis of Truth

I. Michelstaedter and the Two Sides of Modernist Thought

During an interview in October 1936, Italy's greatest interpreter of modernism, Luigi Pirandello, surprisingly grouped together Nietzsche, Weininger, and Michelstaedter, observing that all three had been "broken" by the attempt to grasp the Absolute. Perhaps even more surprising is that Pirandello was not the first to make such an association: in 1927, Julius Evola, scholar of esoteric texts and future collaborator of the Scuola di mistica fascista, had mentioned the same three names, in the same order and with a similar wording: "In Nietzsche, Weininger, and Michelstaedter, we see men who were broken by the unrealized integration of their value into a positive method of power and self-fulfillment ...: the affirmation of the dominion of the I over reality" (*Teoria dell'Individuo assoluto,* 18). Michelstaedter thus stands with Nietzsche, the principal critic of Platonism, intended as the creation of the transcendent world of the *ontos,* and Weininger, the greatest interpreter of the tragic attempt to reactivate that world within a horizon of immanence – that is, of the neo-Kantian version of the Platonic perspective.[1] This philosophical perspective, within which Michelstaedter would often be positioned by scholars, had risen to a position of hegemony in German universities at the end of the nineteenth century, reaching its apex at the beginning of the twentieth (the young Lukács, Georg Simmel, Paul Natorp, and Wilhelm Windelband would be among its principal exponents). This philosophical tendency insisted on the superiority of the Kantian epistemological critique over the ontological one while strongly emphasizing the importance of ethical action as a way of restoring those immanent *values* that had themselves been assailed by epistemology. Ethics, to use the words of the young Lukács in his *The Metaphysics of Tragedy* (1910), allowed the choice of a "form" of existence that opposed the infinite ambiguities and contradictions of the condition of "life." By making an ethical choice, the subject re-established *value* in a reality that even epistemological criticism had shown to be devoid of any immanent value. By means of the ethical choice the subject was able to again give meaning to himself and to his existence. In Weininger's words: "While the earth that we inhabit continually revolves, the human being remains untouched by the cosmic dance … He looks out freely, and gives the spectacle its value, or takes it away" (*A Translation*, 94).

However, Pirandello viewed Nietzsche, Weininger, and Michelstaedter as basically seekers of the Absolute. Dominated by Stirner's "fixed ideas," they inevitably succumbed to a reality that allowed for no reconciliation at all, save within the "fiction" of an operating system of thought that employed those fixed ideas to move across reality and master it through a cynical rationality, recalling Nietzsche's *On Truth and Falsehood in the Extra-Moral Sense*: "The intellect, as a means of preserving the individual, develops its main powers in dissimulation" (247).[2] For Pirandello, I mean, only awareness that truth is mere convention could structure the action of the subject in the real. For Evola, instead, the failure of these three thinkers lay in their inability to channel the desire for the Absolute into the pure egoarchic myth of a man both atomized and powerful, one who was capable of resuscitating reality and disaggregating it in the experiential form of Myth.[3]

The acceptance of relativism and the attempt to salvage a meaningful world from the only place that still seems independent (the interiority of man) are – to varying degrees – the two roads that characterize the various modernist positions. Critics have often associated Michelstaedter with one or the other of these two approaches.[4] For instance, his thought has often been interpreted in relation to an ethical perspective. One of the first to follow this path, Giovanni Amendola, said of him: "The gold vein has surfaced once again … He has felt and communicated the need to be serious and earnest … An ethical and conscious ego" (in "Carlo Michelstaedter," *Etica e biografia*, 167–9). This approach, which has been supported by prominent scholars like Sergio Campailla, Massimo Cacciari, Giuseppe Camerino, Daniela Bini, Giorgio Brianese, and Maria Adelaide Raschini, sees an ethical defence of truth in Michelstaedter's philosophy.

However, associations of Michelstaedter's poetics with a relativistic current that refutes the unitary myths of "bourgeois metaphysics" have been equally numerous (and were especially so during the final years of post-structuralism's cultural predominance).[5] This position, which has been defended in particular by Claudio La Rocca, Guido Guglielmi, Marco Fortunato, and Roberto Salsano, as well as, in a less dogmatic and more complex way, by Thomas Harrison, reads Michelstaedter's philosophy against the backdrop of the emergence of the nihilist crisis by analysing its influence on Michelstaedter's thought in *Persuasion and Rhetoric*. This approach, however, has also led to some readings of Michelstaedter that are entirely unacceptable. Vincenzo Intermite's position, for instance, is an extreme example of the relativist reading of Michelstaedter: his thought is summarized as a Stirnerian-like exaltation of relativity (in opposition to the rigid structures created by bourgeois society). In this comparison, the Stirnerian system of "fixed ideas" is the equivalent of Michelstaedter's rhetoric: "like Stirner and Nietzsche ..., what Michelstaedter's philosophy has in common with that perspective is the anarchic-individualistic character" (Intermite 33). According to this interpretation, modernist perspectives are a revolt against systematic and totalizing bourgeois rationality rather than (as I believe they were for Michelstaedter) a moment internal to it. On the relationship between Stirner and Michelstaedter, Piero Pieri rightly observes:

> Michelstaedter upholds an opposing concept: the individual does not experience the ideas that limit the expansion and full possession of himself as extraneous. He loves and defends them because these ideas structure his identity in the world ... With respect to the optimistic nihilism of Stirner, Michelstaedter tends towards a more elaborate analysis of the relationship between consciousness and ideology. The I assimilates and interiorizes the ideas of the bourgeois age and defends them as though they belonged to his own personal intuition of things. (*Il pensiero della poesia*, 34–5)

Giacomo Debenedetti's affirmation that with Michelstaedter (as with Pirandello) we witness the crisis of the unitary subject,[6] and Eugenio Garin and Carlo Salinari's observation that Pirandello and Michelstaedter were the authors who best understood the epistemological issues of their time, are not meant to be interpreted as a direct identification of the two authors with each other.

Not surprisingly, Garin was the first to bring Lukács into the discussion on Michelstaedter, "a figure to be recontextualized in the same places and time in which Lukács was coming up ... At the bottom of his [Michelstaedter's] analysis there could only be the call for a decision, a change of course, a leap ... The analysis of rhetoric turns into an exhortation to reverse the social context" (*Intellettuali italiani*, 97–100).

Attention to the influence of the social context on thought is one of the points that radically separates Pirandello's relativist position from that of Michelstaedter. In positing the breaking up of total reality into fragments that seemingly cannot be reassembled, Pirandello approaches this phenomenon as if (Marx might say) reality had proceeded from books to history, as if changes in reality had been caused by the epistemological revolution rather than the other way around. Within this revolution Pirandello attempts to resolve (to rationalize) the question of the inauthenticity of life. He tries to resolve the crisis of the symbolic by symbolizing the absence of the symbolic itself. Therefore, though insightful, Roberto Salsano's analysis in *Michelstaedter tra D'Annunzio, Pirandello e il mondo della vita* must be challenged: "in Michelstaedter and Pirandello [we can find] a rooted criticism of the social and cultural status quo" (48).

The similarities Salsano observes between Pirandello's thought and that of Michelstaedter are derived from his observation that they share an interest in several modernist themes closely linked to the "philosophy of the crisis"; however, their respective critiques of the social structure move in completely different if not opposing directions. Pirandello criticizes the social structure for its inability to move beyond the artificial realm of *forms* (conventions), opting instead for a form of relativist immanence expressed (for him) by the ever-changing flux represented by life; for Michelstaedter, by contrast, this sort of relativization is the foundation for societal consensus and convention. For Michelstaedter, relativism cannot exist as long as individuals – atomized – search for consensual unions in order to believe in their presumed ontological stability. Their relativized condition is the foundation for social accords, which are presented as anything but relative.

Michelstaedter rejects any theoretical–epistemological approach and places that approach at the centre of his analysis in a doubly determined relationship with society.[7] *Persuasion and Rhetoric* has caused critics so much difficulty because, for Michelstaedter, the two variegated sides of the issue – the Scylla of relativism and the Charybdis of truth – are both abstractions that tend to conceal and perpetuate the purely theoretical approach that, in both cases, is a "second nature" of reality, overlapping it and determining in thought (i.e., merely in theory) the space of disalienation.

Michelstaedter does not adhere to the anti-ontological camp, nor does he adopt an ethical duty/existence perspective. Instead, he stands as the guilty conscience of modernism: as the point where the epistemological revolution acts against itself and, while not forgetting the results achieved (or that the response to its age must be given in that age itself), is acknowledged as the cultural logic of a time in history, in its critical epistemology of relativist origins as well as in its anti-relativistic ethical stances. Therefore, Michelstaedter does not, as Angela Michelis suggests, "take the road indicated by Nietzsche in which life revolts against culture" (*Carlo Michelstaedter*, 15). As we will see, in Michelstaedter the problem is connected not to an objectification of the real carried out individually by the subject, but rather to the *social* organization of the relative into objectified forms.

Michelstaedter, like his contemporaries, is part of modernism inasmuch as it is the hegemonic culture of his time, a time defined by a post-metaphysical crisis of the established certainties of reality, thought, self, and language (a crisis of the possibility of assuming reality in the symbolisms of the I, of unifyingly subsuming the knowable in consciousness).[8] Most of Michelstaedter's more attentive critics have recognized his participation in the climate of the "crisis of foundations."[9] Yet he is also its negative conscience, the moment when the act of accepting the "flow of life" (the delight of Heraclitean existence beyond all forms)[10] is recognized as an ideological construct, but also the moment of its opposite, when we encounter the various attempts by bourgeois thought to rebuild some sort of stable foundation, as we see in his Italian contemporaries, such as Giovanni Boine, Piero Jahier, and Scipio Slataper. In Michelstaedter, both responses are revealed as part of the same cultural operation, as part of the same abstractive structure, one that reflects – in the "theory" that restabilizes the disaggregation – the forms of social control.[11]

Michelstaedter grasps that the crisis of classical rationality (its inability to posit itself as nature: what the nihilist perspective now actually reveals) is reflected as nature-based thought's capacity for concealment, both in the ideologies willing to leave behind the fetish of Being (pragmatism, relativism, contingentism, etc.) and in religion-based or ethics-based ideologies, which, as we shall see, end up being part of a structure in which Being is relativized and experienced as "social being," reified in theory as the truth of the ideological moment that society expresses and enacts as consent. The binomial pairs of bourgeois thought (life/form; *Kultur/Zivilisation*; universal/particular) are collapsed in Michelstaedter: he sees them working in unison for the preservation of the social status quo; he sees them as being shaped by the social environment in which they originated. He realizes, as we shall see, that specialization (the loss of a vision of totality that leaves reality in fragments, making it impossible to reassemble the different viewpoints of increasingly atomized human beings) and rationalization (the systemic need to recompose these viewpoints in an increasingly predictable and computable mechanized abstraction) work together. Confronted by the transformation of "substance" into convention/fiction (modernist decadence in relation to the concept of objective truth),[12] Michelstaedter not only refuses to consider that function a substance, not only rejects the cynical opportunity to use that function "as if" it were a substance, but also identifies, in the thinking aimed at reconstructing the old idea of substance, a mechanism designed to introduce Being as abstraction, as the cement of a social cohesion that only according to this alienated perspective can be expressed and perpetuated as such, imprinting itself in the hearts of men:

> Abstracted from *necessity*, the laws will make their proclamations through calculation; men, from their own necessities, will conform *by calculation* to the organized system of necessities ... In the diminished life determined by abstraction lies the condition for the existence of the system of abstractions ... Without this, the system could never work *right* – but once it does work right, it too will be *right* ... And in each of them [men] will be reproduced the right image of the system. ("Appendice II," *La persuasione*, 157–9)[13]

To maintain, as some critics have, that Michelstaedter could have arrived at these conclusions from an ahistorical perspective would be inaccurate: "History cannot be destroyed at its roots when a text appeals to readers whose epochal codes have already been oriented by certain readings of Schopenhauer (the inauthentic character of phenomena) and Nietzsche (the crisis of foundations)" (Pieri, "Per una dialettica storica del silenzio," 235). Disconnected from the cultural (and structural) directives of his time, outside the crisis of European consciousness, the season of tragic thought and *Lebensphilosophie*, the age of Ernst Mach, Georg Simmel, and Karl Kraus, outside this complex of ideas that, as Henry Stuart Hughes writes, were "so intertwined as to appear a cultural revolution" (*Consciousness and Society*, 7), Michelstaedter's speculation becomes meaningless. His cultural background was formed by the various ramifications of negative thought that arose in reaction to Hegelianism and Positivism: the transposing of the achievements of thought into fictional models for the construction of the Real (forms, ideologies, linguistic concretions); the conventional unity imposed on the multiple, which now, just when individuals appear increasingly isolated, is seen as a psychological phenomenon (inevitable or useful/utilitarian);[14] the collapse of the traditional philosophical space that the Florence-based intellectuals experienced through the mediation of Henri Bergson and William James; the condemnation of logical/systematic thought as violence against what existed in the flow of "becoming." For the sake of convenience, we can group these various expressions of negative thought under the name of Nietzsche – or, better still, Ernst Mach's hegemonic interpretation of Nietzsche.

By analysing every conceptual concretion (God, law, the self, language) in terms of a bundle of sensations pre-directed by the subjectivity of an individual, Mach determines that scientific action is founded on the economical, instrumental use of these symbolic crystallizations, which synthetically organize the material of experience into independent and methodological abstractions necessary for reconstructing a stable model based on "convention." In other words, empirical appearances (directed by interests and by chance) are established as subsisting units, which Mach calls "elements" (and Hans Vaihinger – the author of *The Philosophy of "As If"* – more naively but more correctly terms "fictions."). This issue, which found its most widely read interpretation in Mach's *Analysis of Sensations* (the Italian translation came out in 1903), was also analysed by one of Michelstaedter's professors, Francesco De Sarlo. In *Il concetto dell'anima nella psicologia contemporanea*, De Sarlo demonstrated that he had absorbed Mach's theories and connected them with the work of Wilhelm Wundt and Alfred Binet (not incidentally, the latter would be a fundamental author for Pirandello):

> The I, which is effectively a composite or a process, is understood as a unity, as the basis for a necessary illusion, inherent to human nature; an illusion that is the form of our consciousness and the condition for our experience. We, who are the contrary, appear to ourselves as a [single] substance, as something that is, rather than something that is continuously becoming. (11)[15]

These "units of measure" – or in Mach's words, "elements" ("object," "mind," "Ego") – are not substantial structures, but relationships of relative stability transmitted through sensations: a combination of elements/aspects of the phenomenal and individual experience of the subject. From this premise it was clearly inevitable that objective truth would be repudiated, as was the development of a sceptical epistemology aimed at subtracting value from any idea of substance, the "I" included: "The 'I' is unsavable" (Mach, *The Analysis of Sensations*, 19). The same affirmation would reappear in Robert Musil's *Diaries*.

Nietzsche portrays this cultural space and time as that of the "wanderer," the man beyond the dream of the *fundamentum veritatis*. The prevalent image is that of Becoming. In becoming, all things (including the subject, who now senses the precariousness of his own ontological and epistemological foundations) reveal their representational nature as a constant oscillation between apparent objectivity and a continuous denial of that objectivity. This denial takes place within an external space of non-dialectical judgment built on binomial pairs (starting with those regarding life and form; living/rigid), which declares the eternal logic of becoming ("flow") as the place of unresolvable contradiction. In this way, the progressive thrust of Mach's becoming aimed at breaking down the objectivistic concretions of Western metaphysics and bourgeois common sense is reified into an epistemological conceptualism that serves as the theoretical "corset" of the relativist perspective. Intellective knowledge epistemologically derived – the kind of knowledge that during the age of imperialism tended increasingly to become the hegemonic form of thought – presents itself as the limit of *all* knowledge, because of its constant failure to fully implement its *own* capacity to conceptualize reality. Non-dialectical conceptualization leads to a dead end, producing a "retreat" from reality. This escape presents itself as the solution to what is seen as the anthropological limit of rational knowledge itself ("there are no facts: only interpretations"). The principle of the perpetual motion of everything conceals the static nature of formal – and merely epistemological – logic. The gradual erosion of objectivistic assumptions (and the corollary attack on the assumed conceptual concretions represented by "subject" and "language") creates the space for a judgment of reality, which is assumed to be an *absence* of judgment because it is equated with the *reality* of a life that denies any concretion of itself besides the one it represents.

The relationship between subject and reality is examined on epistemological grounds as a presupposed identity that has been broken by the attempt to establish objective truths. This Becoming, which is not the objective form of a particular historical period, is then given the traits of Being, that is, the traits of a cosmic and biological nexus: the subject that sees himself becoming projects these data onto reality and believes that only by adapting to them will it be possible for him to avoid betraying reality itself. In this manner the psychological features of a particular, objective historical period become – through the Trojan horse of epistemology – the true (and eternal) reality of the world.

Within the formal logic of such a philosophy, the historical antinomies of the bourgeoisie (elevated to the antinomies of existence in general) are presented as eternal. The struggle waged by this perspective is not directed at eliminating those antinomies,[16] because this would mean fighting against the mode of being of existence itself (which would be an absurdity). Rather, in the epistemological assumption, it presents reality as a simulacrum of itself. These Machian "elements" (i.e., forms) are in fact composites/complexes of sensations that do not represent substantial social structures, but rather relative networks of stability that can be used. Though non-existent, they turn out to be useful, as absolutely necessary "errors," for practical purposes. The abstracting of these elements from the flow for those purposes gained a space of real cultural hegemony, which spread with surprising speed (*The Analysis of Sensations* alone had three new editions during the first four years of the century).[17] This rapid diffusion was related to their organic tie to new modes of technical progress, rooted in the restructured production system (which entailed the combined action of specialization and rationalization). From Mach's perspective, the epistemological–scientific model has become a theory of knowledge that has taken shape concurrently with the way common thought works and has ahistorically always worked. In one of the few notes he dedicates to Mach, Michelstaedter underscores a point that will later turn out to be fundamental to his perspective: "he lacks a historical sense, the awareness of time passed, the difference of the situation." (*Sfugge la vita*, 156) For Mach the randomness of elements is methodically structured (e.g., through the language that organizes them) and abstractly prepared for instrumental exploitation (thus William James, in *Pragmatism*, argues at the same time that life goes beyond logic and that theories are not answers but instruments). According to Mach, science adapts thought to facts, just like the thoughts of all of us do every day, creating *forms* economically.

Such *forms* are none other than mental symbols transmitted in order to identify (and use) a temporary complex of sensations. To the forms that emerge from the becoming we give, temporarily and for practical purposes, the status of Being.

But at this point, modernist philosophers and writers depart from one another (Lukács appropriately titles his foundational essay from 1910 "The Parting of the Ways"): one group exalts the advantages of the relativist perspective while the other attempts through various approaches to reappropriate existence as the space of a *real* Being. For example, Hermann Bahr reads Mach's reduction of the Self through a Nietzschean lens, considering this approach a "philosophy of Impressionism," where the only truth is provided by the immediate sensation of the moment before it is crystallized by the work of the mind (*Expressionism*). In Italy, the writer and painter Ardengo Soffici writes: "Life is a victorious, aimless flowing, without rhyme or reason, that keeps on going, heedless of all the plugs we put up with our morality, our good and evil" ("Giornale di bordo," in *Opere* IV, 7). Soffici expresses appreciation of a world in which all aspects are egalitarian: "To show – as Friedrich Nietzsche (almost a brother) says – 'how a man who has the starkest, most frightful view of reality, who is capable of the "most profound thought," finds, despite all this, no objection to living'" ("Rimbaud," in *Opere* I, 163). This statement sums up the inclination – excellently described by the young Lukács in his essay "Aesthetic Culture" – to superficially equate all of the "particular" aspects of life and abandon all symbolic and hierarchical value in favour of the overwhelming power of moods and their continual surrendering to the inevitably transitory aspects of life:

> In an authentic culture everything is symbolic, because everything expresses ... what is of paramount importance: how the individual reacts to life, how his whole being responds to and confronts life as a whole. The center of aesthetic culture is: the mood ... The essence of mood is its accidental ... the moment when life itself is seen as an endless sequence of transient moods. It was born when objects ceased to exist, because everything was merely an occasion for the mood; when all that was permanent disappeared from life, because the mood proved intolerant of what was permanent and recurrent. It was born when life was stripped of all values, and it now values the products of moods, that is to say, the products

> of fortuitous circumstances devoid of any necessary correlation with values. In a sense the unity of aesthetic culture does exist: as a lack of unity. Aesthetic culture has a central tenet: the peripheral nature of all things. This culture also has a symbol for everything: namely that nothing is symbolic ... Aesthetic culture becomes the art of life; the elevation of life into an art. ("Aesthetic Culture," in *The Lukács Reader*, 148)

Massimo Cacciari has correctly observed Michelstaedter and early Lukács's shared "refusal of aesthetic culture ...: though impressionism more or less represents its origin ... passes through both Machian psychologism ... as well as all of the various vitalistic misrepresentations of Nietzsche's *dura lectio* ... Who exalts the absence of truth as truth and the disappearance of the center as the center ... is not a free man, but the greatest of slaves" ("Interpretazione di Michelstaedter," 22–3).

On the other side of the modernist spectrum, a writer such as Hugo von Hofmannsthal (who followed Mach's courses at university) looks at the Romantic dream of a not-disintegrated truth as an opportunity to rebuild an organic, disalienated space in which *Erfahrung* (true experience) can resume a central role. In this same vein an already mentioned compatriot of Michelstaedter's, Carlo Stuparich, writes:

> Those who must deal with a central knot painfully resist the tendency to cleave, and with an agonizing effort try to concentrate, to neutralize the forces of disintegration, to precipitate all the molecular tensions in its center. The tragedy of modern society. The centripetal force that organizes the chaotic elements, which used to be faith, has dissolved. – The effort must come from the individual. (67)

Yet for Michelstaedter (at least in 1909–10) even this division at the heart of modernist culture is entirely inauthentic. For him, experience, when only epistemologically acquirable, nevertheless continues to follow the mechanized rules of its abstraction. In other words, it continues to leave untouched the structural elements by which it is determined as the categorical systemization of knowledge, and in which ethics represents the instrumental aspects of the ideological level achieved by society: the moment when the subject regains, albeit only speculatively, the forces he perceives as having been estranged from him. For Michelstaedter the point is that since both directions fail to understand themselves as historically determined and to establish disalienation as a dialectical perspective capable of setting "truth" as a constantly evolving historical figure, they remain subjugated to the cultural hegemony that the current social moment expresses, in which truth, as nature, is immobile. For Michelstaedter, in the same way that the relativist perspective provides us with only an abstract vision (established in theory and culture) of human atomization, of the infinite human contrasts that can only be reconciled with reference to the same "stabilized" social being, those theories aimed at the reconstruction of the lost-Being will turn out to be no more than the reified image of an absent Being. As such, they perpetuate themselves through a repetition of the forms of social being, beginning with the desire for immobility that social being expresses. Michelstaedter was among the first to understand that the crisis of values described by modernist philosophy, and the response to that crisis, are really the consequences of a *social* crisis, and that both these crises have as their purpose the protection of the status quo.

For Michelstaedter the separation of the theoretical problem of truth from the operations of the social structure (the autonomy of thought from social praxis) implies the possibility of a theoretical reconciliation that thought can still bring about by replicating the reifying facilities of the social structure, that is, by assigning an abstract form of objectivity determinable through quantified measures to a reality multiplied in entities (not unified by a higher principle) – specialized, sectorized, unstable, and temporal. This reification, which relativists interpret as the persistence of symbolic–metaphysical thought (and which still reifies in the form of an absolutized relativism that is no longer historical), is actually the cancellation, on the level of thought, of the mechanism from which the objectivity originates. As we shall see with Michelstaedter, this is the mechanism that the social structure expresses, at the achieved ideological level, as theory – as "knowledge," which in order to be accepted must become knowledge of current beliefs, of common sense made treacherously abstract by the conditions of material reality.

This is how men begin to depend on an objectivity that they themselves have created, that they themselves have objectified. The time of the "death of God,"[18] Michelstaedter suggests, is the time of an inhuman objectivity. This is not because God is not yet completely dead in the hearts of men, but because the rationality of the new cultural horizon (and what it determines) takes God's place as an abstraction, assigning its own features to everything, to every thing that, wanting to live, takes part in this mimetic nightmare, whose purpose is to present as eternal (immobile) its own volatility: "that which in every case and every manner is called life – is the infinitely various conjoining of *potency* finitely localized in infinitely various aspects – as consciousness, according to which in every case its correlate is stable amid the instability" (*Persuasion*, 16).

The new cultural horizon assumes both the features of the ought-to-be and the features of the ought-to-become, because in the space of knowledge (theory), both are perceived as the place of a conciliatory substantialization. This substantialization, however, is no more than the point where society projects itself as the place of Being beyond its contradictions, beyond relativistic accidentality, because for Michelstaedter, this relativistic accidentality is the very foundation of that abstract social being. It is in this sense, albeit just on the level of ideas, that Michelstaedter had understood the combined work of specialization and rationalization, the social necessity of rationalizing the loss of the vision of the whole in an abstract form. This is why Alberto Asor Rosa claimed that *Persuasion and Rhetoric* was "undoubtedly the most anomalous and remarkable book of the Italian literature" (Asor Rosa, *Letteratura*, 265). Because, in its pages, bourgeois thought (thought still unable to apply its analysis to the mechanisms of labour)[19] confronts the structure of its own alienation and even recognizes itself as abstract ("using words, a war on words"), and recognizes itself as part of a social mechanism directed at distinguishing reality from the image of reality,

> *the world, life, becomes a theory*. Things are no longer or are not as they even are, but for the sake of this theoretical life: ... things are handled like data stripped of any interest, with no reference to life ... To reason means to live this way of *current reality* no longer the necessary relations of reality ... but to transpose one's life into the joining and separating of impersonal data, which may stand one way in the present of our discourse, and may stand in another in the future of our discourse, if now in the present we assume this hypothesis instead of another. Life has fled the discourse ... Thus the events of this diminished life now usurp the words that have meaning in life ... he [man] can each time specify, for the sake of the discourse, in which abstract regard he takes a given thing. (Michelstaedter, "Appendice II," *La persuasione*, 196–7)

This is not nihilism. In Michelstaedter, nihilism is played against itself, which makes it the necessary historical experience of an alienated, atomized world, one that in order to conceal its alienation must turn life into "knowledge about life," precariousness into value (but including the *value* of nihilism itself). Nor is it a form of ethics, because for Michelstaedter ethics would merely be the abstraction that the atomized subject makes of himself in order to give social stability to his own precariousness, having recognized the values expressed by society as the most suitable for bridging the hiatus produced between himself and society, thereby transfiguring a real need into an abstract "duty" – the same duty that, as his father made clear when Carlo left for Florence (October 1905), should inform his whole life: "Remember that any infringement you may make to your honor, even if gilded over by mitigating circumstances, would be a death sentence for your father, who allows no excuse for such transgressions, who has made honor the foundation of his life, honest work his supreme law, and duty his religion" (Alberto Michelstaedter, in Campailla, *Dialoghi*, 13).

II. The *Social* Overcoming of the Aesthetic Perspective

The Michelstaedter home faced the central square of Gorizia, a town close to Venice and Trieste, in a region of Italy occupied at the time by the Austro-Hungarian Empire but whose residents were for the most part pro-Italian. Most of the townspeople were liberal bourgeoisie and quite welcoming of progress (in 1906 a new Transalpine train line would link the town to the great cities of Central Europe); but in their hearts, they continued to live the illusion of a patriarchal provincial "community" – what Stefan Zweig would later refer to as the "world of yesterday": "Before the war, Gorizia presented a quiet, domestic lifestyle lived between salons and churches, a lifestyle that was slightly withdrawn and showy, slightly indulgent and bigoted, that simultaneously brought to mind the age of Goldoni and that of Maria Theresa, with bombastic preachers of that decrepit 'Accademia dei Sonziaci' [*sonziaci* = speakers of *sonziaco*, the language of Gorizia] which had been a distinguished coterie in Gorizia among eighteenth-century Arcadians" (Astori, 8–9).[20]

Carlo was the fourth son in an assimilated Jewish family.[21] His father Alberto cultivated literary interests in his spare time and was well-known in the town's cultural circles. After working as a money-changer, he became an agent with the Trieste-based insurance company Assicurazioni Generali, an integral part of that world of affluence and "preventive security" in which, as Bobi Bazlen recalls, "everything was insured" (248). Forms of mutualism and collective self-protection were already in place years before the introduction of the Austrian welfare state. They had been developed and supported by the members of the liberal bourgeoisie of Italian origin in particular, as a form of opposition to the Viennese government, but also as a bulwark against direct action by the Socialist and Social Democrat trade unions a few years later. Fabrizio Meroi notes that Michelstaedter's father would later attempt to remove a reference to the figure of the insurer – of the "important gentleman" who comes to represent the world of "rhetoric" – from the printed version of *Persuasion and Rhetoric* (*Persuasione ed esistenza*, 141).

Alberto and Carlo represented the clash of generations – between integration into societal structures and a search for authenticity – that Kafka would so emblematically describe.[22] That clash, which would later encompass the individualism of modern consciousness (reality perceived as a form of disaggregation), was more than just psychological. It also marked the beginning of an era of social transition and the emergence of two radically different ways of understanding the relationship between the individual and society:

> You are telling me the worst things I can be told. That I try to reassure myself with casuistic quibbling for having unconsciously sucked up modern ideas, that the differences between my viewpoint and yours are irremediable … All of you keep saying that I have been morally spoiled by modern-day principles. And just because I'm saying that consciousness is individual. (Michelstaedter, letter to father dated 27 June 1907, in *Epistolario*, 234–6)[23]

As is well-known, this conflict was expressed in Habsburg society with particular intensity:

> I see that I have no control over things and people, as I have no control over the ideas that cross my mind, vague, confused …; that I lack moral balance, and therefore that powerful impulse that makes one go through life proudly and confidently, that I lack the intellectual balance that moves one's thoughts straight to the point; because I find that I am living as if in a dream where everything is incomplete and obscure, and when I try to understand, to focus on something that floats around me, it all slips through my fingers … and it seems to me that there is always a heavy veil between myself and reality; and I become more and more convinced that I am a degenerate … Part of this is personal, and part is the disease of the time as far as moral balance is concerned, because we are living in a period of societal transition in which all bonds are coming loose … and the roads of life are no longer clearly drawn towards a certain climax, but are all mixed up and unclear. (Michelstaedter, letter to his sister Paula dated 9 December 1906, in *Epistolario*, 157–8)

Here Michelstaedter seems to grasp the emergence – note the reference to "degeneration," most likely inspired by Max Nordau[24] – of a psychological situation about which all the intellectuals of the time, in Italy and elsewhere, were beginning to express awareness.

What Alberto did not observe in the words of his son was that Carlo was worlds away from an acritical exaltation of individualized consciousness. On the contrary, for Carlo the severing of the tie between individual and society represented a dialectical moment that would not bring about the liberation of the individual, but rather his social enslavement.

Yet Alberto was not an old fogey. A lecture he had given, *On Falsehood* (La menzogna), had even caused some commotion in town. In that talk he argued that falsehood is actually one of the foundations of social life; that the world "sways between relative truth and relative falsehood"; and that it is only by concealing this fact, by separating theory from practice, that social life and its mechanisms (the institutions that regulate it) are made possible: "The moment that the first semblance of society's beginnings sprang forth from the shapeless and wild masses, falsehood was born. Or rather, to be more precise, with *the first falsehood, society was born*" (8–9).[25]

Alberto had chosen to live the bourgeois contradiction: "theory is one thing, practice another!" (Michelstaedter, *Persuasion*, 105). As David Micheletti writes: "For Alberto, falsehood ... is the true sign of man's intelligence, something which is not present in other animals. And it is in direct relation to this capacity to lie that the level of civilization of one population may be measured in comparison with another" ("Il razionalismo delle menti ebraiche," in Sorrentino and Michelis, eds, *E sotto avverso ciel*, 49). Alberto was aware of the new modernist epistemology (i.e., of the idea that all of our truths are abstract and exist for convention only), but his actions were not aimed – as were those of the young Florentine intellectuals, such as Prezzolini and Papini – at exploiting this new perspective, but rather at upholding the societal consensus and conventions then in force. Theoretically, the new epistemology could shake the common belief system, but it could not create a gap between individual consciousness and the collective consciousness in which it resides. Alberto Michelstaedter embodied a bourgeoisie that smiled ironically at its universalistic purpose, at its ability to propose its values as universal, but this smile did not involve any real change of practice. Carlo, by contrast, understood how this gap that had become fodder for the amusement of his father's intellectual circles was actually one and the same with the abyss that the nihilist perspective had opened. Alberto Michelstaedter's position in *La menzogna*, though much simplified, was already a Nietzschean one that presented the exact same elements around which the nihilist tendencies of the beginning of the century would construct and nourish themselves: the connections of ideas to the psychology of the individual; the reduction of truth to necessity and interests; truth that is established as such for convention alone; and so on.

Alberto offered his departing son stern moral advice that would seem to admit no division in the relationship between value/duty and societal morality: "go cheerfully to radiant Florence and immerse yourself in art and literature ... But I hope that your conscience will always remind you that you are not there just to enjoy yourself, but that you have duties to fulfill ... Duty is our guiding light" (cited in Campailla, "Lettere a Carlo" dated 21 October 1905, in *Dialoghi intorno a Michelstaedter*, 10). Yet these principles, Carlo realized, were no longer those of an organic, communitarian world (a world that now existed only as an abstract ideological residue). Rather, they were based on a "fiction" that appeased and distanced the critical and sceptical perspective of the same epistemology that Alberto himself had outlined in *La menzogna*. They functioned to lead one towards an objectivity whose purpose was to allow mimetic participation in the social mechanism, which now had to configure itself as an abstract organicity and draw its "value" from this configuration. Later, in 1909–10, Carlo would write:

> Individual professionals can perfectly handle their trades but do not *know life*; ... yet they do not know whether what they are doing is good, they do not know why and wherefore they live – they do not know themselves: they live without persuasion ... a dull, patchy life ... farmers, cobblers, blacksmiths, merchants, bankers, soldiers, politicians, all carrying out the functions necessary for the individual needs of the city, so that it may go on ... Everyone adapts to the sufficiency of that abstraction of life ... *imitating* ... learning to repeat the obscure actions they see performed by others: the future blacksmith how to handle iron, how to use the hammer, the hero-like attitudes of the blacksmith; the future cobbler how to make tight stitches. ("Appendice II," 150–2)

In 1905, on the train to Florence, eighteen-year-old Carlo had begun to feel the first signs of rebellion swelling up in him, a strange uneasiness that would find expression in a vaguely Dannunzian form of individualism.[26] And so it was first through D'Annunzio that he began to develop the will to resist the standardizing structures of society as a means of forging his own "heroic" personality:

> This evening I went to see D'Annunzio's *Più che l'amore*. – The concept is typically Dannunzian, or rather Nietzschean: The superior man, in his immediate conjunction of love, of enthusiasm, with nature, with the living forces of life, outside of society, thus outside all its moral concepts, has the right to crush, without regard for these concepts, every barrier raised by society between his love and the achievement of his ideal. (letter to Paula dated 12 December 1907, in *Epistolario*, 167)

Here he is contextualizing personal initiative in the model of an energetic life as a response to the "loss of centre," to psychological and social disintegration and the crisis of traditional truths; out of this would arise a *surplus* of an individualism imbued with late-Romantic visions of aesthetically transfiguring reality:

> I want and *am able to* sculpt my life like a work of art, to feel in everything ... an increase in my vitality, and to escape from the necessity of things, idealizing them, mastering them ideally ... Sometimes I feel weak and small and with horror I see the approach of the "stock car" that will transport me into the world as a bourgeois, a triumphant idiot. (letter to Iolanda De Blasi dated 25 April 1907, in *Epistolario*, 202–4)

This would be his perspective up until at least the beginning of 1907.[27] In 1908, however, in "Stelio Effrena (Dialogo della morale e dell'estetica eroica)," the new model of the intellectual he proposed would recognize in the aesthete his own wish – experienced, however, in the form of "contemplative" alienation offered by the artistic model ("As your lips unknowingly speak the truth while they can only speak falsehoods"; in Cerruti: *Carlo Michelstaedter*, 244). It was a desire for liberation, but of the sort that could only be expressed as a farcical and *kitsch* sublimation, following a model that in his final years would take on the negative features of the metaphorical figure of the sophist Callicles:

> "The superior, stronger spirit" – says Plato's Gorgias through the mouth of Callicles – "has the right to assert his personality completely, to *dominate* ..., to crush the inferior will, and the laws instituted by inferior wills for their mutual defense." This is the first enunciation of the individualistic

> principle opposing the social principle … This is the philosophical antithesis at the basis of the problem in [D'Annunzio's] *Più che l'amore* … What a poor thing Gabriele D'Annunzio had done … in the long dialogs only the individualistic thesis is expounded …, [he] gave us neither the handsome hero of a transcendental will … nor the environment … strong in his meanness established as law, – mean, no doubt, but steady and confident in his principles, endowed with the characteristics of moral finiteness. ("'Più che l'amore' di Gabriele D'Annunzio al Teatro di Società," in *La melodia*, 195–7)

Consider the difference between this and another review of *Più che l'amore* written the year before but never published, in which the aesthetic perspective is still positively characterized:

> It is the triumph of individualism. In such a moment, conscience and moral principles are idle words … Corrado Brando … hardened by the wild solitudes of Africa, where he came close to the sources of life above and beyond any social body, is the real model for this individual … He is a hero because of the strength of his character, because of his intellectual value, because of his energy. ("'Più che l'amore' di Gabriele D'Annunzio," in *La melodia*, 180)

This positive characterization is also present in a review of D'Annunzio's *Il piacere* from 1906, in which Michelstaedter wavers between a moral and an aesthetic position:

> Andrea Sp[erelli] is the poet and the artist of form; of music …, of the harmonious voluptuousness … But if we look beyond the outward magnificence … from the moral and social point of view, when *Il piacere* proclaims the absolute dream of personal egoism … and preaches the religion of satisfying any unbridled instinct, it is a despicable work. ("'Il piacere' di Gabriele D'Annunzio," in *La melodia*, 172–3)

The 1908 dialogue "Stelio Effrena" represents the final moment of an ideological crisis that juxtaposes forms of ethical and aesthetic rebellion and recognizes in the latter the foundations for a rebellion against the social environment, which Michelstaedter accepts for its agonistic proposition but then recognizes as compromised by virtue of its belonging to the same social system – as an illusion aimed at mere artistic and contemplative transcendence:

> A: Do not indulge the indolence of our mortal flesh, but rather sublimate it … in this dream of beauty, in the Dionysian orgy … underneath the vain appearances.
>
> B: I am also fascinated by this superior life … but … how does it come about? … You … live a superior life in that you contemplate it … But … if you impress the sign of your dream on your material vitality like you do with other things, how is the materiality of your life different from the materiality of other lives? (Michelstaedter, "Stelio Effrena: Dialogo della morale e dell'estetica eroica," in Cerruti, *Carlo Michelstaedter*, 243–5)

Michelstaedter's reading of D'Annunzio reveals the ambiguity of the heroic dimension of the *aesthetic* superman. He still interprets D'Annunzio's work in relation to the opposition between superman and society. However, this contrast is read not in terms of a tragic effort on the part of the Dannunzian hero to free himself from society's yoke, but rather as a merely internal contrast – that is, in terms of the individual in whom "the potentiality and the necessity of the social environment is contained" ("'Più che l'amore' di Gabriele D'Annnunzio al Teatro di Società," in *La melodia*, 196).

Here, Michelstaedter is critical of D'Annunzio, having recognized that "in his admiration for his superman" (198) he had evoked a reality made up of the subjective elements projected by the superman himself: "Is not the essence of every ancient tragedy the peregrination of the hero along the roads of the conscience … only to fall back down under the laws of the social organism?" ("'Più che l'amore' di Gabriele D'Annunzio," in *La melodia*, 182). The contrast, then, was neither real nor tragic (dialectical, we could say), since it was veiled by an aestheticized perspective to which the real nature of society, as well as its means of repressing individualistic responses, remained extraneous. Due to its inevitable compromise with the same *social* from which it "dreams" of detaching itself, the Dannunzian perspective was inauthentic:

> For this project to excel dramatically it needs the social environment with its laws, its feelings, prejudices, or one of its relentless and convinced representatives who cannot even fathom other ideas, or at least the remains of this world in the soul of the hero … Instead the author bends everyone under the charm of Corrado. (letter to family dated 12 January 1907, in *Epistolario*, 167–8)

Michelstaedter here is beginning to understand the role of social organization in the construction of individualistic responses (even those that are in opposition to its laws). It is precisely the need for a dialectical confrontation between the individual and society that breaks down the aesthetic perspective, contextualizing it in terms of an illusionistic, contemplative, and abstract evasion, which can only be sustained by eliminating the tragic juxtaposition with the environment (society) in which the individual is determined.

For Michelstaedter, D'Annunzio's perspective concealed an ideological relationship with the social structure, because of its organic connection to the new commercial spirit of early industrialism and its complicity with the petite bourgeoisie (intellectual or not), for whom it provided a compensatory, aesthetics-based model for rebuilding, on the new horizon of the metropolis, the space of a nature uncontrolled by the social, a space where the individual could continue to be free. The unresolved dilemma between ethics and aesthetics drove Michelstaedter to abandon D'Annunzio, who now appeared to him as organic to the new social spirit. D'Annunzio's concept of freedom is inevitably marked by the stigma of falsification, having been *produced* by the same structure from which it claims to have liberated itself with such ease. Pieri correctly observes that the presumed instinctual and "natural" liberty of the Dannunzian superman confounds civilization and nature in the image of a supposed and completely artificial liberty: "Bourgeois individuality is offered a path which only agrees with its false mercantile conscience" (*La scienza del tragico*, 71). Therefore, only the very first years of Michelstaedter's work can be characterized as rooted in the "aestheticizing" perspective encountered in D'Annunzio's misleading interpretation of Nietzsche. The second phase of Michelstaedter's thought is characterized by a move towards ethics: "I, on the other hand, feel that is impossible to go on living without some good and some bad at the depths of *my* conscience. And I can guarantee you that all of the Corrado Brandos and Gabrieli [*sic*] D'Annunzios and their *force*, when I read them as men, as what men are supposed to be instead of as works of art, they seem miserable to me" (letter to Iolanda De Blasi dated 14 June 1907, in *Epistolario*, 230).

It is also fundamental to note that through this dialectical relationship with the Dannunzian perspective, Michelstaedter, rejecting D'Annunzio's Nietzsche along with D'Annunzio himself, was able to begin distancing himself from some of the more vital elements of the Nietzschean model, such as his "philosophy of life" and his exaltation of "mood," "sensation," and the "contingent" charged with meaning:

> Out there life is clamoring ... I ask, with the anguish of one who sees the ground he stands on being destroyed, why can I not also abandon myself to the wild impetus of life ... Thus, I believe, spoke one day a Germanic Zarathustra, who was also beastly and tawny. And from him come all the more or less tawny beasts that since then began to infest the world ... [They believe] that their every act becomes pregnant with meaning. ("Di fuori la vita rumoreggia," in *Dialogo della salute e altri scritti*, 185–7)

In his second review of *Più che l'amore*, Michelstaedter would in fact group Nietzsche with Stirner as among the great exponents of sceptical–individualistic thought developed outside the bounds of the ethical prospective. For Michelstaedter, the "understanding of the perpetual flow of things that teaches us to enjoy things in the moment that never returns" (48) – touted by Nino, the antagonist of his *Dialogo della salute* – would represent the point at which life came to consist in the reification of an alienated social foundation.

III. The *Social* Overcoming of Ethical Life and Tragic Thought

Let's go back to 1906. Michelstaedter had enrolled at the Istituto per gli Studi Superiori and was living the life of a student.[28] Unlike his compatriot Scipio Slataper, he had not had the good fortune of being introduced to Giovanni Papini and Giuseppe Prezzolini's world of militant culture. In this period, he made friends with two students of philosophy, Gaetano Chiavacci and Vladimiro Arangio-Ruiz, and wrote his first text, a term paper on Lessing and Baretti (May 1906). In that paper he admits a certain historicism in artistic techniques ("Technique is therefore subject to historical development, to the circumstances of time and place"; *Scritti scolastici*, 3), even while maintaining that philosophy and art are by their very nature purely non-temporal: "Art ... is always one, because there is only one sentiment that belongs to nature, to the world of the absolute ... in brief moments it identifies with nature" (3). This perspective only applies to the early Michelstaedter. It would be incorrect to characterize his later thought as an aesthetic or decadent response that speaks of art as a form of *persuasion*, that breaks down the limits of rhetoric or resists reification: "In its highest expressions this is called apostolate, religion, philosophy, art, education. And the men of these words cover themselves" (*Opere*, 742–3).

But in this term paper Michelstaedter takes a step that will prove decisive, in that it lays the foundations for a personal theory of tragedy: "The argument that settles the matter once and for all … is that unity [is] a natural consequence of the Greek spirit" (*Scritti scolastici*, 8). In other words, Greece (in particular the Greece of Sophocles and Socrates)[29] begins to be seen as a world that is alien to the reified structure of consciousness, as a naturally structured society that can be referred to as an experience of "uniformity between thought and life" ("Tolstoi," in *La melodia*, 209). This world can be contrasted with a society experienced in the form of abstract thought reified into theory, a "second nature," in which individual consciousness is oppressed by the rationalized contingency of need: "In order for my eyes to see … it is necessary that they not be the eyes of hunger, sleep, lust, the eyes of whatever mocks my will, but of a consciousness greater than my will and directed at what can sate me more lastingly (that plants my hopes on solid ground)" (*Opere*, 719).

Michelstaedter expands this analysis in two directions. Now abandoning the Dannunzian model, he proposes the reactivation of the forms of artistic tragedy along a Romantic line that in the years to come would be given contemporary form by the works of Ibsen and Tolstoy.[30] Though his attention to Tolstoy is part of a general European interest in the Russian author at the turn of the century (promoted in particular by Romain Rolland), Michelstaedter – and here the association with Ibsen exemplifies this – detaches Tolstoy from the evangelical–socialist context and injects him into a bitter confrontation of a moral and social character with an explicit tragic value, centred on the dialectical relationship between the individual and society. In this way he turns to an artistic model centred on an ethical good, one that avoids temptations of an impressionistic–aestheticizing quality, having recognized in them the same social mode of operation:

> Ibsen wants man to learn how to break the circle of lies that surrounds him, to learn to want the truth …; he must fight the falsehood inside him … Tolstoy does not want fight from man, but devotion – man must learn to resist the enticements of society, which he considers based on falseness and arrogance; man must pull out and abandon the whole system of life … In contemporary world literature, while others descend in a quest for details – from Oscar Wilde to Gabriele D'Annunzio – Ibsen

> and Tolstoy emerge from the crowd because they are not satisfied with just expressing the superficial sensations of their souls. ("Tolstoi," in *La melodia*, 211–12)[31]

Just as he starts to shape this idea of tragedy as an antagonistic/moral instance, he begins – clearly following Schopenhauer – to analyse the ideological structures of the social mechanism that relate to the will.[32] At this point, through Schopenhauer's analysis of the concepts of "time" and "will," he experiences an epistemological crisis (after experiencing the dialectical confrontation with society). The crisis consists in the ontological breaking apart of the *Grund* within a perspective of temporality expressed as the inane repetition of the mechanism of "willing," which excludes the self-sufficiency of Being: a condition of ontological precariousness that on the ideological level is expressed as a reference to the inauthenticity of the social structure (*Zivilisation*) and its contradictions, *Zivilisation* becoming the conceptual expression of time (temporality). This means that the breaking apart of the ontological *Grund* (the perception of the being as an expression of non-substantiality) is connected to the negativity of the *temporal*, to the destabilization created by becoming, and here in particular by the incessant transformation of the will of the subject. And it is in a temporal dimension that the subject is estranged from that which his will desires: "he finds himself having to combat a desperate battle with time" (*Parmenide ed Eraclito*, 24).

Michelstaedter's response, at this time, echoes the Romantic model of representing symbolic value (the lost image of *unity*) in the tragic conflict between the hero's duty towards himself and his respect for social conventions. Moving beyond Schopenhauer, his response is expressed as a tragic artistic value: "any essential definition of tragedy is a definition of art itself" ("La catarsi tragica," in *La melodia*, 51). While romantically acknowledging the disintegration of the "full" sense of life in the social mechanism, he activates an artistic experience that re-creates a unitary world as a device of thought in which the lost organicity/unity finds a new voice. Though at this point his analysis remains tied to the possibility of an artistic (and theoretical) "reconstruction" of a seemingly disintegrated reality, the juxtaposing of the absolute *value* that the tragic form expresses for him and the disintegration of that value in the social mechanism allows him to begin considering those same values that society presents in terms of a *mere* (and this will be a fundamental point) utilitarian satisfaction:

> Let us look around: – on every side we see the multitude of "those who succeeded," who are on the "high road that leads – as Tolstoy says – to certain profit," ... of which the purpose in life is life itself ...: we live in a world of corpses; corpses that eat, drink, sleep, and talk, but that nonetheless are still corpses. ("Tolstoi," in *La melodia*, 208–9)

In a term paper written for Professor Vitelli (October 1907), "Il coro nella teoria e in alcune sue forme originali in Italia," Michelstaedter attempts to historicize the crisis of the tragic. Considering Sophocles as its highest expression, he describes the fall of the "tragic" both in the symbolic microcosm of the Classical world (Sophocles–Euripides–Horace) and in the broader context of modernist culture. In this narrative, Sophocles (and then Ibsen)[33] expresses the lost moment of universal truth, beyond the "anarchy of chiaroscuro" that bestows ambiguity on the social: the moment when the heroic experience told by tragedy clashes with the negative pole of society from which it has separated:

> Perhaps that is what Sophocles meant when he said he considered men as they should be ... drawn out of dull, real life, where things are all overlapping one another ... provided with all the features that contribute to give universal, ideal truth to the sentiment that drives them, without any overlapping. ("Il coro nella teoria e in alcune sue forme originali in Italia," in *Scritti scolastici*, 124)

Michelstaedter reveals a real social organicity in Sophocles's tragedy, one experienced in the "form of conflict" between the chorus and the hero:

> Harmony becomes moral harmony, equilibrium, balance of principles, of passions. And the knowledge of these becomes the factor of fear and compassion ... [Tragedy] removes them from the contingency of the moment to speak generally, to tell of their value and absolute power ... The voice of the chorus ... does not soothe, it does not mitigate the impression of the action, but rather intensifies its hues and makes more evident the tragic clash between the need for a single passion and the need for moral balance, which must be rebuilt through the catastrophe. ("Il coro nella teoria," in *Scritti scolastici*, 122–3)[34]

The transition to Euripides's expression of the tragic brings with it, instead, a form of psychological disaggregation in which the psychology of the individual itself expresses the disaggregation of society:

> Euripides' tragedies deal with individual organisms that carry within themselves the contrast of differing urges, the agony of doubt, that bear tragic conflict and catastrophe; harmony is no longer to be found in the environment, but in the heart ... psychological tragedy ... Because in everyday life men do not have an ultimate goal that cannot be surrendered at the cost of life, but if they do have an exaggerated passion there are other effects by which it is neutralized. ("Il coro nella teoria," in *Scritti scolastici*, 128–9)

In this tragedy "every man is his own chorus" (*Scritti scolastici*, 56). It is the tragedy of a social disconnection (atomization) that reveals the emergence of individual consciousness as a moment of this social destructuring: "And the chorus? I ask for inhabitants and they respond with individuals ... the environment does not exist and the individual triumphs" (131). This moment is acted out by the hero, whose "reflection" surpasses action (we find the identical principle in Pirandello's *On Humor*),[35] whose reference to a past and future time (memory and foresight) muddles up the present. The "will" is shattered and dispersed into the countless streams of contingency that reflection is able to express, and the contingent "particular" and the multiple triumph: "When man pauses in his action 'reflection' sets in: his position with regard to the past, his position with regard to the future ... All of life is exhausted in these two elements. From their infinite combinations come the infinite sides of life" (*Scritti scolastici*, 51).

At this point Michelstaedter could still be considered from a perspective that places utopia within an ethical framework in which the tragic conclusion appears as the reconciliation of meaning and life. Here he could have completely rejected the Euripidean prospective and hypostatized, formally and aesthetically, the Sophoclean principle as a possible reconstruction of the shattered collective truth and of the broken social unity. However, his next step gives us an idea of how his perspective would now develop. He was moving away from a modernist tragic perspective (in which the *tragic* is in opposition to social and epistemological ambiguity) towards a concept of tragedy tied to an idea of life that is much more material than (merely) cultural. In fact, Euripidean disaggregation is not followed by dispersion, by fragmentation, by ambiguous contingency, but by solid morality. This, however, is not the "community" morality of the Sophoclean chorus expressed in the "form of conflict," but the morality of isolated individuals who justify their material, contingent, and becoming wills as adaptations to what on the ethical level is expressed by a chorus become society.[36] Thus in Michelstaedter the epistemological crisis is linked to what "rationalizes" it and is already related to the social structure:

> They stand before the chorus ... but in it they find not the contingency of reality, but rather the ideal form of consciousness that comes from the people, and from which they repeat their origin ... The material interest of the people considered as an entity is none other than moral interest, its selfishness is love of justice, whatever is good for it is good, whatever is bad for it is evil ... A multitude of people becomes a society precisely by associating the interests of individuals, assuming as a canon of social defense that which was formerly a criterion of individual defense: thus personal selfishness become[s] justice, what was bad for the individual becomes evil in general ... Every infringement of its moral laws is personal damage to this collective entity ... While for the aggregate it is a material condition of existence, for the individual mind it is a moral principle ... The chorus ... only invokes the triumph of laws for the laws, only the good of the city. (*Scritti scolastici*, 124–6)

In "Euripidean" time the "chorus ... cannot help repeating common places" ("La catarsi tragica," in *La melodia*, 56). It can only respond to the person by referring him back to the precepts of society.

Therefore, with his analysis of the tragic, Michelstaedter is already mapping out the direction in which his intellectual reflections will take him. The existential condition of atomized individuals in a disaggregated society is sublimated in the minds of those same individuals into principles of a moral nature that the same society conveys in an act of surreptitious reaggregation:

> Since the concept of society cannot be defined if not with the transformation of material interest into moral interest for the society as a society, ... while for the whole it is a material condition of existence, for the individual mind it is a moral principle. (*Scritti scolastici* 125)

2 The Individual Will/Need and the Social Second Nature

I. The Light of Will and the "Direct Mode," or Michelstaedter's Version of Specialization

With the passage through Euripides's mechanism of the tragic – which is clearly the moment of modernity, the moment in which the organic tie between individual and society is severed, the time of social atomization – even the will, Michelstaedter says, is individualized: "*the will is at every point a will for determinate things*" (*Persuasion*, 15). Will cannot be expressed as a noumenal structure of reality; we cannot assume it to be the metaphysical principle of the *Wille* or an abstraction of the "determinate wills." Michelstaedter's analysis of the mechanism of the tragic in Euripides allows him to move beyond Schopenhauer's interpretation of the will. The will cannot designate an ontological principle of life, but it *can* a modality of life, which Michelstaedter will describe in the first pages of *Persuasion and Rhetoric*, using the metaphor of the "weight":

> A weight hangs suspended from a hook, being suspended, is suffers because it cannot fall: ... we free it from its dependence, letting it go so that it might satisfy its hunger for what lies below ... But at none of the points attained is it content to stop; it still wants to fall ... Nor will any future point be such as to render it content ... Every time a point is made present, it will be emptied of all attraction, no longer being below; thus does it *want at every point the point below it*, and those attract it more and more. It is always drawn by an equal hunger. (*Persuasion*, 9)[1]

The weight's will (which is also its need) does not allow it to *consist* at any point. It is condemned to continuous movement (to continue to *tend towards something*), to continue to pursue the possession of other things – that is, correlation. The will is inevitably a non-being, a form of lacking, because it is unable to escape the logic of correlativity. The will of the subject always includes an object (the object of desire). As such, the will can only appear as power (*potenza*), the power the isolated subject expresses as a temporal relationship with an object, as a momentary (hence inevitably fictitious) attribution of value that the subject, in the act of *willing*, believes can be stably determined.[2]

This is what Michelstaedter refers to as the "direct mode." In his relationship with the object, the subject – following the necessity imposed by his own will[3] – affirms himself as power (in the relationship). For the duration of that willing, he ontologically absolutizes the real as a whole in the desired object (he considers the desired object as all of reality). He even absolutizes himself – his will – in the contingency of his relationship with that object: "the illusion that the will to be has an essence in itself in its potential form as a persistent *power* outside of contingency" (*Sfugge la vita*, 130). Michelstaedter defines this as the "affirmation of inadequate individuality." It represents the moment in which the subject finds the sense of the world and himself through the "taste" of things alone, through the interpretation of the real as a whole on the basis of that taste: "the *taste* of things ... will represent for me this illusion, since in every thing I will feel that it is right with regard to the continuation of my life in that way, and with that specific content" (*Parmenide ed Eraclito*, 15).

Determined in such a way, the consciousness of the subject constitutes only a limited satisfaction: the "illusion of persuasion." The contingency of the relationship, which is expressed as the will for "pleasure" and as self-preservation through the satisfaction of that will, crystallizes itself through this illusion by feigning an absolute subject in what – by satisfying the subject's needs – appears to him as absolute reality, containing in itself (as supratemporal meaning) his whole *persona*:

> The organism is gradually determined in relation to different things – but there is the inherent sense in each determination that it does not occur for itself but rather inasmuch as it is necessary for the continuation of the organism. This is the sweet taste that everything in life has ... Inasmuch

> as something is pleasant, the whole person is therein *involved*. – And as it converges on that thing as its *own*, so it draws therefrom the illusion of individuality. What I like, what is useful to me: that is my conscience: that is my reality. (Michelstaedter, "Dialogo della salute," in *Dialogo della salute*, 44)

Therefore, the consciousness of the individual subject (and his consciousness of himself as subject) is nothing more than the state of need of the same subject; that need is what determines his disposition towards the real, superimposing his own consciousness on the object in the moment in which it is desired. This understanding of "consciousness" in Michelstaedter should have been enough to dissuade critics who sought to link him to Bergson on the basis of his idea of "time": for Michelstaedter there can be no separation between "spatiality" as a characteristic of things and "duration" as a characteristic of consciousness, because spatiality has already invaded consciousness insofar as it continuously redefines itself in relation to the desired object. Consciousness, in its subjugation to will/need, is already reified in the object, in the correlation with the object. This is why for Michelstaedter the relationship I–World cannot simply be understood as a cognitive and unidirectional experience. For him, subjective consciousness is formed by the world through the medium of possibilities of *consistency* (in a social role, for example) that the real offers the subject.[4] As such, the cognitive act, inasmuch as it is dictated by the need of the subject, will always be the reification of itself in a real that expresses the forms of that need. Consciousness inserts itself into the space in which the relationship between the subject and the object is torn, reconstructing that relationship in abstract forms alone, with the foresight that these conditions will repeat themselves and that this will allow the subject to satisfy his need:

> Man attributes to things that do not have in themselves an absolute value as determined things … an absolute value … The things that are necessary for him to satisfy his needs become a reality for him because he can rely on them for the future. This reliance for the future is the actual reality in every present: consciousness. (*Parmenide ed Eraclito*, 49)

The world will then be represented according to the will/need, subject to time, of each single individual:

> The world of each is *the* world; and that world's value is the correlative of its *valency* ... His *certain end*, his *reason for being*, the *sense* that each act has for him, again are nothing but his self-continuation ... is none other than *the will of himself in the future* ... But while lacking himself in the present he wills himself in the future – which he *cannot* do but along the way of singular determinations organized so as to make him continue wanting in such a manner in the future. He circles around the way of singular needs and escapes himself always. He cannot *possess himself*, have reason for himself, inasmuch as it is *necessary* for him to attribute value to his own *persona*, which is determined in things, and to the things he needs in order to continue. For by such things he is *distracted in time* along the way ... And man, all while rejoicing in the affirmation, senses that this *persona* is not his, that he does not possess it ... He senses other infinite wills, ... he senses the flow of what is outside his power ... The known (finite) weave of illusory individuality, where pleasure casts its light, is not so tight that the obscurity of the (infinite) unknown does not penetrate. And his pleasure is contaminated by a *dull and continuous* pain. (*Persuasion*, 23–5)

The subject believes he is ontologically safeguarding himself by representing himself in the possession of the object. Thus the object, through the will of possession, becomes a representation of the presumed absoluteness of the subject himself. This is also why, in Michelstaedter, we find a theory regarding the disappearance of the I, just as we do in the most important interpreters of modernism: "this which I call 'I,' but which I am not." (Michelstaedter, "Risveglio," in *Poesie*, 69). But Michelstaedter – and herein lies a fundamental difference – does not arrive at the decay of the I through a sceptical–relativist perspective that reduces it to a bundle of sensations, to mere form (as in Mach). On the contrary, in Michelstaedter the I places the motives for its own ontological significance – and as a consequence the ontological significance of the real – in the object towards which the will moves it (correlation), and in its inability to ontologically affirm itself, it disappears:

> The anguish of the mystery is what ... grips the heart of man when ... he wants to raise his head out of the river of relativity and he realizes that this means leaving himself. Since his entire being is none other than dispositions in relation to other things, things in which his "I" is contained. (*Parmenide ed Eraclito*, 23)

Therefore the I is non-existent since each time it bases its own identity (or its own cognitive capacity, which is one and the same thing) on the possession of things illuminated by its will: "that which you want is to be absolute, and the whole of your will is nothing more than contingency" (*Il prediletto*, 125) The will casts light on only a limited and contingent space of the real (the space occupied by the relationship between itself and the object), but in that moment that space (interpreted as a *possession* of the object) is the whole of reality for the subject. The will, for Michelstaedter, expresses the theoretical point of view of *specialization*, the reduction of the real to the limited space of a specific task/desire:

> It [the subject] is deprived by time of *consisting* at every point ... *There is no possession of any thing* – only *changing with regard* to a thing, *entering into a relation* to a thing. Each thing *has* inasmuch as *it is had. Determinacy is an attribution of value: consciousness*. Each thing at every point does not possess but is the will for determinate possession: that is, a determinate attribution of value: a determinate consciousness. At that point of the present when it enters *into a relation* with a given thing, it believes it is in the act of possession, but it is only a finite *potenza* [power] ... We isolate a single determination of the will, for example, the stomach of a body, as if it lived for its own self: the stomach is all hunger, the attribution of value to food, the consciousness of the world insofar as it is edible ... When two substances combine chemically, each satisfying the determinacy of the other, each departs from its nature, altered in reciprocal absorption. (*Persuasion*, 15–17)

The will expresses a possibility of possession that the subject interprets as *value*, because for the duration of that desire/willing, the characteristics of the desired object (whose possession should guarantee pleasure) represent the way in which the subject interprets all of reality. If I am hungry, I am all stomach, and so on:

> What is the real taste of things? ... It is necessary that it's not the eye of hunger, tiredness, libido that taunts my will, but a vaster consciousness than this will of mine, which would aim at something that would satisfy me in the long term (deposit its hope in a stable place). ("I professionisti della filosofia," in *Dialogo sulla salute*, 200)

Naturally, this "hunger" (need) is not exhausted in the simple tending towards objects, because from this perspective, other human beings as well are considered suitable objects for satisfying momentary needs: "he must sate his hunger with his correlative as a cure for being able to have hunger again, until the day arrives in which other chains of ... determinations, of causes override it, and ... it steadily moves ahead transforming itself without end" (*Parmenide ed Eraclito*, 30–1). Significantly, Michelstaedter continues to use the word "hunger" also with regard to interpersonal relationships: "Nor can a man seeking refuge in the *persona* he loves satisfy his hunger" (*Persuasion*, 10). The functioning of the will that determines, over and over, the consciousness of the subject is analogously repeated in relationships both with objects, in the strictest sense of the word, and with other human beings:

> It is mine because it represents the certainty of being able to satisfy my hunger in eating it ... And loved ones in the same manner are necessary ... But a mutual need always restrains you ... Thus each time the animal sees the thing as *his*, and he leaps towards it to sate all of his hunger ... – but he only sates his hunger in relation to that thing. ("Il dialogo della salute," in *Dialogo della salute*, 38–42)

As Marco Fortunato correctly noted: "in the moment in which he is dominated by his hunger, he could care less if the vast non-edible portion of the world is there or not" (*Aporie della decisione*, 49). In that moment, the real in its entirety *is* that which is expressed in the will to possess. Michelstaedter's persuasion, by contrast, does not aim to satisfy the hunger of the single, momentary need; rather, it works to counteract the problem of hunger itself: "he must be sufficient to the hunger of the world, not to the *flavor* of that man" (*Persuasion*, 52).

Michelstaedter, distancing himself once again from contemporary interpretations of a Heraclitean stamp, relies on Heraclitus's teachings to describe the partial and specialized vision that allows for the reconciliation of the particular case into abstract forms of the particular and momentary will. Michelstaedter – who includes Heraclitus among the great "persuaded" – cites the Pre-Socratic philosopher (in particular *Fragment*, 26: "A person in the night kindles a light for himself") in order to clarify what he has defined as "determined will." This is the "light" – metaphorically lit by the god of *philospychia* (love of life) – that gives the subject the ontological illusion of *consisting* in that determined will, of determining himself ontologically in the partial vision connected to the momentary will/need of the object:

> He [the god of *philospychia*] illuminates the things that are useful, and he makes them shine as long as the thing is useful ... The entire future of the animal shines in that light ... The animal who is only in part satisfied, turns to where another light appears to him – that the benevolent god lights for him ... It leads him across the obscurity of things in its illuminated wake, so that he can *continue*. ("Dialogo della salute," in *Dialogo della salute*, 42)

Thus Michelstaedter's theory of pleasure is closely tied to his interpretation of "will" and "correlativity" (the interconnectedness of *willing* subjects). For the subject the things of the world exist in relation to his will to possess, which promises pleasure – pleasure that in turn corresponds to the ontological guarantee that possession itself promises: "The affirmation of things that bring pleasure is the inadequate affirmation of possession, the inadequate affirmation of individuality" (*Sfugge la vita*, 134). The will to possess a single determined thing promises (as foreknowledge of the future) the enjoyment of the entire reality and thus the eternal ontological *consistency* of the subject by means of the satisfaction of that desire: "The satisfaction of the determinate deficiencies allows the complex of determinations to remain deficient ... because the *criterion* of that determination's self-affirmation is *the foresight of the others*" (*Persuasion*, 16). This provides the subject with the illusion of consciousness, which is one and the same as the illusion of ontological consistency: "The sweet music of life that things whisper to the *healthy* man, that each one he sees as his own and each one says to him *'you are'*" ("Dialogo della salute," in *Dialogo della salute*, 53).

The subject tries to take hold of his own pleasure in a relationship with the object so as to ensure his ontological consistency (and the "names" he gives to things are part of the same mechanism) as well as his freedom. This freedom is the ability to want that which gives you pleasure. The perspective of pleasure ends, however, with possession itself (as with the "weight"), annulling itself in the desire for (in temporality) a new possession: "The thing that I wanted is nothing for me in the moment in which I possess it because I no longer have any desire to have it in that moment but in the moment that follows. And every moment annulls itself in the past while the will projects itself on the future" (*Sfugge la vita*, 128).[5]

Pleasure, however, is also dominated by correlativity (of the relationship), and thus the pleasure of the subject is subordinate to the equally relative universe of the will of others. Only on the social level ("connective mode") can the will of others be subdued, rationalized, and stabilized into abstract forms to which all people can refer, but this stabilizing of the will(s) of others also implies stabilizing the will of the subject who *wills*. The possibility of pleasure would mean adapting to that which the social consensus has established as pleasure. Michelstaedter explains the entire mechanism in the form of a fable:

> Once upon a time there was a fortunate town ... It was paradise on earth ... A strange fate hung over that town ... Perhaps it was the same pleasant air that contained within it the seeds of evil. – It is true that from that strange air another particularity of that blessed town was born: that crystalline water that poured forth from every angle of the shaded springs and lured everyone to touch their lips to it lost its goodness as soon as any man had it in his mouth, so that other water always attracted him leaving him unable to satisfy himself. And the same was true of the fruit and the women – and of every other thing: as such prescient men guaranteed themselves the springs, they guaranteed themselves a greater abundance of fruit through more work, they guaranteed themselves women through pacts, not imagining each time that [as] they were about to use them that they would find themselves in the same circumstances. ("Era il paradiso terrestre," in *La melodia*, 151–2)

This partial and utilitarian vision in relation to that which the world offers represents Michelstaedter's analysis of the epistemological phenomenon of "specialization," that is, the impossibility of seeing all of reality together (totality), a vision reduced to the partial and contingent towards which the momentary need/pleasure pulls us: "everyone finds the taste of bread different after a meal than before" ("I professionisti della filosofia," in *Dialogo della salute*, 199).[6] The will's instrument for cognitively grasping the real is nothing more than the determination generated by the consciousness following its need. Therefore, that real is only a partial angle illuminated by the need, and as such it appears differently every time. The world will be interpreted differently each time according to the momentary desire for pleasure of each person.

For Michelstaedter, need/will necessarily expresses itself in the contingency (i.e., not in the relativist contrast between thought as absolute and life as flux). Indeed, his theory of consciousness inserts itself into the moment of involuntary abstraction carried out by the subject, recognizing the sublimation of momentary needs into absolute values as a form of reconciliation of the individual subject's need into the larger structures of the social need (what Michelstaedter will call the "connective mode"). Michelstaedter will define this as a passage from "taste" (*sapore*: the simple desire of the subject to obtain pleasure) to "knowledge" (*sapere*: the adaptation of the "taste" desired by the subject in the pre-existing social structures).

Instead, in the "direct mode" that we are analysing, the presumed ontological *consistency* that the possession of the object offers to the subject is continuously being shattered. First, because his desire for the object exists in the realm of temporality, which modifies both the desire and the object itself: "men who attribute essence to a determined thing negate its essence when it is transformed according to its nature" (*Parmenide ed Eraclito*, 17). Second, because "objects" (this includes living beings) are *willing* in turn. As such the ontological security/insurance that should arise is continuously postponed and placed at risk.

The functioning of the determined will of the individual subject, the unity of sense of self that the subject experiences in determining all of reality on the contingent basis of his will, opens the way to a real that is founded on – this is why Michelstaedter claims that the real is "the sum of things willed/desired" – the continuous attempt of one entity to overpower the others. In this system, each subject views the other as the means (a thing among things) by which to stabilize its own ontological instability.

If in the "direct mode" reality is the continuous contrast of subjective abstractions dictated by the will, and if the reason the subject expresses (the value he gives to his actions) is only "a particular objective which becomes a dominant form when contemplated singularly" (*Sfugge la vita*, 171), then reality for each subject will be that which adapts to that desire, so as to realize its "usefulness": "He *comprehends* what he *can grasp*" (*Persuasion*, 24) As such, the value of every thing *contained in the real* comes to be based on its possible use only.

What the will expresses, in the contingent structures of "temporality" and the correlative "relationship," becomes for the subject what is "just," because that is all the subject sees. It is the source of his illusory *consisting*: he considers as a whole the limited space his will illuminates (specialization). A different subject, equally prey to this specializing vision, will do the same: for all subjects, reality, considered in this form, becomes a set of usable things, a set of objects (means) to attach to their perception in order to satisfy their need and thereby ontologically *consist*: "But the others want to talk and not listen, – and so they all slaughter and contradict each other" ("Dialogo della salute," in *Dialogo della salute*, 55). The system of correlative flowing is not the expression of a relational *eros*, but the *neikos* (contrast) of a continuous attempt at domination driven by need/will, whereby everyone, depending on what is useful to each, asserts himself with violence, reifying reality:

> The flower sees the propagation of its pollen in the bee, while the bee sees sweet food for its larvae in the flower. In the embrace of the two organisms each sees "itself as if in a mirror" ... Neither knows whether its affirmation coincides with the other's or whether conversely its affirmation deprives the other of the future – killing it; each knows only that this is good for it and uses the other as a means to its own end, material for its own life, while it is itself material for the other's life ... And when coincidence does not provide for the continuation of both, when the cog of one large or small gear does not fit into the cavities of another or vice versa, *inimical violence* manifests itself. For where one affirms itself the other cannot, and if both do not perish in the struggle, one must concede or succumb ... In the other's eye he senses the obscurity of a power that transcends him. (*Persuasion*, 32–3)

II. The Vortex of Correlativity, or Michelstaedter's Version of Relativism

The functioning of the will locks the individual within the mechanism of correlativity. The mechanism of correlativity is a relational system in which every thing is contingent for two reasons: first, because what the subject interprets as value is merely the momentary affirmation of his will/need; and second, because the implementation of that value can only come about through a relationship with another subject: "it is not an autonomous system, but the expression of a succession of relationships that constitute both consciousness and correlate together, which reciprocally determine one another" (La Rocca, 46)

For the subject, the object is instrumental. Being instrumental, it ontologically reconfirms the subject. The subject actually confers value – not on the object, however, but on the "relationship" of himself with the object. Therefore the reification that the functioning of the subject's will carries out on the object (in the "direct mode") actually represents the reification of the entry into contact (the relationship) of the subject with that object. The objectivity attained (the ontological value that the will looks for through pleasure) is that same relationship. The subject, then, will place the implementation of his will in the object (rather than in himself, as he imagines). In the "direct mode" every subject is in this way confronted by another subject, who considers him as a thing; and every subject is a thing since he bases the satisfaction of his will (and as such his ontological consistency) not in himself, but rather in the characteristics of the object he would like to make his own. This is the mechanism that Michelstaedter describes with his metaphorical "dialogue with the foot," in which the possession of the object (the "foot") translates into subjugation to the characteristics of it: "The owner has never walked! Never walked! ... Why did you, utterly still, say 'walk.' And I, poor devil, would begin to manoeuvre ... Is walking not a property of yours?" ("Appendice II," 160–1).

Within the system of correlativity, the relationships between the subject and the objects suitable for satisfying his desire (i.e., his need) are objectified. This assumed objectivity is an indication of the ontological *inconsistency* of the subject himself, who is incapable of consisting ontologically (in the "direct mode") outside of the framework of relationships: "if my living is the will to be – that is, the lack of being – the world that I experience, the things that are real for me, in their correlativity to my will, must also be non-beings, and I will never acquire any real essence from the relationship in which I find myself with them" (Fratta, 32).

The continuous dissatisfaction of the will drives the subject to attempt to regulate, in a subjective manner (without yet relying on social structures), the contingent elements that he believes are thwarting his possession. In other words, the subject acts with the intention of reifying the will of other subjects. The movement the *neikos* (contrast) expresses as "need" is determined as the epistemological willingness to use whatever is abstractly contained in reality (the ability to exploit what reality makes available, including other men):

> I believe, the man who glanced into the mind of the average man would find there a truly strange and deformed image of the world and of men and himself ... He would see there, for example, the taste of food and the odor and impression of taking in food, and the maker and seller of food, mixed all in a single complex of obscure dispositions; and in connection with this – if one were dealing with a clerk – another complex with paper façades, rows of calculations, tabulation surfaces ... while in the middle would be

> shadows of men, some without heads, others without legs (marks of recognition: legs, noses), some marked by a "yes," others by a "no," and the impression of a kiss or gnashing of teeth ... along with an infernal jumble of names, information, words, numbers ... But through the whole tangle he would see the pangs of insatiable hunger. (*Persuasion*, 127–8)

In the *neikos* the subject's need (his desire for pleasure: the light shone by the god of *philopsychia*) lives with no care for the will of the object:

> Chlorine, for example, has always been so gluttonous that it is completely dead, but if we bring it back to life by placing it in the *proximity* of hydrogen, it lives only for the hydrogen. Hydrogen is the single value of the world to it: the world; its life is uniting with hydrogen ... But once love is satisfied, *that light too shall be extinguished* ... Their love is not for the satisfied life, not for being persuaded, but for the mutual need that ignores another's life ... for each has seen in the other only its own self-assertion. (*Persuasion*, 13–14)

Michelstaedter describes the violent action of affirmation using an apologue titled *Paolino*. At the beginning of the story, the main character, a young boy, is anxious to obtain the status of "man," to participate in the social consensus (in the social knowledge)[7] with his own determined place in it. Particularly fond of one of the family hens, Paolino is distraught when he sees the family cook preparing to slaughter the animal. The violent affirmation of dominance over an other (the hen) in the correlative universe in which the subject wants to satisfy his personal pleasure (here it is "hunger") is associated by the cook with the process of becoming an adult: "Paolino ... these are tantrums for a baby not men" (in *La melodia*, 159).[8]

Reality is the expression of a continuous attempt at domination in which the need to affirm one's need (and thereby *consist* ontologically) constantly collides (*neikos*) with the wills/needs of other individuals: "both in the defense of the right to exist of that which they hold to be true and determined *just because they arrived* there, as well as by destructing the truth of others in their self-affirmation" ("Appendice VI").

Therefore, every subject tries, with violence, to subjugate others (the *objects*) to his own perception, epistemology, ethics, will, and reason:

> Everyone can show you how the causes, the needs behind his act or demand, result as mathematically just: the stone is right in falling when the earth

> attracts it, the oppressed ant is right in protesting when the stone weighs on it; ... everybody has the right to live ... each affirmation is just to its need. But no one *is just* ... If he is the son of certain causes and needs, he does not have *reason* in himself; and the affirmation of whichever *persona* he has is always, because irrational, *violent*. In whatever manner he asks to continue, the necessities of his existence speak in him, and insofar as he affirms as *just* what *is just to him*, he denies what is just to others. (*Persuasion*, 45–7)

Understood in this way, *reason* is not based on justice. Here the correlative of contrasting and contingent needs (in which every individual considers others as objects, as things, annexable to his own will) is a space of violent acts (also, cognitively speaking, "forms") of individual subjects who are prey to their needs:

> He *wants* something, he affirms the mode, the *persona* of his will. At the point where he places a real thing outside himself, he expresses the flavor that things have for him, his consciousness, his knowing – whichever it may be. In his illusion he says that what "*is for him*" simply "is"; he calls it good or bad insofar as it pleases or displeases him ... But if his *persona* were real, had reason in itself, the thing it affirms would be ... real and absolute just as it is ... But because he *needs to reaffirm it* with his affirmation of his knowing, he presents it as *not real in itself* – and presents his own *persona*, its correlate, as insufficient. Now with the reaffirmation of his insufficient *persona* he presumes to attribute value to this thing. (*Persuasion*, 67)

Michelstaedter will use the image of fog as a metaphor to describe this system: "the fog of correlative mutations spreads" ("Appendice II," 181); "the fog of things that are and are not" ("Dialogo della salute," in *Dialogo della salute*, 80). A multiplicity of wills that mutually determine one another in an infinite system of relationships in which what appears as possession, as a determination of value, is only the momentary (temporal) relationship established by the will itself: "Men attribute essence to things as they see them and insofar as they enter into relation with them, insofar as they need them" (*Parmenide ed Eraclito*, 40).

Existence consists of these entwined relationships among wills that are constantly transforming and always in search of the objects they want to possess. Reality becomes "the sum of willed things" (*Opere*, 759), which endlessly redetermine themselves as value, since the willed object becomes, for the subject and for the duration of his willing, the whole of his reality.

Nevertheless Michelstaedter realizes that stopping at an explanation of the problem in epistemological terms is an integral part of the problem itself, because it corresponds to the determination of "sufficiency" that purports to subsume reality into a theoretical space (e.g., the metaphysical principle of the *Wille*) that presents the same reified structure – the same *need* – of the mechanism of the determinate will. In other words, it is not a matter of rejecting Schopenhauer's view because of the metaphysics implicit in his system (this is the nihilist point of view), since using the will as an epistemological picklock for a cognitive analysis, which re-presents a reconciled (albeit pessimistically) reality, means providing a theoretical justification for the motif of "deficiency" (the constant willing in time) that the determinate will continually reiterates:

> Life is will to live, will is deficiency, deficiency is pain, every life is pain. But every creature that lives believes it is alive and that it has life; and for every creature pain is always mute and continuous so that it does not call it pain – but it calls pain the revelations of non-existence of its believed possession ... So even its pain is called according to its own illusion ... It laments the loss of the thing, not its losability: the unreality of possession. And in order to live it turns to new things ... But whoever really wants life refuses to live in relation to those things ... Wanting true possession, the mute, obscure suffering of all things takes shape and unfolds in him. His life is a refusal and a fight against all the temptations of illusory satisfactions. ("Pessimista è l'imperfetto pessimista," in *La melodia*, 115–16)

Regarding Schopenhauer's pessimism, Michelstaedter in fact will write:

> As it often happens with him, he limits himself to putting the error in logical terms that make it appear a mathematical problem, and he doesn't care to show the necessity of the error implied in the general principle of life that let live those who had denied any reason for living. And in fact that's what happened to him, who lived a long life professing pessimism. ("Appunti su Aristotele," in *Opere*, 839–40)[9]

Michelstaedter characterizes Schopenhauer's *noluntas* (non-will) – the experience of "quiet," of a space alien to the tearing of empirical life – not simply as a consolatory myth, but as a reiteration of the precondition for the separation of life from thought, in which life is attributed with the stable features of theory in an attempt to stabilize it. In our world, in Euripides's world, there is no place for "a healthy individual who is *one* thing, not two" (*Scritti scolastici*, 55) – life and thought – because the epistemological destructuring requires a doubling of the empirical instance into an abstract "form" of *theorein*, a form that the new chorus (society) can convey (and we will see how) both in the guise of Becoming (the vanity of the world, the delight of the "flow," etc.) and in that of the ethical *ought-to-be*. These abstract forms are those in which society itself comes to be expressed (science, art, philosophy, etc.), being the result of a separation of theory and practice – an abstract determination, in the sphere of knowledge, of a determinate will therein acknowledged as stable:

> But wherein lies the reason for the beauty of a gesture? Evidently within a stronger beam in which the personality is better revealed. At the bottom of this work of art is the criterion of the value of the personality – *the moral criterion* ...; whenever an individual envisages moral perfection or senses an artistic harmony he gives shape – to the extent allowed by his personal capacities – to the aspiration for truth found in every man: his interest is a universal interest ... it is a *good* act ... But you might object: if we examine this man's moral view we will find that it has the form made necessary and defined by the place he occupies in life: it is the result of his particular interests ... so the interest is the interest of utilitarianistically coordinating the various elements of his nature. ("Il coraggio," in *La melodia*, 48–9)

Thus the road to any theoretical reconciliation (even pessimism, even *ataraxy*) is barred, because any theoretical reconciliation would reproduce the fictitious conjunction between the universal and the particular, the rationalization of the determinate will, this time expressed in the form of a theory:

> to establish as the imperative for modern man the freedom of man in nature: that is your heroic philosophy and morality ... *Freedom*? What is the freedom of man in nature? It is the freedom that all parts of the universe have, because they live in accordance with their own law without realizing it ... Then where is the freedom of man? It's in his thought, by God! ... Going through every degree of humanity up to universality, it achieves the contemplation of eternity ... To know: to know oneself and in oneself the universe: to reason out the universe and give it a name ... They say: in moments of grace one communicates with things, one perceives

> them in their true being ... Not so. This communication and this interest is another fiction of man's spirit of self-preservation that one can never get rid of ... So then, what does this contemplation and domination of the infinite come down to? To "reasoning." And this was perfectly pointed out by Kant ... Should this be freedom? or is freedom in the pictures that the arts make of you, complacent of these powers of yours? ... The flood of sounds that symphonies pour over you titillating the ear and the soul ... for this final fiction of our egoism? ("Di fuori la vita rumoreggia," in *La melodia*, 187–8)

It is not a matter of choosing between life and form, between the flow of life and the fortress of ethics: Michelstaedter realizes that the two perspectives can only work if put together. The flow can be rationalized in a fortress, and at the base of the fortress we still find the flow. The world of social disruption, the system of correlativity that atomizes individuals into desiring mechanisms and keeps them in constant conditions of accidentality, is the Euripidean cosmos of disintegration and violence: the will that has to satisfy a need – what for a man is temporarily all of reality – is clearly liable to clash with the will of others. Yet the unrealized "organic" connection of individual consciousness with collective consciousness cannot lead to the absence of social systematicity. On the contrary, it can only result in an instrumental systematicity that abstracts within itself that individuality as the sum of partial mechanisms. Through theory (through the separation of life and knowledge) these individualities are forced to unify themselves into an abstracted whole that presents social morality as individual morality and the contrasting relativity of individuals as an abstract form of peace, that is, as a "categorization" of Being.

This moment marks the passage from the "direct mode" to the "connective mode": for the subject this will mean transposing his own determined will onto those structures in which it may be best satisfied, where it will be least exposed to contingency, to the pain provoked by the fracturing of the ontological illusion. The "connective mode," by contrast, will allow for the sum of the wills to be made uniform, reducing friction (*neikos*) between them and thereby reducing the possibility of shattering the ontological illusion of the "direct mode":

> The security of necessary things consists of the power to ensure the future affirmation of one's own determination in the face of all other external and hostile determinations (forces) ... In such matter my fellow creatures are

> also included: ... in order *to continue* they impose on the rest of matter the same form I impose on it. (*Persuasion*, 112)

Stopping at an analysis of the "direct mode," it might be possible to confuse Michelstaedter for an existentialist. Yet the individual determined wills – seemingly irreconcilable with one another – will come back together in the "connective mode" as a *unit*, made possible by the agglomeration of the wills themselves. The agonistic atomization/disorganization of the "direct mode" – in which the "you are" that the object *says* to the subject in light of its "utility" is inevitably exposed to the risk of coming undone – will be rationalized in the security (also surreptitiously ontological) offered by the social and ideological structures to which the subject will find it useful to subjugate himself. The reification of the object in the "direct mode" will be transformed into a voluntary auto-reification on the part of the subject in relation to the structures of society.

III. The Organization (Abstraction) of Relativity

In April 1908 Michelstaedter attended a conference on education held by the sociologist Scipio Sighele from which he drew a series of reflections that would later become central to his work:

> [A child's] fantastic power is closely related to this isolating capacity that makes of every act and every moment a little world in itself ... In the satisfaction of his every momentary desire the child sees the absolutely necessary premise for his happiness and well-being ... The transition from child to man is but the development of his "capacity" for desire ... As a child grows into a man, so grows his ability to understand the value of distant things as if they were actually present, and to appreciate their "ideal" value ... Every act acquires a certain meaning which is its moral value ... Thus the ideal value of every act is essentially its "moral" value. This is of course the extreme limit; it is the conceptual man, the *homunculus* of ethics. ("Sull'educazione del fanciullo," in *Opere*, 638–9)

Around this time, Michelstaedter began to develop a Kierkegaardian-type theory of melancholy that would become pivotal to *Persuasion and Rhetoric* under the term "deficiency."[10] As Antonello Perli writes, an awareness of one's "ontological inconsistency" (30) is what provokes the individual to lash out agonistically against a reality that falsely portrays consistency. In that moment, "deficiency" – as the lack of an objective towards which to tend – reveals itself to be a psychological reaction:

> Over ... things time has passed; it took pleasure in spoiling them, to show that they were just an illusion ... illusions that are all the products of human work (inasmuch as they are the purposes feigned by illusion, or have served to that end). Drawn out of their vital point – the point where they were connected to a man's illusion or to a larger network of illusions – they reveal their vanity ... They reveal with uncommon effectiveness the vanity of all forms of human activity, a small tear in the "veil of Maya" – then life resumes its course. (Michelstaedter, "La malinconia," in *La melodia*, 77–8)

Melancholy is the tendency to see the world as ruin, a place of ontological groundlessness in which the illusory nature of the relationship expressed by the subject on the object is revealed, thus exposing the insubstantiality of the subject himself, who had fictitiously sought his own ontological subsistence in the object:

> *Melancholy* and boredom, which men localize in things as if there were melancholic or boring things, are the same terror of the infinite, when the weave of illusion is in some manner interrupted ... *Pain* of loss, of a determinate injury ... is rather terror at the revelation of the impotency of one's own illusion ... And once the voice of pleasure, which tells it *you are*, is interrupted, he senses only the dull, painful murmur, now made distinct, which says: *you are not*. (*Persuasion* 29–32)[11]

Melancholy unmasks the ontological illusion. Melancholy is the most prominent analogical symptom to emanate from the pain expressed in a particular relationship when that relationship is not perceived as "sufficiency." When the evolving nature of the relationship is revealed, the subject, who had felt stable in that relationship, is once again placed at the mercy of chance. He is exposed to the accidents of life, which shatter the ontological illusion by obstructing the desiring mechanism of the will. Correlativity, which functions as an aggregate of partial desiring systems, is clearly unable to shield these systems from the relentless blows of accidentality. Thus the ontological form of existence – a form the subject experiences on each occasion in the partial view illuminated by his will/need – is constantly under attack: "Just as every individual existence means the negation of all the rest, so every thought of the individual exists only insofar as it negates the thoughts of others ... killing for its own benefit the life of other centers (inasmuch as they are centers)" ("Delle particelle avversative," in *Dialogo della salute e altri scritti*, 197).

The system of correlativity, being subject to the contingency of contrasting wills, is, as we said, a system of violence and insecurity: "but a slight breath is enough to tear them down forever and show them how uncertain their foundation was in the face of necessity, which they were under the illusion of already having overcome ... A single snag can break the web of calculated forces and allow violence [to] burst into life" (*Sfugge la vita*, 161). This violence must then be subsumed into a perfectible cultural code (rhetoric, in its various forms) in which the will can always be found as an abstract, socialized form of itself: the "connective mode." This line of thought had already appeared in embryonic form in a letter Michelstaedter wrote to his family in June 1907:

> When this absoluteness of things is inside him, he can project it as universal over everybody else. And then, again, this is his law alone, and not instead an abstract *good* outside of him, which, having no abstract existence since it is an empirical given, would have him refer the control of his actions to the opinions of others, or to written law. And then he would not do good because he would feel that he could do nothing but good, but he would do so in obeisance to the opinions of others, and for fear of the law. (*Epistolario*, 230)

He would further develop this topic in his final term paper (June 1908), rooting his thesis in a "crack" he had located in the mechanisms of linguistic eloquence expressed by the semantic nuclei "persuasion" and "rhetoric":

> Rhetoric ... requires taking into account the contingent (practical, historical) interest of the matter: the interest it has for the subject being addressed by the speaker ... It does not ask that accidental subject the profound universal essence of the matter but wants to put the issue in a favorable light before whatever moral or material criterion is prevalent in the subject ... it is the science of ordering the representation of the state of things so as to be able to apply to them the terms of a formula that already exists in the code (or mentality, or system of interests) to which the speaker is appealing – ... a result having undisputed value for the subject and achieving the outcome desired by the speaker ... That science ... is the certain knowledge of the conditions of the moment, the perfect knowledge of the subject and of what has value for him. (*Scritti scolastici*, 189–91)[12]

As Giorgio Colli has written: "in dialectics the struggle was for knowledge; in rhetoric *the struggle is for knowledge aimed at power*" (102). Rhetoric works in the rift created between truth and subject (modernism), tying the contingency that the subject expresses as will and that he lives as a "rational resolution" (*Opere*, 689) – as value that the will makes appear as meaning – to the abstracted content of the speaker's "code," a code that has already categorized truth and the characteristic modes of relativity into abstract entities and orders of knowledge.

Rhetoric has the task of organizing the will/need in an environment so that the subject may identify the form most suitable for his ontological subsistence, for his "continuation" (the most secure stabilization of the constantly unstable "direct mode"), and for his categorization of reality in the modes of rhetoric (in the modes of that environment). Rhetoric organizes Becoming and calls it Being. It organizes the violence of correlativity in an abstract system: through knowledge (language, science, philosophy), an individual who lives the correlativity of contingency places himself outside himself as a "well-grounded" subject, and is abstracted in the security allowed by the categorization of contingency, which he interprets as objectivity: "[Common man] finds all he needs in an established form, he believes that he knows life when he has learned the norms of this form and obtains without danger what he needs. – He is a slave of contingencies ...: all he knows is that he wants this and this, and that his security depends on this form" (*Sfugge la vita* 158).

The ontological fragmentation of Being, which according to the well-known definition of Aristotelian metaphysics is expressed in manifold ways, became the foundation for Michelstaedter's analysis of the Schopenhauerian (and then modernist) assumption of temporality in relation to the will. Always expressing itself as "power" (*potenza*), the will determines in a "deficient" manner the ontological consistency of a subject: "If this power that wanting-to-be could really be, experience should have an *absolute value* outside time and space, outside will and life ... And if it were absolute it would have no need for experience to become so. That is, the *I* should not be a power but a *being*" ("La filosofia domanda il valore delle cose," in *La melodia*, 97).

The subject takes on different roles in this system. He is the object of other subjects (a thing among things). But in his relationship with the object, he also pretends to be an absolute subject, splitting himself in two. He recognizes himself as stable not only in the present moment of the relationship but also in the coordinates of the past and the future (memory and foresight), in order to stabilize the relationship outside time and correlativity and reduce the possibility (the risk) of recognizing himself as "deficient":

> He finds this sweet taste in each thing, which he feels as *his own* because it is useful for his continuation, and in each affirming himself with its potency, he draws from it the flattery *"You are."* So that, time after time, in the *presentness of his affirmation*, he feels superior to the present moment and to the relation belonging to it ... He always feels the same amid diverse times and things: he says, *"I am."* And at the same time *his* things, which surround him and await his future, are the *only reality*, absolute and indisputable ... He does not say, "This is for me" but "This is"; he does not say, "I like this" but "It's good," because in fact the I for whom the thing is or is good is his consciousness, *his pleasure*, his *presentness*, which for him is fixed, absolute, outside time ... His presentness in pleasure (or displeasure) has *organized the foresight* of what is suitable to the organism's continuation, which creates from afar the future proximity necessary to the future affirmation. For this reason things are not indifferent but subject to judgment with regard *to an end*. This end, which is in his consciousness, is indisputable to him, fixed ... What he *does* is not random but *certain and reasonably subordinate* to the end. Just as he says, *"I am,"* so he says, "I know what I *do* because I do it; I don't act by chance but with full consciousness and persuasion." *Thus does what lives persuade itself that whatever life it lives is life.* (*Persuasion*, 22–3)[13]

As explained earlier, in the correlative flux the wills of subjects assert themselves in an attempt to oppress other wills, that is, to annex them and make them their own. Michelstaedter's vision of the social sphere is one of alienation and "exchange" described in the same (non-progressive) terms as Hegel's master–slave dialectic, understood as an organized system of "chance events" that ensures its own continuation.[14] His readings of Hegel, starting with his considerations on subjective epistemologies, allow him to interpret the system of social relations from a particular perspective. Hegel helps him sort out the terms of the relationship between theories of consciousness and the structures of society. Men, writes Michelstaedter, "contend for the security of being able to violate nature and make use of the accumulation of past labor" (*Persuasion*, 113).[15] Whoever wins the battle affirms his individuality and forces the other to locate his own ontological consistency in the duty of serving the "needs" of the master. In this sense, unlike in

Hegel, master and slave integrate each other in a double-mechanism of abstraction that ultimately coincides with the social structure itself, that is, with the mechanism that constantly redetermines, through rhetoric/knowledge, the modes in which individuals give satisfaction to their will. Though the condition of accidentality (violence) between men persists in its contingency, in the utilitarian mechanism that reifies everything in the interest of pleasure (thing among things), this condition is disguised (to prevent the explosion of uncontrolled violence/suffering that could lead to its destruction) through abstraction. Contingency is abstracted into a law of contingency that satisfies subjects' needs through a mechanism of constant redetermination aimed at producing increasingly similar needs among them:

> Can you hear the voice of society? It's like a tremendous buzzing – but if you set your ear to listen to individual sounds, you will hear voices of impatience, of excitement, voices of revelers without joy, of command without form … And if you look into their eyes, you will see … the fear and anguish of the hunted beast … Can you hear the machine creaking at the seams? – But don't worry – it won't break down – that's the way it works. ("Dialogo della salute," in *Dialogo della salute*, 72–3)

As other-than-oneself, the subject presumes a false totality that he believes to be created by himself and reflective of himself but that is only an abstraction of himself in his reified relationship with reality. That subject, as we have seen, is anything but whole (he is the fictitiously "sufficient" form of himself created by the will in its unstable relationship with things).[16] As such, he must always give stability to this possession, to this relationship, because the experience through which the subject establishes himself is always precarious in the correlativity of contrasting wills (in the *neikos*), always susceptible to the irruption of pain, to the ontological insubstantiality that ruptures the illusion of being persuaded. That is why memory and foresight (the foundations of knowledge) come into play, leading to a separation between the subject and his life and establishing a "second nature."

Through memory the subject acknowledges the regularity of the system of relations and declares those relations to be theory (through memory he builds tools for grasping reality). We are worlds apart from the neo-Kantianism of the early twentieth century, according to which memory is the ability of individuality to rediscover itself beyond the "meaningless" flow of relationships. The difference is that, in Michelstaedter, that individuality is dominated by need and reacts to this with a wanting-to-be that also always means wanting-to-know (wanting to categorize reality). Individuality in Michelstaedter is expressed as "lacking." The subject uses memory (what he already knows) to tap his own knowledge; that memory, however, is not really his memory, but rather memory reconciled in order to gain satisfaction (the adaptation of his individual needs to forms of *knowledge* shared by society), a satisfaction that is, however, premeditated and permitted by society: "good memory, that sickness which drives the organism to take in, to conserve without assimilating, and without expelling extraneous material. Rhetoric is a form of poison" ("Appendice II" 151).

Through foresight, instead, the unstable will that the relationship with the object expresses – a will that can never fully satisfy the subject (but that lends him apparent ontological consistency) – is eternalized (made secure) in the future as the eternal return of that will, as the analogical foresight of the reoccurring of the same need (and thus of the conditions necessary for its satisfaction, which must be preserved):

> For the self-affirmation of another determination: each contains the foresight of the others. The will feeds on the future in each empty present ... The promised sweetness of the future, the determinations of other things, the foresight of the given future, all live in the present *taste* ... Thus, as he moves in the turning of things that give him pleasure, man pivots on the fulcrum given ... and attends to his own continuation without *troubling about it*, because pleasure troubles the future for him. (*Persuasion*, 21–2)[17]

But such foresight, which is always determined by the need the individual's will expresses (a will that always remains unsatisfied, given the impossibility of *completing* the ontological need of the subject), is only efficient if the social structures remain the same. In this system, foresight about the future actually remains ... foresight about the present. This is the present that man wants to preserve, and to that end, he progressively adapts himself to the present social structures. This reduces foresight to the defence of those conditions that allow for that same foresight. Successful foresight becomes more likely the more reality is rationalized, since foreseeing the *useful* towards which the will of the subject will strive becomes more feasible. This is the basis of man's calculatory and contemplative relation towards the real.

IV. The "Connective Mode"

The conceptualization of reality begins in the "connective mode," where subjects no longer place themselves in self-deceiving, self-affirming relationships with objects ("direct mode"), but rather seek "security" and ontological consistency in broader structures. Though these structures are still constructed on the "deficiency" that the subject's needs express, they are completely extraneous to the subject and take the form of laws, codes, and knowledge:

> But how does this *knowing* affirm itself alongside life ...? When man says, "this is," he directly affirms his own *persona*, his own reality ... When man says, "I know this is," he affirms *himself* in the face of his own reality ..., he places a real thing outside himself, he expresses the flavor that things have for him, his consciousness, his knowing – whichever it may be ... When man says, "I know this is," he "wants himself wanting"; he again affirms his *persona* in the face of an element of reality that is nothing but the affirmation of his very *persona*. He places his *persona* as real outside of himself in any affirmation. (*Persuasion* 66–7)

The passage from the "direct mode" to the "connective mode" serves as the cornerstone of Michelstaedter's philosophy. The "connective mode" describes the rationalization of individual wills, subject to correlativity and therefore *neikos*, within the sphere of social regulation. As previously noted, the correlative flux represents the space in which the subjective abstraction of man in search of pleasure (and of the ontological and epistemological reassurance tied to it: "the illusion of persuasion") is continuously thwarted both by the temporality in which his relationships are experienced and by the will of other subjects. Therefore, in the "direct mode" the subject's real "deficiency" has the possibility of continuously re-presenting itself (melancholy): "he feels it like a pain in the moments in which his power is not sufficient or he is jolted by chance" (*Il prediletto punto*, 101). The role of the "connective mode" is not to do away with the conflictual system of relationships between beings but rather to construct, in light of the irrationality of the will/need and the correlative system, a uniform framework within which the different wills of subjects can relate to one another. It is not a matter of finding agreement among subjects, but of obligating other subjects to adapt to the prevailing wills of society. The "connective mode" entails organizing subjects' wills in order to suppress the emergence of deficiency:

> If they are well organized in the environment they never need to compromise, but rather they quickly realize that those modes, for their position are more favorable to life: in short, they will have a code of those things that are useful and damaging to their position, they will call them good and bad. ("Sapienza e felicità," in *Opere*, 70)

The "connective mode" marks the point at which the *neikos* takes on the appearance of the *philia*: "when everyone, socially trained, in wanting for himself, shall want for society, because his negation of others will be an affirmation of societal life" (*Persuasion*, 136–7). The sphere of the "connective mode" is no longer – in appearance – the space of violence and subjugation that the *neikos* represented: it is the organization of this space. It is the moment in which the subject no longer merely directs his will towards an *object*; rather, in an attempt to avoid conflict with the wills of other individuals (a conflict in which he might end up yielding), he turns to the prevailing network of social wills, that is, to the hegemonic ideological structures of society. The problematic reification of other individuals becomes the auto-reification of the subject into those values that are shared throughout society: "in appeasing his companions ... he finds the illusion of individuality" ("Dialogo della salute," in *Dialogo della salute*, 56). *Neikos* is no longer expressed in the subjective struggle, but it is much more efficient because it is rooted in the lives of social consensus. Subject to rhetoric, the individual will no longer wants to subjugate others to his determined will, but rather to force them to yield to the will of society (and he will be assisted in this by an entire system: rhetoric): "on this common weakness they have created a security out of reciprocal convention. – It is the realm of rhetoric" (*Persuasion*, 111).

Michelstaedter refers to this as the attribution of "*substance* and the absolute to the modes of correlativity" ("Appendice II," 179). The irrational/contingent sphere of correlative existence is still present, but it is abstracted (stabilized) into a form of social being. In this manner, "absolute substance is tacitly attributed ... to the irrational" ("Appendice II," 181). The freedom of the individual is merely the constantly relative form of his need/will; his social perspective tells us the manner in which he adapts the satisfaction of that need to a social system:

> It is not being but becoming ... In every moment in time there is the predetermination of existing future relations ... The concatenation of causes over time – has no goal ... But the aggregate seems free only because we

> see each element contribute organically to the continuation of the whole (whereby we accord it an individual essence). The whole ... is the sum of their *necessities* ... He predicts, calculates, and subordinates his needs to a rule of life so that his actions do not appear to be driven by these needs but by his free will towards an absolute goal ... But when this realiz[ation] is replaced by the particular realization of individual goals, then the concept of the goal is pure abstraction, because we are not talking about a goal but of an each-time goal, and the form is nothing more than the sum of the material itself, the sum of the necessities. (*Sfugge la vita*, 168–71)

So the System itself – the same System that early twentieth-century relativist philosophy attacked as being separate from reality – becomes the expression of relativism, the relativism of individual necessities that are abstracted, socially, in the words with which society elevates them to universal values (morality, progress, freedom, art, and so on). They are crystallized, not as forms of metaphysical thought to be destroyed by "life," but as reified thought drawing its forms from that same relativized life – life alienated by the will/need patterns of individuals who are both isolated and instrumentally ("usefully") interrelated to one another. The resultant reality, at its base, is that created through correlative needs, but it is now abstracted in the forms of knowledge (fictitiously separated from the contingency of life) and is experienced as more stable: "[he] grants the name of 'duty' and 'truth' to the any weakness." ("La via della salute," in *Dialogo della salute*, 194). Michelstaedter's objectivity is monstrous not because it is separated from the contingent becoming but because it contains the becoming within itself, because it is the abstraction of the contingent becoming.

In the "connective mode," individuals are no longer linked in the expression of their subjective power, but rather in the "second nature" (abstraction) represented by the ideological organization of the sum of individual wills (the organization of a "bad infinity"). Clearly this interpretation does not constitute an actual social agreement. It is not even an expression of the majority's vision of such an agreement. Rather, it corresponds to the will of those who have power in society – those whom Michelstaedter defines "the gang of the evil." It is an abstract form of the *neikos* itself: the point at which contrasting (and correlating) wills adapt to abstract and reified forms within a framework of values that covers all of reality. Naturally, though the world of relativity and contingency (the flux of correlation) acquires the social value of objectivity, it always remains that of correlative needs (the world of contrasting subjectivities), now abstracted in an expression of the will of those who control society. These systems of objectivity shield the subject from the pain associated with discovering one's ontological inconsistency within the system of correlativity. They limit the possible emergence of moments of "deficiency," the only moments in which demand for real ontological consistency – the elimination of violence and domination from the world – may come forth. These absolute networks (forms of "second nature") now become Being, yet they are nothing more than the current ideological structure, that is, the abstraction of correlative relationships warped in the direction of the will of those who direct the ideologies of society: "The finite science of the infinite relations of things, that ... forcibly adapts events – and everything is called absolute life" ("Appendice II," 184). Thus that absolute is not one of Stirner's "fixed ideas," or the Platonic–Christian principle of the "will of truth" formulated by Nietzsche, or one of Mach's "conceptual monsters of objectivity," but rather the same relativity remodulated in abstract form.

The move from the direct to the connective mode represents a passage from subjective abstraction (always insufficient, always exposed to pain) to a forced adaptation to a system in which the relative is abstracted. For Michelstaedter, this abstraction relates to both currents of modernist thought (as it reassembles itself). In other words, such a social abstraction can be accounted for by relativist systems of absolute contingency as well as by contrasting notions of a lost truth. Once the relationship between these philosophies and the formation (and establishment) of the social structure has been revealed, their binomial opposition begins to dissolve.

3 Rhetoric's Paths

I. Rhetoric in Language: Michelstaedter's *Sprachkritik* and Giuseppe Prezzolini

Among the many nets that men cast in an attempt to objectify reality (and themselves in the process), language is one of the most prevalent. As Giorgio Brianese has observed, a clear awareness of this is demonstrated by Michelstaedter, whose "two key concepts denote, first and foremost, two modalities of linguistics and communication" (*L'arco e il destino*, 113).

When speaking, the subject organizes reality from his subjective position. He takes possession of reality through language. By speaking, the subject affirms his individuality as absolute and as existing beyond his will:

> The limits of a speaker's *power* are the limits of reality; this is not given as a reality that exists according to the speaker's will, but as an *absolute* reality ... Every *concept is arbitrarily concluded*. This is because in what he says the subject imagines himself as an absolute *Subject*. Everything that is said has a *Subject* who pretends to be absolute. ("Appendice I," 135)

Yet this does not mean that the limits of language are the limits of knowledge. Knowledge is inherently marked by its limits, arising both in the "direct mode" and in the "connective mode": in the former, in the specializing presupposition enacted by the subject's will; in the latter, in what increasingly directs the needs of all individuals towards the domestication and the "natural" uniformity of those needs in the form of *rhetorical* structures. Michelstaedter understands the step from the direct to the connective mode in relation to the passage from Plato to Aristotle. Both philosophers describe how elements of a relative character are bestowed with substance, yet in the case of Aristotle this substance is reinforced by societal consensus, making it infinitely more powerful:

> The intuition of a particular objective which considered individually becomes the dominant form. But the vital elements of this form build the syllogism of its recognition in words that cover the abysses of an unobserved relativity, ... it bestows a presumption of substance on a complex of relativity. Then Arist. must create a system of unity, he abstracts this existence and these relative objectives and arrives at the characteristic modes of relativity, the categories of existence ... an abstract unity ... he speaks of nothing but the essence of particular objectives and abstract systems. ("La trascendenza di Platone e quella di Aristotele," in *Opere*, 690)

For Michelstaedter, the limits of language are inherently part of the structures of alienation: language repeats and helps stabilize the social relationships abstracted in the societal knowledge that regulates them.

Michelstaedter's analysis of the concept of "persuasion" in relation to language differs greatly from the nihilist approaches of his time, such as Prezzolini's. Indeed, Alberto Asor Rosa suggested reading *Persuasion and Rhetoric* as a response to Prezzolini's *L'arte di persuadere* (1907).[1] In his analysis Asor Rosa reconstructed the cultural context in which Prezzolini wrote his volume – the extreme subjectivism of Ernst Mach, Henri Poincaré, Bergson, and others – and noted the dual scope of Prezzolini's analysis. He observed how Prezzolini's essentially nihilist theory of "fiction" and "masks," aimed at exposing the falsity of social life's conventions – conventional shared truths – was accompanied by an exaltation of the heroic powers of persuasion. According to Prezzolini, the art of persuasion is the capacity of the intellectual to exploit the collapse of the idea of objective truth and shared values in order to realize his own work of persuasion, in order to create consensus around his own convictions, convictions that the intellectual understands as having been built on a hollow foundation: "fiction, masking, come to be the basis for a subsequent step, in which the realization of his own strength convinces him of the possibility of 'revolution'" (Asor Rosa, "Ritratto dell'intellettuale da giovane," 13). Prezzolini manipulates the ontological collapse by twisting his critique of the epistemological perspective (the impossibility of arriving at an objective truth) into an instrument for cynically exploiting fictional (conventional) truths: "A new conception of scientific activity and its value. Born in Germany with Mach; Poincaré in his books was its most popular and brilliant exponent … These men developed the idea that science is an economic convention for action" (Prezzolini, *Il Cattolicismo rosso*, 98).

From an epistemological perspective, the radical subjectification of the laws of science (and history), which excluded – together with the possibility of any collective agreement – the possibility of any pragmatic modification of the real (because praxis is merely a reflection of an inherently fictional theoretical base), implied the eternal continuation of the current mode of operation of life in society (and the ideas formed in it). Greatly distanced from the now scarcely utilizable solutions of the feudal Right, with their absolute truths, the intellectual bourgeoisie of the age of imperialism opt for a different ideological immobilization of historical progress. The immutable values of previous ages ("feudal") are no longer exalted by intellectuals, who now affirm their impossibility as they move towards an ideological vision in which historical progress is emptied of meaning and seen to be irreconcilable with the flow of life itself. In this vision, every objective advancement (e.g., scientific theory) is inevitably dictated by the psychological needs of the individual: "Problems of a universal nature all admit a preliminary condition that casts doubt on the point of arrival" (Prezzolini, *Faville di un ribelle*, 41–2).[2] As such, agreement is impossible. Not only will no two men ever understand the same thing (they will only pretend to do so for the sake of convention), but even the individual himself is in constant mutation, so much so that thought (and language) are unable to keep up: "the psyche is incommensurable with language … and *language is the impoverishment of thought* … If we observe that in our consciousness no color ever presents itself twice in the same identical hue … the same language that hides this heterogeneity from our consciousness, might also be obscuring the distinctiveness of our minds with respect to others" ("Il linguaggio come causa d'errore," in *Studi e capricci*, 70–4).

However, in Prezzolini's model, those intellectuals who have understood the mechanism have the potential to exploit the terrain left open by nihilist theories. Naturally, they cannot create objectivities or real values. This is impossible for everyone within the model. However, in understanding the mechanism by which fictional truths are developed, they can persuade others to believe them. This is a crucial point in Prezzolini's argument, for it implies that those intellectuals who have understood the mechanism cannot be "persuaded." This, of course, is the corollary of Prezzolini's theory: if praxis is always dictated by the subjective/psychological motivations of the subject, if it is always the speculative and individual sphere that drives collective actions, the collective movement (praxis in the Marxian sense) must always be considered a reaction to theoretical and cultural modifications. In this vision, the presumed autonomy of the intellectual exposes him to the risk of not realizing that he himself has been subjected to persuasion; of not recognizing that the entire nihilist epistemology itself is determined by an external praxis, that is, by social–material elements.

Whether or not Michelstaedter had read *L'arte di persuadere* (which is not improbable), a comparison of these two texts and their treatment of epistemological theory, language, and the mechanisms of consensus provides us with a better understanding of the position of Italian intellectuals in the early 1900s with respect to those of the so-called "philosophy of the crisis" (and *Sprachkritik* as one of its by-products). Moreover, it demonstrates the degree to which the philosophy of the crisis was able to offer itself as a crucial instrument of consensus at in the early years of mass societies.

Sprachkritik is the idea that language is not simply an instrument for conveying meaning and communicating; rather, it is an insurmountable barrier that separates human beings from the reality of existence. This idea appears in the European intellectual debate around the same time that the integrity of the Subject is being irreversibly shattered and Nietzsche is proclaiming the death of God. Indeed, Nietzsche announces the "crisis of foundations" in *Untimely Meditations* with a keen awareness of the petrifying effect that verbal acts have on the incessant fluidity of life, which refutes linguistic and symbolic organization.

The death of God, the destruction of the symbolic world above that instils meaning in our contingent actions and words, is an indication that the subject is no longer able to organize the multiplicity of phenomena without realizing the fictitiousness of his act of organizing, without seeing that act as a compulsion directed at constricting the multiplicity of life into a non-existent synthesis. With the disintegration of the idea of a *fundamentum veritatis*, the breakdown of language is inevitable; if the relationship between subject and reality becomes problematic, so must the instrument that expresses this relationship. Just as the subject's conceptual acts are perceived as attempts to force into an abstract unity the "anarchy of atoms" – another expression coined by Nietzsche – that is now life, the presupposed totality expressed by words and sentences comes to be seen as a straitjacket that restricts the emergence of reality: "the inability to contain in words the spreading of life, which shatters even words" (Magris, *L'anello di Clarisse*, 39).

Among the Italian authors of the time, Giuseppe Prezzolini was the first to elaborate his own *Sprachkritik*. He was also the most informed about the debate taking place on the topic outside of Italy. Besides being familiar with debates on the topic in Austria, he was especially influenced by what was happening in France, where he would travel at the start of the century to hear Bergson's lectures:

> I learned about Iginio Petrone, Boutroux, Bergson, about the critique of sciences and the new solutions proposed in relation to the problems of determinism and free will: which from their principal hypothesis take the name "philosophy of contingency" ... It seemed like I had found the key to the universe. (*L'italiano inutile*, 66)

The ideas of the protagonists of the "philosophy of contingency" (Émile Boutroux, Félix Ravaisson, Charles Renouvier), and those proponents of a new scientific epistemology, such as Richard Avenarius and Henri Poincaré, resonated with Prezzolini. His thought developed in dialogue with both the development of a sceptical-relativist–type epistemology and an extreme perspective of subjectivism,[3] which, following the ideas of William James, allows for the subject to change the world through his own physical and psychological transformation:

> To change the world without the assistance of one's limbs or of other people, but through thought alone ... Blue-tinted glasses make things look blue, jaundice makes them look yellow ... All these different ways of acting on the self result in changing the world. Those who stop believing in God perceive the universe differently from when they believed, indeed they see it differently ... If then they change and believe in science, they also change the world. (Prezzolini, *L'arte di persuadere*, 61–2)

Prezzolini's theories were not unlike those being developed by his friend Giovanni Papini, who would publish a significant excerpt of Bergson's writings in 1910; nor were they out of step with the general current in Europe, where these debates were spreading like wildfire (Pirandello was emblematic of this trend in Italy).[4] All conceptual constructions come to be seen as the immobilization and abstract reduction of the possibilities inherent in life[5] – a violent, forced immobility aimed at taking over reality by sacrificing everything that does not fit into this or that philosophical discourse and its rational postulates, which – being pre-determined by the psychology of this or that philosopher – are not actually rational: "he believes himself to be in command of images, to be placing them at the service of a social or material idea; but it is actually the images and the sentiments that are in command of him" (Prezzolini, "Il linguaggio come causa d'errore," in *Studi e capricci*, 84). From a diary entry in 1903, it is clear that Prezzolini had understood the importance of language for his interpretation: "in life ... at no point of it do we find the fixed point ..., to the great despair of those who study life and would like to find logic in it, just as grammarians find rules in languages, and rationalists order in the world" ("Vita intima," in *Faville*, 62). However, the barrier between language and life extends beyond the mere recognition of the insufficiency of linguistic expression for marking the separation between conceptual constructions and the incessant "flux" of life itself, which is extraneous to the principles of identification inevitably involved in language and its immobilizing force.

Language creates fictitious regularity where there can be none, not only because the words of every human being refer to his unique psychological make-up (to his unique understanding of the world), but also because the very same psychological make-up of every human being is unique in each moment of his existence. Language is therefore a "cause of error" because it typically sacrifices the particular – the infinite possibilities that life expresses – for the sake of a universal that is actually an artificial construct, an abstraction:

> Words are our enemies ...; they betray us like faithless ambassadors, and deceive us like malignant interpreters ... The sounds we produce were credited with creating mythologies; they seemed to be not the work of man, but gods ... Times have changed. More than the gift of God, language seems to be the gift of a cunning, wicked devil, who used it to cast discord and deceit in the world. ("Il linguaggio come causa d'errore," in *Studi e capricci*, 65–6)

Prezzolini develops a binary structure in which the particularity of the Subject continuously risks being subjugated to the concentrations of thought and language (Mach's "economy of thought") that are necessary for life: "Words, like general ideas, are a necessary error" ("Il linguaggio come causa d'errore," in *Studi e capricci*, 77). This "economy of words" represents a simulacrum of the real whose fictionality can be used by the individual to persuade others. This individual cannot really come to an agreement with others (their agreement only expresses an artificial convention), but he can "suggest" – leveraging his knowledge of the psychological structures of those whom he wants to convince – an agreement, the implementation of a convergence.

Prezzolini, of course, has no interest in reading this phenomenon in a historical perspective, or in interpreting it as an integral part of the breakdown of societal cohesion in an age in which society is becoming increasingly atomized. On the contrary, interpreting the matter from an epistemological perspective alone,[6] he concludes that no "communitarian" action is possible because the relationships of men are always built on their trust in false abstraction. Therefore, a *real* agreement among them is quite impossible: "Communion among men is always external, factitious, and deceptive" ("Il linguaggio come causa d'errore," in *Studi e capricci*, 83).

Prezzolini turns words into generalizations that are alienated from the mind that created them, into forms that are irreconcilable with the mobility of life: "life ... cannot be understood in the form of a definition that freezes it" (*Il Cattolicismo rosso*, 102).

Language therefore "suggests" rather than communicates; it evokes pre-formed images and sensations in the minds of the speaker and the listener (creating regularity through memory). As such, language can only express "lies," because the distance between words and things, between concept and reality, is immeasurable. Having realized that language, like every scientific theory or philosophical system, is actually an impoverishment of reality performed for reasons of "economy," of "utility," Prezzolini looks down cynically on mankind's futile bustling about in the phantasmagoria of reality and uses his awareness of the system – his new epistemological perspective – to develop his own attempts at convincing, hence *l'arte di persuadere* (the art of persuasion).

What Prezzolini calls "the art of persuasion" is in fact a practical application of the new epistemological perspective: if every linguistic expression is a falsification dictated by the psychological need to temporarily immobilize what is constantly moving, then the task of the persuader is to apply that very principle to the highest degree. The persuader, who knows that all verbal acts (and conceptual acts) are directed by one's own momentary psychological situation, itself determined by the contingent situation of the speaker, must adapt to that contingency in order to produce the desired effect on the listener: "*it is the need to adapt to the listeners that one intends to persuade*. The artist of persuasion must be a diviner of men ... He will have to gather information on their nature, wear their souls, study their tastes." (*L'arte di persuadere*, 42–3) The task of the persuader – who knows that reality is constantly changing – is to take possession of the psychological convictions of his interlocutor in order to produce his desired effect:

> Words are nothing more than an *indication and suggestion*, and they can only speak to what has already been formed in the soul of the listener ... They refer above all to the *phantom, the feeling, the value* that things awake in us ... Now this vision differs in each mind; it is not the same in the mind of who is speaking and who is listening. (*L'arte di persuadere*, 68)

The persuader will be able to enter this condition precisely because he no longer sees "lying" as the betrayal of an original Self. On the contrary, he sees his actions as part of the contingent change that he now controls, to which he is no longer subjugated. In controlling his interactions, he persuades others, and persuading others, he modifies the world. For if words can only communicate what is already formed in the mind of the listener, if they do not have a universal but only a contingent value, they may be used for purposes of persuasion by those who have "understood the game."

In surveying the pragmatic manner that Prezzolini proposes for exploiting the collapse of language, the principle of authority returns again and again. According to him, in order to be convincing one must always adapt to the most common ideas, to the most authoritative figures, to dogmatic and unproven statements, and so on. In Prezzolini this adaptation is always presented as the free choice of the persuader who has "understood the game." But in viewing this new epistemological approach as an autonomous cultural development, unconnected to current historical conditions, Prezzolini fails to recognize that the very approach itself (according to its own rules/principles) may have been determined (persuaded) by something external to it. He sees a reality in which the epistemological collapse of shared social values and theoretical modes of action has paved the way for a climate of social atomization in which the intellectual – who is no longer dominated by the phantasmagoric and immutable values of the universal/absolute – is able to steer reality, to control minds and make space for his own individuality. What Prezzolini does not consider is that over time, the widespread authoritative beliefs that are used for the purpose of persuasion spread exponentially – the persuader, in order to persuade, will be forced to refer to the hegemonic values in place – and eventually erase the free will of the personal perspective. The relativist presupposition thus reveals itself to be subversive from the cultural point of view alone. The linguistic–conceptual breakdown is a product of the atomization of society caused by the new systems of production in the age of imperialism (human beings, increasingly alienated from one another, are no longer able to refer to a shared value system). Intellectuals exalt this existential situation as a new (and cynical) space of freedom, as an overturning of the former philosophical order, which mirrored the old form of social organization. Yet in doing so, they again propose that very same universalistic tendency of positioning the bourgeois intellectual as the interpreter (and guide) of the world while simultaneously refusing to acknowledge that society, in order to protect itself and continue, must rearticulate the forms of that breakdown into presumed units. In order to do so they must replace Truth with the impersonal "they say," with forms proposed by authorities and majorities, the same forms to which the persuader, to carry on his game and persuade, will be unwillingly forced to refer. In other words, what Prezzolini misses is the effect that societal consensus has on the intellectual: it divests him of autonomy.

The arguments put forward by both Michelstaedter and Prezzolini converge on five main points. First, for both thinkers, language is a net the subject casts over the real in an attempt to consolidate it, counting on the mechanisms of memory and foreknowledge (past and future) that create presumed regularities and the fictional consistency of the subject himself.

Second, they both believe that scientific production functions in exactly the same way as language, creating "economic" regularities (always in a Machian sense) that are devoid of absolute truth:

> *In order to construct a lie that has the greatest probability of being accepted, you must observe the same rules as the scientist does in forming his scientific theories;* lies and scientific theories respond to the same intellectual needs (Mach, Avenarius, Petzoldt). (Prezzolini, *L'arte di persuadere*, 32)

Third, for both, the mechanisms of persuasion depend not only on "who is speaking" but indeed above all on "who is listening." The persuader's ability lies in his capacity to make use of what the listener wants to hear.

Fourth, the relationship between who is talking and who is listening must always be based on the principle of authority, on what is most commonly and widely believed:

> It must be *in agreement with the facts* or with the greatest number of facts ... Many people refuse to do or think something until you can demonstrate that it is done and thought by all; then they become ashamed that they had not done or thought it before. (*L'arte di persuadere*, 36)

Fifth and finally, for both, the mechanism simultaneously brings about a progressive reduction of social conflict, while placing subjects in a situation of interrelatedness in which one individual is capable exploiting the other. On the one hand, "throughout the social machine these lies are needed to reduce the friction, like a sort of oil that dampens the squeaking of the gears" (*L'arte di persuadere*, 30–1). But on the other,

> the artist of persuasion must possess many terms in order to disguise himself at will and speak the language of the person whom he wants to persuade; these represent a variety of particular tools with which he can act on this or that man, like a pianist touching a key knows that he is striking one string and not another. (*L'arte di persuadere*, 69)

Clearly, for Prezzolini, only the persuader (the intellectual) ever exploits others as instruments. He alone has understood and makes use of the new nihilist episteme. But having failed to connect the actual modifications taking place in society with this perspective, Prezzolini sees this perfected epistemology as having modified the real and as permitting the action of the persuader. Yet those "keys" and "strings" represent the hegemonic system of consensus in society, to which the persuader is obliged to refer, which turns his attempts at consensus (persuasion) into a form of adaptation – and reinforcement – of the pre-existing system of consensus. Thus the rhetorician's freedom is limited to the "freedom" to adapt to that which is already hegemonic (authoritative). In its presumed autonomy from praxis and history, the subjectivist principle that dominates Prezzolini's theories (and those of many other intellectuals of the time) – and that turns the world into a space of unlimited potential for the individual – turns out itself to be subaltern. Persuading comes to represent convincing in the name of that which is already in vogue; the exaltation of extreme freedom that relativism allows amounts to no more than believing the same truths in which society already believes.

Michelstaedter writes: "To persuade others I have to make my reality 'reasonable' ... And it happens that people blame the means of communication and the circumstances of isolation instead of the irrationality of their reality" (*Opere*, 742). In Michelstaedter it is not language that structures the world – it's the world, the world that men have objectified against themselves, that structures the language that then gives form to reality. The linguistic system produces a system of autonomous signs in which to arrange one's will/need: "*to imagine in our words real proof of that which we say each time* ... Words and expressions only exist so that he who speaks them may give meaning to the complex of determinations present in his consciousness" ("Appendice III," 221). Words are not simply artificial definitions. They are accompanied by a desire (a need) whose potential realization creates a false sense of ontological "sufficiency" ("direct mode"): "Every word spoken is the voice of sufficiency: when someone speaks, he affirms his own illusory individuality as absolute" ("Appendice I"). That same subject then adapts ("connective mode") his own need to the wider structures of social ideologies: "we speak out of hunger, we desperately seek with our words the support that we are missing within ourselves" ("Dialogo della salute," in *Dialogo della salute*, 92). In Michelstaedter's poem "I figli del mare," the protagonists "come to know the words that are worthwhile knowing" (*Poesie*, 80), that society transmits and to which the subject must adapt.[7]

Language, a product of society, offers the subject, who must situate his "need" in the extended structures of the "connective mode," a system of separated and abstract signs in which he can reconfirm himself ontologically. As such, Michelstaedter's linguistic analysis can only be tangentially considered an example of *Sprachkritik*, whose characteristics Claudio La Rocca precisely described: "For Nietzsche, Rilke, Hofmannsthal, Bergson, Mauthner, 'life' seems inevitably to exceed every linguistic form ... 'The expressive modes of language' – maintained Nietzsche – are not useful for describing 'becoming'" (*Nichilismo e retorica*, 39).[8]

However, with Michelstaedter we are not dealing with a critique of language as a challenge to the rational/metaphysical structures that limit language's capacity to express life (the crack that is created between signified and signifier with the "crisis of foundations"). He is not concerned with saving "becoming" from the abstraction of "forms," because those forms *are* the abstraction, the categorization of becoming, of the multiple. His thought is post-metaphysical in a sense that is different from Nietzsche. Once he has determined the weapons of social control, he identifies the space of becoming as itself one of these weapons. We are not dealing with Musil's *Young Torless's* "life beyond words," nor are we with the impossibility, observed by Hofmannsthal (in *The Lord Chandos Letter*), of language containing a reality now expressed in a pluralistic and contradictory manner.[9]

In Michelstaedter, linguistic categories express a relationship with social ideologies. Like social ideologies, language is in movement, in constant contrast, while also moving towards a progressive standardization and therefore towards a state of stabilization in which the same structures are infinitely repeated, guaranteeing the subject the easiest path to satisfying his will/need and confirming his ontological consistency. The point here is not to call attention to the crystallization of language, underscoring its nihilist postulate, as Prezzolini does, nor is it to analytically refute the nominalistic confusions of language (for Michelstaedter, language will always be increasingly perfected through the progressive social agreement). The general critique of language and the nihilist historical backdrop that fuelled it together form the base of Michelstaedter's perspective; that said, he recognizes the two dominant perspectives that stem from this critique – the acceptance of language as a convention/artifice, and the search for a language "beyond words" – as corresponding to the usual mechanism of perpetuating a form of societal security that is simultaneously created by man and directed against him. The words are, that is to say, the words spoken by "will/need": "Then if the truth ... regarding bread were exhausted by his relationship with his stomach, the proposition would have never been made because as for the stomach it would have been persuaded with bread and would have asked for ... nothing more" (*Parmenide ed Eraclito*, 31).

These words implicitly signify the insufficiency of the relationship with the object. They are the words of need, both in the "direct mode" and in the "connective mode":

> It is a question of being satisfied. If one is sufficient to himself in the modes of life offered by society, he can be satisfied by signifying conventional things for his everyday use, in conventional modes, and abandoning himself to repeating without understanding what others in such circumstances say ... The organic life of language that pulsates equally in every word

> and combination of words dulls and disintegrates – as a function of the individual human life – when man's organized foresight (individual security) is reduced by societal security to a single point. (*Persuasion*, 134–5)

Language is one of the systems of social security that establishes itself as an abstraction: it is the linguistic expression of the world of *doxa*, of the contrast of opinions abstracted into *epistemes*, into "absolute knowledge": "When common men take philosophical positions, they make abstractions of words, giving general value to their limited concepts as though they were an absolute concept" (Michelstaedter, *L'anima ignuda*, 52). Yet such forms of absolute knowledge are nothing more than societal consensus intended to surreptitiously overcome the violence of relationships of exchange between individuals (*neikos*), making this exchange non-conflictual, but only by forcibly equating the needs of everyone with the same social consensus.

Like knowledge, language offers the subject a system within which to stabilize his needs; and like knowledge, this stabilization must pass from the "direct mode" to the "connective mode" in order to acquire a more solid appearance of autonomy (the mask of Being), that is, in order to mediate an "exchange" so as to avoid social disaggregation. For Michelstaedter, social organization has absorbed the needs of men, alienating both their language and their thought, scattering all of the residual forms of autonomy of the subject. The subject no longer needs to be persuaded because the forms of rhetoric take the place of his persuasion and permit him to participate in the "absolute." This participation, which is clearly artificial, leads to a division of the "deficient" life of the subject and his language–knowledge sphere: "Words are not tools of the trade: they are *technical terms* ... and when he must look out across this fog of life, he no longer sees clearly, nor finds the precise word, because he has grown so weak by relying on the ease of established positions" ("Appendice II," 196–8). Words are one of the means by which the subject adapts to pre-existing conditions. As with "foresight," the future discloses itself as a "voluntary" repetition of pre-existing relationships, structures, and words:

> As such everyone, believing to be living their own lives, move others and are moved by others and are given a clear way to live among others ... And we can thank Aristotle, who with infinite patience collected the words of men and ... compiled the first code of knowledge of life. ("Appendice VI," 299–300)

Language lends an appearance of substantiality to relationships in which the subject imagines himself to be absolute (i.e., language rationalizes the "specializing" vision of the will). However, subjugated by need, this relationship is interpreted by the subject as value, first as an immediate and inadequate satisfaction, and then in the reifying structures of society in which that value (insecure in the "direct mode") is reified as "shared" knowledge through "the socio-ideological codifications that convey dialogue" (Benussi Frandoli, 111). This is why for Michelstaedter – in contrast to Prezzolini – the crisis of language does not descend from theory (epistemology) to determine the praxis of individuals; rather it is steered by praxis and by the social theory that arranges individual needs into theoretical and linguistic forms. Taviani is mistaken when she writes that "words" are rejected because they "conceal the age-old authority of *logos*" (*Michelstaedter*, 45); rather, words are rejected as expressions of social correlativity (needs in contrast), abstracted into the socially hegemonic forms of knowledge – of language – in the "connective mode." Words are still part of the "hunger" of the subject: "this phrase is spoken in order to correspond to the need to sate my will for longer than ... bread does ... with my stomach" (Michelstaedter, *Parmenide ed Eraclito*, 32). Words are yet another attempt to objectify, to alienate in abstract forms, the need of the subject, that is, his desire to ontologically possess the real, since the ontological consistency of the subject in the world of rhetoric is based solely on the injustice and contingency of the correlative relationship.

But in the world of rhetoric, satisfaction only comes through adaptation, not to the *logos* but rather to the Aristotelian theory of the *logoi*, that is, to an idea of existence that, dominated by the relative needs of life, individuates its substance (its truth) in these same relative needs, from those that have become most prevalent in society. And for Michelstaedter these opinions do not prevail by chance. Society and its ideologies (language included) are guided by those who control (the "gang of the evil") "property" and "money": "words ... are continuously adapted and dictated by the current consortiums of power in the form of jargon" (Spampinato, 246).

For Michelstaedter, these types of ideological products (language included) represent an attempt to attribute substance to the modes of relativity, that is, "theory premade by the public voice" ("Appendice III," 218).

In Marxian terms, we could say that linguistic expression in Michelstaedter is a commodity. Giving rise to episodes of conflict for its possession (in the contrasting correlativity of needs), it must be expressed on a social level as an abstracted form of itself, that is, as a reified structure that allows individuals to subjugate themselves to its value in society in an apparently non-conflictual manner. As individuals find it easier to satisfy their linguistic needs (as with other types of needs) by making direct reference to the established social language – interpreting all along their adaption to this system as a free choice – external forms of violence disappear. Language bestows a presumed ontological consistency on that which correlativity expresses as the complex of wills, as the adaptation of individual wills to the prevalent ideas of social knowledge; "since no one can make his world be the world of others, everyone feigns words that contain the absolute world" (*Il prediletto punto*, 194). Therefore,

> for everyday use everyone says "table," "chair," "square," "sky," "hill," and so on, or "Marco," "Filippo," "Gregorio," ... but if they want to say what they are, the image of them dissolves into received bits of information ... and referring to them with words, people do not communicate or express them but signify them to others in a manner satisfactory for life's everyday uses. Just as a man turns a lever or presses a button of a machine to have certain reactions ... though he does not know whence they proceed and he does not know how to create them – so he relates to them only by means of the conventional sign. Thus does the man in society act: he finds the conventional sign on the keyboard prepared like a note on a piano. And conventional signs join together in conventional ways, in made-up complexes. He plays not his own melody but phrases *prescribed* by others. (*Persuasion*, 129–30)

Linguistic transformation is the construction of a homogeneous outcome directed at creating a political confirmation in which the actions and reactions of speakers are gradually adjusted to the stabilization of rules and judgments of correctness or incorrectness. In this sense, Michelstaedter understood the modernists' emphasis on the crisis of language as a move to establish modernist cultural hegemony by locating the development and resolution of the crisis within the sphere of epistemology alone, rather than in the separation of language from praxis, that is, from the "deficient" life of the subject: "he could not ... reverse the language of crisis into the crisis of language: from Michelstaedter's point of view, Persuasion ... is not compromised together with the rhetoric of 'certainty' or the rhetoric of 'crisis'" (Campailla, *Scrittori giuliani*, 117). Language is not born ontologically separated from life; rather, language is manipulated (it is part of the master–slave relationship) in order to transform it into a more and more perfect abstraction in which men can find satisfaction, reified as knowledge, to their needs: "as soon as I say I know, I have already been defeated" (in *Opere*, 727).

Therefore, the limits of language are not those expressed by Wittgenstein, but rather the limits of society, that is, the repetition in linguistic acts of that which society presents as its *knowledge*, the prevailing values to which the subject must adapt himself in order to satisfy his needs. Language is not a form of linguistic re-elaboration of ideas that have been historically transmitted to us through language; rather, for Michelstaedter, those ideas are socially readapted into societal knowledge in order to serve the very same societal knowledge in place.

Ideology resides in language as a repetition of the societal ideology expressed in current forms of knowledge. Through language, as through knowledge, the subject confirms his participation in the "absolute." But that existence is only the social existence of that particular historical moment, which, in directing the needs of the individual, situates those needs within its ontological *entity*. In this way it forces the individual to unwittingly adapt to the (historical) forms of its authority, presenting the forms of current social relationships as external (and eternal) nexuses.

In this sense, the whole sphere of theory (knowledge) becomes the system through which men sublimate the "condition of the struggle for survival" (Franchi, 27) – the clash of wills/needs – in a context in which society, completely disarticulated and polarized, is rearticulated as abstraction: "And so men give names to the secure manifestations of life, they aspire to their forms in order to obtain their *personas* and joys; concerned about this life that slips from their hands, they enslave themselves to it" ("Dialogo della salute," in *Dialogo della* salute, 63–4). "Names" (words) are not revealed to be the metaphysical detritus left in the wake of life's destructive flux, but rather one of those social "rearticulations" that indicate the disaggregation at work in society:

> *The application of these names, the closing of the circle of definitions* is the sufficient life of the wise man ... And the arrangements and qualities and regularities: *the changes recognized in a given regard*, so placed in position and provided with names ... are the *world* ... But he who calls this deficiency life and in the recognition of those causes and determinations and changes presumes to find the reason of things may rightfully call the world of δυναμισ [*dunamis*] his absolute world. ("Appendice II," 186–7)

In this abstraction, reality once again appears as the place of Being. However, foreshadowing Heidegger, it is actually no more than a matter of "gossip," which, spreading in ever widening and increasingly abstract circles (therefore seemingly more and more suited to the needs of all), increases its authority. In some ways this argument still seems to be connected with the notion of the contrast between *Kultur* and *Zivilisation*, in which material and economic progress go hand in hand with the dissolution of "natural" and organic social ties, pushing man to the margins of society and forcing him to adopt a behaviour of mere action and reaction in the face of a system that he does not comprehend and that is beyond him.[10] However, in Michelstaedter this contrast is expressed not as the classic opposition of Being and Becoming, but rather in relation to the mechanisms and historicity of social forms. Being (authenticity), or *Kultur*, is no longer an organic *plenum* but a deficiency; while *Zivilisation* (inauthentic forms) is no longer seen as a disruptive mechanism, but rather as a structure capable of creating "elements" that are more solid, more rigid, with which the subject confirms himself:

> *What is necessary is to signify* ... The conjunction of names makes it possible to *signify* – and names are the *signs* of things and the voice of the elements of knowledge ... Abstract relations can determine one another in order to constitute knowledge which the philosopher elaborates through reasoning ... What I determine of something is a mutation ...: it is still the manifestation of the correlativity ... But now ... is not a *non-being*, but a being in relation to *other* things ... I have given substance ... to the indication of a relationship: I have given substance to the mutation, to the infinite correlativity, to non-being. ("Appendice II," 182–3)

In the "connective mode," language is expressed in the form of *theory*, it is the abstracted rearticulation that holds society in place, functioning, through "conversation," as "exchange," as the value of things separated from the things themselves. Thus Michelstaedter is a critic of language insofar as he is a critic of society. Language for him is just one of the infinite ways, albeit one of the most powerful, in which societal *knowledge* is transmitted among individuals, forcing them to depend on a series of broader social ideologies formed by those who dominate society. The subject's adaptation, in an attempt to satisfy his needs, leads to an impoverishment of his linguistic capacities. This is not because language necessarily represents a crystallization of life's flux (as in Prezzolini), but rather because language is reified in those ideologies that are most widespread. In contrast to what Manfreda has written, Michelstaedter does not "condemn ... language's inability to *arrive at*, to express the essence of living" ("Note sull'idea di linguaggio nella *Persuasione*," in Sorrentino and Michelis, eds, *E sotto avverso ciel*, 224). On the contrary, language is constructed through the same alienation as life. It is one of the representations through which the subject imagines his consistency – first in the "direct mode" and subsequently at the level of social consensus.

The individual who wants to make himself understood (to win an argument or satisfy a need) will come to understand that this is most easily done by adapting himself to that which his interlocutor is ready to hear, that is, to his *values* and his *words*. But this victory means that the subject has adapted himself to the structures of language and the societal consensus rooted in them in order to lend more force (authority) to his argument. As such, for Michelstaedter, "those who pretend persuasion in their words and search for those words ... [are] either a vile person or a rhetorician" (*La melodia*, 141); so words "cover the abysses of an unobserved relativity" and rhetoric is "the kingdom of words without content" (*Parmenide ed Eraclito*, 68). Those words that involve an adaptation into forms of societal consensus, being founded on the individual's will to satisfy a momentary need, are not even worthy of being said, because all they express is the will of the subject to satisfy that momentary and contingent need by adapting himself to the *security* offered by social institutions (and words): "the 'sufficiency' crystallized in the words and institutions of men" ("Appendice II," 216). These words only express the contingent isolation of the individual who is forced to adapt to the "absolute" forms of society.

II. The Abstractions of the Social Machine and the Master–Slave Dialectic

Individuals are prey to the needs they recognize as value. They are dominated by what they interpret as "useful," by that which is illuminated for them by their wills, in what Michelstaedter refers to as the mechanism of *philopsychia*:

> In the indifferent haze of things the god *makes* the one thing the organism needs shine; and the organism struggles toward it as if to satiate all its

> hunger, as if that thing could provide all its life: *absolute persuasion*. But the knowing god extinguishes the light when its abuse would remove its usefulness, and the animal, satiated only with regard to that thing, turns toward another light ... Then the light reappears without respite like lightning on a summer night. And in that light *the animal's entire future gleams* ... This benevolent and prudent god is the god of philopsychia and the *light* is *pleasure*. (*Persuasion*, 20)

In this mechanism, in which men are exposed to conflict with other individuals, there is the constant risk that the presumed ontological consistency obtained through the temporary satisfaction of the will may be shattered. Only through a social "agreement" are the different wills rearticulated in a cohesive system expressed as the rationalization of contingency into an increasingly crystallized and subject-independent system of knowledge. In Michelstaedter, this correlative exchange of wills/desires is expressed as a form of conversation in which men transmit "words." In the "direct mode" these words correspond to their desire to subjugate the desire/will of others, while in the "connective mode" they coincide with the one subject's will to force another to adapt to the will of society. In both cases the ideologies transmitted by the conversation are abstracted from their real value. In both moments, these ideologies rest on an underlying base of complete contingency, that is, the complete irrationality of the correlative system: "*Socrates* ... denied *knowledge* to the man distracted in relationships" ("Appendice II," 174).

Michelstaedter understood the objectified knowledge resulting from the mechanism of *philopsychia* in relation to the disengaging of exchange-value from use-value that takes place with the circulation of commodities:

> Mysticism, spiritualism, pragmatism, individualism, rationalism, solipsism; every system, every school, are all, in the name of absolute truth, the voice of *philopsychia* ... that by putting a poultice on the pain to alleviate it and lessen its sensitivity grants in exchange a divine or philosophical coloring to the any life ... "The spirit is in all things, beneath my apparent activity there is the spirit, my hands work and exist in time but my spirit communicates with what is outside of all time and space" ... This is the god of *philopsychia* advertising himself, like a modern-day merchant, granting the "absolute *persona*," all his finest qualities to whoever buys his commodities. ("La via della salute," in *Dialogo della salute*, 193–4)

Objectified knowledge, separated from life (from "deficiency"), tends to progressively perfect itself as abstraction. Individuals become interdependent as the will of each is always based, in the system correlativity, on a relationship aimed at subjugating the other to this will, in which the other is seen as something available to be used. Only in the "connective mode" these relationships of interdependence are integrated with one another, subordinating themselves to an external structure: rhetoric. This external structure takes on the appearance of a natural law and ends up conditioning them completely. However, since behind these wills (and the relationships of wills) there are real men, they themselves become dependent on the system that mediates the contrasts between them, that abstracts them into a stabilized form.

The exchange of wills, in contrast, serves as the base for the abstraction of these same wills. As such, the system – presented as natural and randomly established – is actually determined by the dominant wills of society. Put another way, the contrast of wills is expressed as ideology and societal cohesion – as a relativist exchange of contrasting wills that is reformulated as an absolutistic abstraction of that relativity.

Therefore, that abstraction is the theoretical (and abstracted) form of that same will/desire; it is the relationships of power between men, abstracted as objective *knowledge* and endowed with a natural appearance.

What was a simple reification of the object on the part of the subject in the "direct mode," becomes the abstract rationalization of the same reification in the "connective mode." Individual wills are domesticated through "adaptation to a code of rights and duties" (*Persuasion*, 110) before which men – in order to find in it what is "useful" for them (and in doing so retrieve ontological consistency) – are reduced to mechanisms:

> But here we find individuals reduced to mechanisms, foresight actuated in the organism, not however, as we might expect, as victims of their weakness, in the grip of chance, but as "sufficient" and as certain as divinity. Their degeneration is called civil education, their hunger is the activity of progress, their fear is morality, their violence and egoistic hatred is the sword of justice ... They have made themselves a force from their weakness, for by speculating on this common weakness they have created a security out of reciprocal convention. (*Persuasion*, 110–11)

The individual does not perceive social ideas as limitations on his freedom. On the contrary, he turns to them because they structure his *being* in the world: "And men believe in free will because they have settled into their state of servitude so much that they declare the chain that ties their wrists and their jailer to be the one truth … But here precisely lies the ultimate mockery of inexorable necessity. He cannot untie what he did not tie himself" (Michelstaedter, "Da un notes," in *Opere*, 632).

Theoretically overcoming contingency in an illusion of "sufficiency," the subject's need is reflected in society by the ideological, administrative, and practical structures (insurance, welfare, pensions, etc.)[11] that harness him to a (large-scale) generalization of his need(s). Yet these needs are now rationalized so as to minimize the possibility of "accidents," of contrasts of wills/needs that might make the individual aware of his ontological "deficiency": the pain that would lead him to recognize rhetoric's insubstantiality, its "second nature," by pointing to the ontological fracture between Being and will/need. This rationalization reduces the individual to a "machine." He is only able to follow the directions of the system that he himself has created and that is increasingly alienated from itself.

Michelstaedter unequivocally expresses his criticism as a historical rejection of the social structures and policies put in place by the bourgeoisie, making direct reference to class conflict. In particular, in his "Discorso al popolo" (autumn of 1909) he addresses a crowd of protesting workers after observing their appreciation for an airplane, underscoring the connection between exploitation and the bourgeoisie's extolling of technological progress:

> If tomorrow you were to reassemble … to triumphantly assert your will to go all the way, … against the authorities established by law, against the authorities established by money, against the government and the bourgeoisie – that ideal by which today you are moved, my brothers, the admirable instrument that you are applauding would measure its strength against you … The bourgeois society … silently prepares its weapons, and masks them under the shining cloak of humanity and progress, and you – you applaud them! … – But the day you acquire full awareness of your rights and your strength … that day, brothers, the humanity and progress of the bourgeoisie will reveal their true colors, and will surround you in a ring of fire and steel, showing no pity for the rebellious slaves … You will remain slaves forever unless you manage to unmask the miserable hypocrisy of bourgeois power that covers its defenses with flowers … Brothers, you have applauded the symbol of the power that crushes you. – But you shall rouse yourselves from your inaction … and then you will

> be invincible, then this hollow construction of bourgeois power ... will collapse together with all its laws, its institutions, its vain science, its hypocritical morality ... scientists, functionaries, soldiers will be extinct races, in the new world. And there will come a world where *man* reigns, man of work, man healthy in body and mind, man who has no need for unjust laws ...: but his faith, and common work, and a community united by brotherly love – will be his government and his law ... Farewell brothers – long live work and justice – death to the bourgeoisie (*La melodia*, 85–8)

At the other end of the political spectrum, we find the "important gentleman" described in *Persuasion and Rhetoric*, whose basic functions are conveniently situated in the mechanisms (material as well as ideological) offered by the social structure:

> One must take advantage of this marvelous comfort of living, and select from the increased variety of pleasure ... One must allow the body something and the spirit something ... It's one thing to get satisfaction from literature, science, art, and philosophy in pleasant conversations – but serious life is something else ... And I enter the temple of civilization to accomplish my work with a heart tempered by objectivity! ... And the holy institutions speak through me ... There's a pension: the State doesn't abandon its faithful ... I belong to a welfare fund ... I am insured against theft ... against fire ... I'm insured in case of death ... I'm secure in a locked vault. (103–5)

Social structures, aimed at reducing the importance of "foresight," create a sense of "security" that lulls the subject into a state of increasing contemplative atrophy, reducing him to a cog in the mechanism.[12] The subject recognizes the calculated relationship with the social institutions as the most secure way to obtain what is useful to him, evading the risk of contingency, because satisfying what is momentarily useful means for the subject confirming himself ontologically (Michelstaedter's theory of pleasure). As a consequence his actions will no longer transcend these institutions: "and that which he calls 'I' is nothing more than the same cog forced to turn" (*Sfugge la vita*, 127). The search for "security" within the structures of society inevitably places the subject at the service of society, pressing him to limit his behaviour in terms of the prospective development of those same social structures:

> Indeed, to the degree that each man is limited to the moment, society extends its foresight in space and time ... "to be attached to file" in

> a socially useful manner, to think – each in his own little place – about his own little life. But this is only possible in such a determinate manner that every other in turn might do as much, rotating on his own pivot and tasting a little at a time through his teeth the teeth of the interconnected wheels … inasmuch as through their life lives the great organism, with its complex and exquisite foresight, crystallized in the delicate and powerful minds who eliminate from the field of life every contingency … Likewise, in exchange for the determinate labor a man performs for society, which is familiar and instinctive to him in manner but obscure in reason and in end, society lavishes on him *sine cura* all that is necessary for him. (*Persuasion*, 111–12)[13]

Thus the world based on divided labour, embodied in the particular sphere of activity in which every man must remain in order to maintain his livelihood, becomes the place of a social illusion that expresses servitude in forms of security. On the epistemological level, separated from the real conditions of life, this social illusion expresses the transposition of ontological recognition – what the individual was seeking in the object signifying his need ("direct mode") – onto society's abstract code of needs (and duties). This passage represents the culmination of Michelstaedter's particular reading of the master–slave dialectic:

> Society takes me, teaches me how to move my hands according to established rules and, for this miserable labor of my miserable machine, flatters me, saying I am a person … Men have found in society a better master than individual masters because it does not demand of them a variety of labor, a power sufficient to security before nature, but only a small, simple bit of labor, familiar and obscure, provided one performs it in the necessary manner … The concern for [this] security enslaves man in every act. From the moment he wants to say, "This is legally mine," he has by means of *his own future* made himself a slave *to the future of all the* others: *he is matter* (personal [mobile] property). But in exchange, society does what no master would: it makes its slaves participants in its own authority by transforming their labor into money and giving money the force of law … In this manner, everyone in organized society violates everyone else by means of the omnipotence of the organization. Everyone is matter and form, slave and master at one and the same time. (*Persuasion*, 116–18)[14]

The subject's willingness to continue – and the impossibility of eliminating the extreme contingency of every relationship, a contingency that is expressed as the desire for preservation – leads him to codify ideological (and practical: insurances, welfare, etc.) superstructures, which become the "forms" in which the subject unconsciously orders his life and his consciousness. The forms of security – that is, the forms of violence (in the "direct mode": the possession of the object; in the "connective mode": forced social adaptation) – are crystallized in the reified structures of social knowledge to which the subject finds himself subaltern. The creation of objectified structures around him allows him to limit his capacity for "foresight" to the increasingly defined (calculatory) schemes those structures require as adaptation: his activity becomes limited to calculating the evolution of that same social functioning. The subject's behaviour is reduced to calculating the occasions those structures offer for gradually eliminating accidental elements (the very same behaviour that Michelstaedter attributes to science/technology). Indeed, what Michelstaedter calls the "loss of vitality" is man's retreat and transition into a contemplative dimension in the face of a system that dominates him. This transition shares many characteristics with that of the development of Taylorism and the rationalization of labour:

> Every substitution of machines for manual work dulls by that amount the hands of man, for they were trained to know how to do things from thought directed toward determinate necessities; and by means of the contrivance in which that thought was crystallized once and for all, they are rendered useless and lose the intelligence of those necessities. Thus, for instance, have blacksmiths become dulled in our days. At one time they knew how to forge from a block of iron whatever object you might have wished using fire, hammer, and chisel, whereas today they barely know how to adapt and screw together the ready-made pieces from the factories. (*Persuasion*, 123)

The specializing vision of the "direct mode" (placing all of reality in the desired object) now becomes the rationalization of the same mechanism within social knowledge:

> The illusion of ONE exclusive rationality of motive and of the *precise* value of the objective ... This reason can only be the intuition of a particular objective, which becomes dominant when contemplated singularly ... When Arist. must create a system of unity ... the characteristic modes of relativity appear to him as the categories of existence. (*Sfugge la vita*, 171–2)

The subject finds himself inserted like a mechanized part into a mechanized system ("ends up losing his power to react ... He is almost reduced to a mechanism"). He finds himself within a system that has been prepared beforehand, over which he exercises no influence, and to which – atrophying and losing vitality – he is forced to adapt himself in a calculating manner, that is, by foreseeing the occasions for "pleasure" and the risks of "pain" (ontological inconsistency) that the same system offers (and social institutions such as insurances mirror this epistemological process on a material level). Moreover, in his progressive adaptation to the social system, the subject's same capacity for foresight becomes more limited:

> The more an individual adapts to circumstantial contingencies, that much less is *his* sufficiency ... Much narrower is the sphere of foresight and limited the sufficiency of the individual who, for his own security, has entrusted himself to social foresight. Within the social individual, absolute social security corresponds to a foresight that is reduced to the instant and point such that, at every new insufficient contingency, the individual would perish wretchedly if he were removed from the bosom of society. (*Persuasion*, 120–1)[15]

In exchange for his "bit of labor," everything society has developed as forms of security will be at his disposal. But all of it will only be cognitively accessible according to a useful/harmful binary, in a perspective that becomes increasingly alien to the needs of his fellow men:

> What does he know about the things he brushes in passing, the things on which he supports himself in order to go forward? What does he know about how they live or what they want or what they are? This alone he knows – whether they are hard or soft for him, difficult or easy, favorable or hostile. He ignores what is just to others, making use of things and people ... insofar as they are useful to his going ... His interests go no further than his own life needs, this nearly inorganic will to live – this man nevertheless, enjoys, in exchange for his tiny learned task and his submission, the security of all that human ingenuity has accumulated in society. (*Persuasion*, 126–35)

As the reference to welfare and insurances illustrates, for Michelstaedter the mechanism of progressive rationalization characteristic of the "connective mode" extends below the cultural level and is rooted in a series of precise material elements. Thus on the one hand, Property becomes the manner in which the subject (the subject–master) exercises his right to exploit an increasingly reliable foresight on reality: "The field represents the security of having these fruits in the future ... Rights do not determine property except with regard to security towards other men" ("Dialogo della salute," in *Dialogo della salute*, 37–8). Others must adapt to this foresight in the form of duty recognized as value. On the other hand, Money (and by now this should not come as a surprise) is the means by which social violence is communicated; it is the abstract instrument (a symbol of the loss of vitality) with which the subject expresses (imposes) his right to interpret/use reality (also against others): "With money one has everything that human ingenuity, accumulated by society and corresponding to an extraordinary form of individuality, has to give – whether it be things that one must otherwise take with bodily force, or things otherwise acquired ... through 'persuasion'" (*Opere*, 872).

Thus in the "connective mode" we are still within the space of correlativity and *neikos* (contrast). From a prominently ideological point of view, the subject's affirmation of his individuality means that "affirming the 'property of thought' is more important to men than their 'interest in thought'" – since "the affirmation of intellectual property requires the negation of the intellectuality of others" ("Delle particelle avversative," in *Dialogo della salute*, 198). Similarly, from a material perspective, property becomes "violence toward man" (*Persuasion*, 112). Property, in other words, is the possibility of satisfying one's momentary needs, offered to the subject–worker by the subject–"owner," who assimilates the former into himself, that is, who gives him a security that, however, means adapting himself to the needs of the owner.

Michelstaedter, then, understands the "slave" and the "master" as being related in unison to the forms of the social structure. But in addition to the pain that affects both (in the rhetorical system, neither's needs can truly be satisfied), Michelstaedter observes the occurrence of a form of exploitation that, in its materiality (money and property), is also epistemological: reality is interpreted by everyone according to the categories of those who dominate reality. He who owns property forces the other to adapt to his needs:

> One has affirmed his individuality before the other, and the other has his *future cropped* and is at the *mercy* of the victor in that he wants to live and cannot take advantage of his own labor power. The other then gives him

> the means of living, provided that he works for him. Thus has man subordinated his fellow creature to his own security ... And this latter, the slave, is matter before the master – he is a *thing* ... The hand of the slave is not forced to turn the mill grindstone, but it does so in order that the body should have food to eat ... The master makes use *of the slave through his form, through his labor power*. He makes him feel that his *right* to exist coincides with the sum of duties toward the master; his *security* is conditioned by his uninterrupted adherence to the needs of the master. (*Persuasion*, 113–14)

Differently than in Hegel, in Michelstaedter slave and master end up integrating their social needs. However, contrary to the interpretation that most critics of Michelstaedter have given, his reading is not some sort of misinterpretation of Hegel that equates the two figures. Rather, in Michelstaedter the needs to which the slave (worker) adapts, in the forms of social security and ideology, are no longer *his*: they are those of the master, transmitted – in the societal organization ("connective mode") – through a progressive levelling out of ideologies. The subject–master dictates the rules that rationalize (abstract) the correlativity of contrasts. Indeed, it is this connection between the functioning of society and the needs of the strongest that allows Michelstaedter to interpret social life as a form of struggle against society. For Michelstaedter, the irrational side of this societal conformation is identified not with the presence of the proletariat (as it is in the Marxist perspective), but rather with the "pain" of the lone individual who perceives himself as unappeased in what he defines at the social level as the creaking the system's cogs. Yet the self-alienation of the master and that of the slave must be distinguished from each other, in that the second is compelled to adapt to the first.

Money represents for Michelstaedter the parallel of this progressive levelling. Unbound to an immediate use-value, it allows for an infinite possibility of relations/exchanges that are, in appearance, less and less conflicting. Likewise, the various ideological positions become increasingly comparable as they more and more fall prey to the abstraction that fictitiously unites, from top to bottom, the social fabric: "*Money*, the actual means of communicating the societal violence by which each is the master of the work of others: ... the drive belt turning the machine's wheels – it shall be like a divinity raised up to heaven, becoming perfectly nominal, an *abstraction*, when the wheels are so well adjusted that the wheels of each shall enter into the wheels of the other without the need of transmission" (*Persuasion*, 137).[16]

Therefore, the abstraction that takes place does not happen merely on a subjective level (by the individual through his cognitive faculties). The communication of social violence – the individual's need to adapt to the hegemonic values of society, the recognition in them of security and of the easiest means of satisfying his needs/desires – is actualized through money. This is why language, another space of ideological adjustment, is equated with money, in the same way that structures such as retirement, insurance, salaries – also criticized by Michelstaedter – should be understood.

Money separates man from himself; it forces him to identify the satisfaction of his needs with the prevalent needs of society, which are transmitted as abstractions and are inevitably defined by those who control society – that is, by those who possess, among other things, money itself, the possession of which provides the material force to allow determined opinions and ideologies to prevail over others.[17]

The creation of ideological products (knowledge expressed in linguistic form), conceived on the grounds of selfish need (what is useful "for me"), is accompanied by the development of abstract and categorized counterparts (more and more perfect, more and more homogeneous) that are extraneous to the original ideological products. Individuals refer to these ideologies – these abstractions established by the knowledge of those who rule society through property and money – in order to conceal their contingent condition, in order to relate harmoniously to one another, while all along remaining polarized within the same underlying system of violence that correlativity represents. Moreover, the irrationality of the subject's determinate will ("direct mode"), his "irrational" life, is veiled as the will becomes increasingly unable to conceive of itself outside of the adaptation to what it is presented with by knowledge as Being, and incapable of understanding the mechanism that ties it to the whole system, which conceals "deficiency" in abstract forms.

Critical of this progressive social "integration," Michelstaedter looks for a response in the thought of ancient Greece and the category of *totality*: a category that social knowledge cannot really possess since it is nothing more than the abstraction of contingent needs. Michelstaedter understands the category of totality as the need to not conceal the "deficiency" of the need the subject lives in his personal experience in favour of what he abstractly conceives. So he proposes viewing the system of abstractions as something (to put it in Vico's words) created by men from what is most common to their own material condition – as something that mere theory cannot solve, but only disguise:

> this knowledge is the arbitrarily finite enumeration of the infinite ways in which men feign happiness, good, evil, and so on, and the manifestations of their passions, virtues, characters, as they distinctly appear and are called in present life (not defined according to what they mean for the individual) ... Rhetoric is thus the register of what men say they want most often ... and then of the declarations that are most repeated, the artifices most resorted to, etc.: all the fragments of life, the materiality of relationships, progressively ordered according to this or that word (good, evil, virtue, etc.) like the colored pieces of glass in a kaleidoscope. But in reality they are the remains of the wreckage of philosophy. ("Appendice VI," 298–9)

Philosophy itself becomes a mere catalogue, rationalized and abstracted, of human needs. It becomes a generalization, on the level of social consensus, of forms derived from the contrast of men's wills/needs: the cognitive form that rationalization assumes on a large scale based on the conflicting nature of social relationships, now abstracted in the progressive uniformity of those needs.

III. The Wreckage of Greek Philosophy and the Road to Persuasion

> Starting tomorrow I'll go back to writing rubbish, regularly, and then I'll be "a student writing his thesis," a wheel in the mechanism, a decent person, and that nobody will look at me with wonder and irony, and I'll have nothing to be ashamed of. (Michelstaedter, letter to his sister Paula dated 5 May 1909, in *Epistolario*, 367)

In the philosophy of the ancient Greeks, Michelstaedter finds both a space of totality – the ability of the Pre-Socratics and Socrates to keep life and thought united – and one in which, through Plato and then Aristotle, a path is opened to rationalization, to abstraction.[18] In *Persuasion and Rhetoric*, Michelstaedter's Greece, in its progressive decadence, is no longer an organic and natural society. Instead, like the industrial society of his time, for Michelstaedter Greece is already fractured and disaggregated. What he calls "rhetoric" is tantamount to the forming of a "second nature" on which men must depend. It is an ideological formation that, through the "laws" determined by knowledge, grants men the contemplative space for satisfying needs that are none other than that which the ideological composition, abstracting the life process in itself, constantly determines as a necessity and its unattainable satisfaction:

> Their power pretends to be finite, and finite the possession they wanted, their will being persuaded in whatever repeated present moment. Facing whatsoever limited, finite relation, they do not live it as a simple correlation but pretend to be men with persuasion; ... they need to attribute value to things in the very act of seeking them and at the same time *need* to say their life is not in those things but *is free in persuasion and outside such needs*. Thus they do not confess that the value of these things lies in regard to their finite need; but there, deep down, is the *absolute* value in which they affirm themselves as absolute. They are still things among things, slaves of this and that ..., in the sway of their needs, fearful of the future, enemies of every other will, unjust toward any other's demand. They still affirm at every point their inadequate *persona*. But this is all appearance; it is not their *persona*. Deep down their absolute *persona* remains, affirming itself absolutely in absolute value ... The man stops and says, *I know* ... And through his knowing he is outside time, space, continual necessity; he is free, *absolute*. He lives on what is given him, of which he does not have reason in himself, but in his absolute knowledge he has Reason ... In his Absolute he has the End; ... Freedom, Possession, Justice. Thus does he carry the Absolute with him on the streets of the city. He is no longer one but *two*: a body ... and a soul. (*Persuasion* 63–5)

From a modernist perspective, Michelstaedter understands the Nietzschean argument that reality is theoretically duplicated (the real world and the apparent world), but he rejects both the *Erlebnis* of the eternal flow of things (*amor fati*) and the limiting of the concept of value to the horizon of subjectivity. For Michelstaedter, both are connected to the subject's material life, which is expressed: (1) as a constant *lack* of self within the system of correlativity:

> If we say it is *one, it must contain all things in itself* ... If it does not contain all things in itself, it lacks something; – it will have this thing in the future: – its future is in this thing: in the present it is no more in itself than it is in this thing: *it is no longer one*; if it lacks one thing it lacks everything, because it lacks itself ... in its place there are *relations*: the irrational indifferent fog of correlativity – because this is the lack of life (or fear of death,

> as you please) ... [He is] the man who lacks everything, who in order to be changes in time. ("Appendice II," 164)

and (2) as the subject's search for ontological consistency, which ultimately leads him to alienate himself in the objectified structures of society:

> A light puff is enough to show how insecure was their foundation, how inadequate their security, in the face of the necessity that they deluded themselves that they had overcome. When a man sinks below and touches bottom ...: he feels unjustly struck down, while the others sense the compassion of fear. And together they protest against destiny ...: as if that man had had the right to be confident, as if, his feet firmly planted, he had conquered his place in the sun ... having eliminated contingencies from his life, and based "his hope on a firm foundation." Because their personal comfort is their reality, the calamity that interrupts it is a transcendent force: the devil ... This is why the constant effort of society aims at tightening the plot to strengthen it by means of communal weakness and make it secure against every eventuality. (*Persuasion*, 139–40)

Thus "persuasion" develops with the revelation that the wheels of the structures are squeaky, that behind them cries the pain of the subject who realizes he has not reached any form of ontological consistency, who is reminded of his "deficiency" and is thereby prevented from obliviously continuing down the road of alienation:

> For as long as man lives, *he* is here, and the *world* is there. For as long as *he* lives he wants to possess it. For a long as he lives he affirms himself in some manner. He *gives* and demands. He enters the ring of relations – and it is always *he here* and *there the world, different from him* ... Thus must he give in order to have the reason of self and have it in himself in order to give it ...: *and, making his own life always richer in negations, create himself and the world* ... This is what the Oracle of Delphi said when it said: Γνοσι Σεαυτον [know thyself]. (*Persuasion*, 50–3)

Persuasion is the dialectic point at which thought recognizes the ideology that structures it, and negates it. At the same time, if it is unable to situate itself in the material reality – in the deficient, irrational life of the subject – it negates itself. Persuasion is the negation of the determinate forms of the will that cover the depths of contingency; it is the *melancholic* negation of any instrumental relationship with what is contained in reality:

> when the weave of illusion thins, disintegrates, tears asunder, then men, *made impotent*, feel themselves in the sway of what is *outside their power*, *of what they do not know … They find themselves wanting to flee death, having lost their usual way, which feigns finite things from which to flee all while seeking finite things* … when the edge of the weave is lifted … they too know frightful moments … They awake, open their eyes wide in the dark, … man finds himself once more without first name and last, wife or loved ones, things to do, clothes … In anguish you seek a plank with which to save yourself, a solid point; everything decomposes, everything yields, flees, draws away; and the sarcastic sneer dominates all: "Ooooooooohhh … nothing, nothing, nothing, I know you're nothing; … I know you can do nothing, nothing, nothing …" … You feel long dead and yet live and fear death … and you suffer each moment the pain of death. This pain is common to all things that live and do not have life in themselves, living without persuasion, fearing death in living. (*Persuasion* 26–9)[19]

Michelstaedter describes the beginning of this process in the "Esempio storico," which appears in the central part of *Persuasion and Rhetoric*. His description centres on the passage from Socrates to Plato, and then to Aristotle, in the form of a narrative of progressive compromise between Being and the forms of empiricism.

After Socrates, in "his love for liberty" (77), has expressed his hatred of gravity (the fact of being subject to the correlative forces of gravity), Plato finds a stratagem for deceiving gravity (but "*without losing weight, body, life*," 78). He builds a steel air balloon filled with the Absolute and takes his disciples up into the sky to see how things are in their universal forms, far from the correlativity (contingency) that dominates the earth:

> With this admirable system he would rise up without losing his own weight, without lessening his own life … "See how we rise up *solely through the will of the absolute*," Plato exclaimed to his disciples who were with him … "It is by *its virtue* that we go toward the sun, where gravity no longer rules, and from the bonds of the latter, we free ourselves little by little." (78)

"But Aristotle takes just one more step" (*Opere*, 866); he notices that his teacher keeps looking down,[20] and he realizes that Socrates is no longer there to remind Plato that there is no Good in what, lacking Being, only wants to continue in the forms of the empirical, which are the forms of correlative violence: "specific objectives that become universal ideas" (*L'anima ignuda*, 63). While in Plato there is still a distance between the world of the absolute and that of life (it will be this looking down – this nostalgia for the world of life – that will cause him to lose the game),[21] with Aristotle "the everyday things of life" acquire substantial value: "for Aristotle ... knowledge is the *knowledge of opinions*" ("Appendice V," 246). In Michelstaedter's metaphor, after reflecting on the matter (after developing a "technique," a method), Aristotle proposes to Plato that he take some of that absolute down to the ground, to put it in the things of the earth and call them, in theory, absolute:

> He made within himself a resolution for finding the means of returning to the earth. From that day he set about studying the ingenious machine ... Soon he had acquired a minute knowledge of all the *mechanisms* ... Plato looked long into his myopic eyes with his own far-seeing eyes, and he saw that he was being betrayed ... Plato ... could not avoid the conclusion, ... For him, too, after all, the vertiginous height, the unbreathable air, the lack of all the dear things of life, ... carried a sinister sense of void. (*Persuasion*, 81–2)

While Plato dies during the descent, Aristotle returns to earth to preach the absolute in the forms of relativity – to dress up, in Michelstaedter's words, the "near" in the categories of the "far":

> All the people ran to take from him the *goods* that *came from the* absolute. He was a practical spirit and took the goods that were most in fashion, and which lent themselves to the eye, needs, and taste of the public, and placed on them a brand name with the logo "lightness." And the public was happy to be able to say *the goods came from the sky and to use them just as if they'd been goods of this earth*. (*Persuasion*, 83–4)

For Michelstaedter, this process leads man to separate life from himself, classifying the external world (in which he recognizes an ontological self) in the forms of foresight and organization: in the forms of instrumental reason.

Greek philosophy becomes the battleground for a very contemporary ideological clash centred around the ability to resist the forms of abstraction in which the "system of names covers the room of individual misery with mirrors" (*Persuasion*, 70). Through Socrates,

Michelstaedter emphasizes the authentic side of existence. This is not the Romantic dream of a lost truth. Rather, it is the historical position of he who, having realized the workings of the cultural ideologies that structure his consciousness, negates them. He does so, not in the name of transcendence, but in opposition to the fictitious union between the universal and the particular that those structures transmit. At this point, in relation to the Romantic position, Michelstaedter only accepts the existence of an unbalanced dialectic between the individual and society, that is, the progressive reduction of the individual to an *abstract* entity, socially quantifiable and as such forced to adapt itself to social quantification.

Socrates emphasized the ability, in perceiving one's "deficiency," to recognize the origin of the injustice that the individual will expresses as need (specialization) and organizes into abstract forms (rationalization) – the forms created by those who dominate society – thereby perpetuating that injustice in the name of value:

> I tell you: tomorrow you will certainly be dead. It doesn't matter? Are you thinking about fame? About your family? But your memory dies with you, with you your family is dead. Are you thinking about your ideals? You want to make a will? You want a headstone? But tomorrow those too are dead, dead. All men die with you ... Do you turn to god? There is no god, god dies with you. The kingdom of heaven crumbles with you ... Tomorrow *everything* is finished ... Well, then the god of today is no longer yesterday's, no longer the country, the good, the bad, friends ... You want to eat? No, you cannot. The taste of food is no longer the same; honey is bitter, milk is sour, ... and the odor ... *it reeks of the dead*. You want a woman to comfort you in your last moments? No, worse, *it is dead flesh*. You want to enjoy the sun, air, light, sky? Enjoy?! The sun is a rotten orange, ... you cannot move a finger, cannot remain standing. The god who kept you standing, made your day clear and your food sweet ... he betrays you now and abandons you because the thread of your *philopsychia* is broken. (*Persuasion*, 37–8)

Socrates asks for justice, not for rights (which are the abstract concept of the former, adapted to the "modes of relativity": a fictitious union between universal and particular). He expresses the need to persist on the road of "deficiency," which negates the possibility of persuasion for those who are distracted by the fog of correlativity. Aristotle, on the other hand, finds his voice in that very fog: "As such Aristotle is invincible like the fog itself, from which his voice speaks forth" ("Appendice II," 220), from which he constructs his "rational" categories.[22] And it will be from this fog that a falsely rational abstraction of irrationality emerges, that is, the knowledge that joins together individual determinate wills. Socrates, instead, does not assign value to the abstraction of contrasting wills of relative entities in contrast. He does not believe he can accommodate his "deficiency" in the abstract forms that feign "sufficiency":

> Socrates, who experiences this deficiency in a deeper, stronger manner; who is not satisfied with what may satisfy others; who sees it clearly not only in the adversities of chance but in the very flow of life, in human happiness ... Socrates can speak to me closely and clearly with the distant voice of the pain I feel myself. He can guide me to take back all the cursing I've done in my life, to recollect all the moments of helplessness, in what my illusion, in its modes and its names that presume *certain happiness* – brings to the contingencies where it will show itself insufficient. And all the things that with their irresistible attractiveness make me slave to the blind circle of my delusion, he can show me to be vain and fragile ... and therefore [he can] break, using parts of my own life, the limited circle of my *foresight*. ("Il prediletto punto d'appoggio della dialettica socratica," in *La melodia*, 102–3)[23]

Socrates knows this requires breaking down the specializing vision that makes the subject view the world in the forms expressed by his "need" ("direct mode"), which are also the same forms of contingency that, in exposing the subject to pain, must be ensured by rationalization ("connective mode"):

> Men ... willingly renounce self-affirmation in determinate modes, provided that their renunciation has a name, a guise, a *persona* through which they may be given a vaster future ... For the sake of a name, for the semblance of a *persona*, men willingly sacrifice their determinate demand ...: *thus does rhetoric flourish irresistibly*. (*Persuasion*, 95)

The voice of deficiency, the same voice that hopes to find peace in the possession of objects in the correlative flux, will end up finding artificial peace in the "connective mode." In the "connective mode" the forms of social objectivity take the place of the subject's individuality. Meanwhile, the individuality of the subject is reified in the same forms of social knowledge. As realized by Aristotle, who adapts his "goods" to whatever is most in vogue, "the criterion is consent" ("I professionisti della filosofia," in *Dialogo della salute*, 199). The subject is forced to adapt the irrational forms of his will, in which he institutes himself as an ontological subject, to those of societal consensus, in order to stabilize himself out of contingency:

> Men talk to affirm themselves, but because they talk they depend on whoever is listening, and the listener can grant them the joy of their affirmation by approving, or take it away by disapproving ... to delude themselves that their individuality remains intact in contingency, for their need to exist (in the approbation of others) ...: and so is formed the "intellectual" κοινονιαι [groups] and in general every coming together of interlocutors, ... insofar as individuality is illusory, affirmation is inadequate. ("Il bisogno della comunicazione," in *Dialogo della salute*, 204–5)

Michelstaedter's Socrates asks to draw "near what is remote," to break the mechanism of memory and foresight where the pain of instability pretends to be stable, because only by completely acknowledging this mechanism (which doesn't mean accepting it) will it be possible to take the road that leads to overcoming it:

> He will see that what men suffer for is not hunger, thirst, disease, or misfortune ... He will see that obtuse pain suffers in them in every present, equally empty, in abundance or privation ... and they will taste the joy of a fuller present in the impossible ... They will see that ... hunger is not hunger, bread is not bread; for they will experience their hunger in another manner, and other bread will have been offered to them. (*Persuasion*, 54)

Bringing close what is remote requires appealing to the "deficiency" the subject experiences. It means causing this "deficiency" to emerge. The persuaded will be able to "give distant things in proximate appearances so that even he who lives only on the latter finds in them a sense he did not know" (*Persuasion*, 56). The persuaded will be able to let his own negative truth immanently shine, thus overcoming the confusion of "closeness" and "remoteness" that forces the subject to move within the limited circulation of occasions of possession offered to him by rhetoric, identifying in these, however, the possibility of ontological value: "And I am condemned to always obey the appeal of finite relationships in which my limited consciousness imagines satisfaction in the place of my deficiency – in the ways and paths under the names as they are presented to me, as they appear to me from up close" ("Il prediletto punto," in *La melodia*, 102).

Aristotle, by contrast, realizes the "criterion of the *'close view'*" ("Appendice II," 99), that is, the ontological function of things as they are in everyday life. From the regularity of these things (from their most prevalent function in society), he extracts the categories of Being:

> Now we can have the close certainties from the mouths of men who announce their ends in life, and attribute sufficiency to this every time: it is not a conspiracy of determinations of life at the service of life, but a catalogue of different established ends. ("Appendice II," 216)

Aristotle established a criterion by which Plato's *ideas* become forms of life endowed with substantial being. He extracts "the 'necessity of a *rule*' from the plurality of contrasting objectives (and wills)" ("Appendice II," 215) From the complex of opinions in contrast, Aristotle extracts the "theories of life" ("Appendice II," 216) For Michelstaedter, these theories are "empirical" and "dogmatic" at once – as he writes to Enrico Mreule in a letter – because they are the reification of the structures of relativity (of contingency) into abstract forms.

These theories are not simply an abstract form of *logos* or traditional Reason. Rather, they are the rationalization of contingency, relativity, fragmentation, and disaggregation themselves. Elevated in society to the level of absolute knowledge and value, they are nothing more than the forms of interpretation (opinions) that are most widespread in society. As Roland Barthes wrote: "For Aristotle, public opinion is the first and last datum" (*La retorica antica*, 147). For Aristotle, "the real is the current" (Michelstaedter, "Appendice V," 265).

Rhetoric cannot really bestow closeness on remote things. It can only call close things remote. It can only organize already existing elements into forms of *knowledge* (of theory), and in doing so, elevate those that are prevalent in society – based on their supposed value in the correlative determination of things – to the level of ontological rules. Theory at this point no longer expresses the consciousness of the "deficiency," but rather *sells* "sufficiency" by passing off the categories of the relative as Being. These categories of the relative are created from the complex of men's needs – thus, theory disguises the world of needs as the world of freedoms, by dressing up every contingency as theory. The objective of this application of theory is to silence the voice of "deficiency."

Michelstaedter's point is in total contrast to Pirandello's "Philosophy of the Remote" (*filosofia del lontano*), that is, the subject's ability to consider the ontologies of the world as "forms" alone, as mere economical organizations of the relative, as described in *On Humor*. This is because he identifies this philosophical approach as yet another development of rhetoric – as one of the many lights illuminated by the god of *philopsychia* in order to give the subject the illusion of consisting ontologically. Socially speaking, it is the myth of an atomized individual who is subject to correlativity but who, considering himself autonomous, believes in the possibility of not being ruled by the forces of social consensus. For Michelstaedter, the subject cannot laterally position himself in relation to the real, because by believing himself to be autonomous to the real he only increases the potential for it to dominate him:

> No man is born naked any longer: everyone comes with a coat ... This form, this straitjacket or rhetorical coat, is woven from all the things of societal life ... The consciousness of each man rests in the possession of any degree of such knowledge: each man (1) has learned a skill or procures for himself a title; (2) knows how to earn his livelihood by means of this; (3) knows to what extent he may earn it before others and how to demand support against the outrages of others; (4) knows what kind of feeling and what manner of respect he should have toward others; (5) knows how he must behave and within what limits act toward them; (6) knows the way, the theory of the environment, with which to prevent or redress troubles, and beyond this, how to consult men who are masters of such theory. (*Persuasion*, 138–9)

For Michelstaedter – who never loses sight of the power of social consensus because he knows that it determines thought and not vice versa – the stance of an individual who affirms the illusory nature of every societal ideology does not represent a critical perspective towards society, but rather another variant (another type of superman) of the subject who imagines himself illuminated and free. For Michelstaedter, the beginning of the process of liberation consists in recognizing one's lack of autonomy, one's subjugation to societal authority. Without this recognition, the subject will be completely conditioned by the real, because he will interpret his own developments (theoretical ones included) as actions without any dialectical relationship with the social consensus.

On the other hand, what Michelstaedter calls "swimming against the current" (*Opere*, 735) is the rejection of any theoretical social settlement.

It is the task of rational thinking, which, heeding the voice of its "deficiency," returns to its duty, to "forge a path when there is no road" (*Persuasion*, 43). This requires recognition of one's position as a cog in the violent mechanism of the system (in the abstraction of the violence), a denouncement of the system's inherent negative truth: "Then you will have distant things as close" ("La giustizia," in *Opere*, 733).

The persuaded negates altogether the categorization of the specific particular (the abstraction of the complex of social needs), recognizing in it the voice of the individual need once it has been adapted to the functioning mechanisms of society. Persuasion is the ability to see both the mechanism of the determined will ("direct mode") and its accommodation in the ideologies of society ("connective mode") as an expression of a process of crystallization that contains within itself the underlying contingency.

This is an unending journey that can never take place: "Can you imagine anything more comical than this man who speaks of a peaceful happiness to be found after climbing Calvary; ... then, once you get back from the trip you're entitled to the *paix du ciel*. One who climbs Calvary does not come back down" (*Epistolario*, 396). Persuasion is not a position of stoicism:

> The stoic *wants to be he who needs no* contingencies ...: he lives to say that he needs nothing to live. – In relation to all "indifferent" things he says, "I am, even without this thing." ... But if these things were not, he could no longer say that they are indifferent to him, and would draw no enjoyment from a life free of them. Let us put the Stoic alone on a mountaintop to live on roots, and let us take away not only the presence but even the memory of everything that life does to others, and then we will see ... The things of the world, even by being denied, are necessary for his life, and what is necessary is not indifferent. (Michelstaedter, in De Leo, *Michelstaedter filosofo del "frammento,"* 69)

Nor is persuasion related to the developments of *ataraxia* and asceticism: "And just as the philosophical delusion is vain, so is the apostolic delusion, the theory of the sacrifice ..., vain is askesis, fakirism, vain are all the optimistic games of this impotent humanity that is attached to its need to live" (Michelstaedter, *Sfugge la vita*, 120).

Persuasion only exists as the voice of an imbalance that denies society a fulcrum (persuasion mystifies sublimation by upholding Justice) because it sees in it the violence of contingency expressed as Being: "in the negation of relativity ... at that point justice was justice because there was nothing unjust any more" (*Opere*, 864). But there is no "harbour" ("the harbour is the fury of the sea," *Poesie*, 82), only an endless indictment that assails every haven (every "illusion of persuasion"), that refuses every ultimate synthesis, while bearing all the pain of its deficiency:

> There are no respites on the way of persuasion. *Life is all one long hard thing* ... [The persuaded] must still see in the other the *persona* who denies, suffers, has not, the *persona* he feels in himself; and respecting in him this *persona*, he must deny seeming value and bring distant things nearer, making even more distant things live in the present. (*Persuasion*, 52)

On the road to persuasion, every advance must be submitted to the test of "sufficiency": "the philosophy of the highest good will still always be a form of optimism" ("Il bene," il *La melodia*, 84). Michelstaedter expresses this same sentiment in his last poem to his friend Argia Cassini, when he writes: "Not Argia, but Senia I called you, / for never settling into an easy rest" (*Poesie*, 93). Persuasion expresses not peace (*argia*) but rather a perpetual sense of homelessness, the permanent feeling of being in a foreign land (*xenia*). No epiphany, no voice of myth, resonates with the persuaded. Any "haven" would be nothing more than the abstract and relative rationalization of the momentary will, of the momentary need. Even the pursuit of death is no more than another of *philopsychia*'s deceptions:

> Those who die as you say want to deceive destiny with a calculation – but they deceive themselves. – Since death is not a response that is *free* from need – a consciousness not subjugated to time, ... his reasoning is not based on the absence of needs ... but rather by the presence of *need*, unsatisfied in *some of its determined parts.* ("Il dialogo della salute," in *Dialogo della salute*, 74–5)

The absence of totality is evoked in the continuous rejection of its determined and contradictory forms, and the limits of these become the limits of the concrete social situation. Persuasion "does not involve proceeding but ... resisting" (Michelstaedter, "Il prediletto," in *La melodia*, 103). It is the moment in which the subject's request for justice no longer lies in the determinations of the need or in the social abstractions of it. Rather, this request becomes an incalculable debt for having taken part in the violence of the world, and as such, a different perspective from which to interpret existence: "the way of persuasion ... is hyperbolic ... Because you participate in the violence of all things, all of this violence is part of your debt to justice. All of your activity must go toward eradicating this" (*Persuasion*, 47–8).

Persuasion cannot be a method either, because methods are forms of calculation for adapting to society, to its continuous ambiguity rationalized into stable forms: "The way is no longer the *way* since the ways and the means are the eternal flow and clash of things that are and are not. But health derives from that which *consists* in the middle of this ... With the words of fog – life, death, more or less, before and after, [you] cannot speak of it" ("Dialogo della salute," in *Dialogo della salute*, 85–6).

For Michelstaedter, persuasion is the endless activity that preserves truth as "absence" against the historical–ideological moment that society expresses in time: "the value of man is measured, it seems to me, not by the form of life he conducts, but by those forms which he rejects" (*Opere*, 785). Hence the activity of the persuaded man is far from out of history if his task is to continually identify what the achieved societal forms try to express, in an absolute manner, as the end of history, as an insuperable social situation, as a static *condition humaine*. There can be no settlement. This is the negative response to the utopia, the never-ending dissolution of the fetishistic structures with which, in the form of knowledge, society expresses itself. Michelstaedter cannot make an object, a commodity, out of persuasion:

> And for spirit I do not mean a holy spirit that in whatever way a man believes may be given to him ... and the activity is not just any work; ... and reason is not ratiocinating about the arbitrariness or not of concepts; for the "I alone" I do not mean any illusion of individuality. ("La via della salute," in *Dialogo sulla salute*, 193)

Persuasion cannot take the form of a theoretical solution, because this would imply "sufficiency," a fictitious union of the relative and the absolute: "I can always sufficiently preach. And applying in every point my theoretical effort, that is my person, as a reality outside of me, always have a world that is alive and substantial, in a point ... the general and the particular ... movement and stability" ("Appendice II," 210). This sufficiency would cover the abysses of the relative with categorizations of being and would become part of the game of violence in which the different theories clash with one another for social predominance.

Nevertheless men grow tired along this road and "ask for a blindfold" (*Persuasion*, 63). They are afflicted by the same pain that forced Plato to look down from the balloon: the desire to heal the fracture between the world of ideas and the phenomenal world. Men want to establish a positive relationship between Being and the world in order to continue in their alleged "sufficiency." And as that relationship, in the "direct mode," is always subject to the irrationality of the *neikos*, which can show it to be an illusion, it must now be predicated in the world of *doxa*. The more it is protected against the risk of unmasking, the more it is generalized and in tune with current beliefs and common sense.

The task of knowledge then, as for Aristotle when he disembarks from the balloon, will be to elevate this common sense to itself:

> They no longer hear the voice of things telling them, "You are," and amidst the obscurity they do not have the *courage* to endure, but each seeks his companion's hand and says, "I am, you are, we are," so that the other might act the mirror and tell him, "you are, I am, we are"; and together they repeat, "we are, we are, because we know, because we can tell each other the words of knowledge, of free and absolute consciousness." *Thus do they stupefy one another* ... and with words they nourish their boredom, making for themselves a poultice for the pain; with words they show what they do not know and what they need in order to soothe the pain or make themselves numb to it ... Men put themselves into a *cognitive attitude and make knowledge*. (*Persuasion*, 68–9)

There is no longer the voice of "deficiency" (the utopia projected towards what not yet *is*). Through theory, value enters into the forms of the "any life": it covers "the depths of unfathomed relativity" (*Opere*, 690) and proclaims as true whatever is more common, because whatever is more common, being believed by the majority, is what best protects all of society from the irruption of contrasts, of contingency. Rhetoric is not interested in removing contingency from life. Rhetoric, instead, shrouds contingency with the categories of being, to which it adds the "finite." This is still the voice of need expressed as will and foresight. However, foresight is now in unison, through knowledge, with the foresight of society as a whole, because the common reaction to the reality expressed by the will is separated from the vital interest of the subject (where the voice of "deficiency" irrupts) and, based on the common historical result of the senses and of morality (convention, adaptation), is called truth:

> The just man ... always feels his *infinite debt* to justice, his distance from the point of his true life ... Plato ... pauses as if he had found it, and from here he starts building reality facing backwards towards the relativity from which he came ... He needs ... the positive signs to build his positive system of relativity, as a norm of values. (*Il prediletto punto*, 152–3)

Michelstaedter's Plato is at the midpoint between Socrates and Aristotle, the point where the combined reference to *agathon* (the absolute good) and the subject's deficient life is fictitiously recomposed along a theoretical path (separated from deficient life) that pretends to "install the relative in the temples of the absolute" (Peluso, in Campailla, *Un'altra società*, 180). The separation is remedied not in the endless activity that speaks to men about the lack of Being in opposing the prevailing ideological moment, but in the systematic overlapping of the universal and the particular, the manifold brought to unity in the modes of categories, that is, theorizing about reality through common sense, accepting the prevailing ideological moment as truth. Feeling the pain of contingency, Plato is unable to resist and attributes "sufficiency" to what is irrational; he attributes to non-being the names of being and is overcome by *philopsychia*: "he cannot draw near what is remote, but he *says the things that are near* and calls them remote – so they may be accepted by short-sighted men while preserving *the name of remote things*: of absolute knowledge" ("Appendice II," 176).[24]

The fragments of irrational life are "abstracted" and combined with ideas through reason: "In this mirror of relativity he contemplates his motionless figure" (*L'anima ignuda*, 61). Thus, entity implies non-entity, the immobility of wisdom conserves in itself the movement of the will/need, and thought, now far from the horror of "flowing" that the life of the individual determines in the *neikos*, surreptitiously appropriates Being. In this sense we can say that Michelstaedter attributes to Plato the features that Nietzsche, in *The Birth of Tragedy*, antedates to Socrates. Yet there is no Dionysian moment for those on the road to persuasion, no "loyalty to the earth," only an infinite debt to Justice with the goal of releasing men from their contingent and relative conditions.[25]

Plato, however, does not ask for justice. Instead, he asks himself what it is. He separates life from knowledge and thinks he can know without being persuaded in that moment (without having directly experienced persuasion as a "deficiency"): "Plato renounces his life and, feigning it sufficient in its 'any' content, puts himself in a cognitive attitude. And in relation to his illusory reality, with his illusory *persona* he reaffirms himself as an individual sufficient for absolute life – one who possesses persuasion, as an individual who *knows* or *has* the way to *know*" ("Appendice II," 144).

In this way justice also becomes nothing more than "an abstraction of all of the particular justices" (*Il prediletto punto*, 153), the attribution of the value of being to the concept of justice that is predominant in society. This is the objective of rhetoric.

As Michelstaedter writes, in *Phaedrus* Plato cloaked close things with the names of things remote, imagining "the reality of an absolute world and in himself the finite power of reaching it" ("Appendice II," 171). Thus, *Phaedrus* is an apology for the Socratic dialectic, but also its betrayal, the point at which "the dialectic has already become rhetoric" ("Appendice II," 172), the moment in which the Socratic way has become saturated with the illusion of sufficiency: "this *more stable locus* does not exist, nor can anyone point it out to his companion, telling him, 'sit, there you will be happy, free, strong, there you will know good'" (*La melodia*, 103). In *Phaedrus*, the Socratic way is no longer the infinite movement towards justice, which, asking for Being, negates every advancement and shows the deficiency of that which lives, but a positive science that theorizes on how to obtain Being:

> He turned intuition not toward *Being*, things, life, activity and justice, … He turned it toward the reactions in as much as they allow him a *persona* … His dialectic is either debated between aporias reducing it to an exercise of method, … or it gives way to a *dogmatism* that classifies, catalogues, distinguishes, gives to everything its place in the system. ("Politico," in *L'anima ignuda*, 67–8)[26]

This is not just the problem of thought absorbing Being, of reason subsuming life. Rather, it involves inserting Being into the dominant categories of social thought, of social being.

While Socrates "was able to bring remote life close" ("Il prediletto punto," in *La melodia*, 104) in reference to the *deficiency* of the subject, in his later writings Plato (followed by Aristotle) superimposed "remote" and "close," structuring the presence of remote things within words. No longer creating the unbridgeable space (as it still existed for Michelstaedter in Plato's *Gorgias*) between the remote world and the empirical world, he began to organize "the ways of correlative being," the ways in which "the variety of things, transforming, continues, and according to which it is given meaning, … the ways of *the lack of being*"

("Appendice II," 180n), that is, the categories of the multiple that cover the reality of non-being and that lead the subject to consider the relationships that are already prevalent in society as truths. In this way, truth is obtained from the plurality of objectives. Thus any irrational will, any need, can be "sufficient" when it is able to adapt to the established categories that organize it into a social consortium (the system of relativity), that organize it into a *city* – the crystallization of those needs, a *Republic* having all the traits of the bourgeois state:

> Under the power of the city everyone is bound by the harsh necessities of life, and keeps to his place not for the present good but out of concern for the future ... *His raison d'être are his material needs*, and it is only *out of self-interest* that he satisfies them in the life imposed by the city ... Accepting as free life what revolves around basic needs, we establish in the city the freedom of being slaves; once the principle of violence affirming the need to continue is accepted as just, *every affirmation is just for every need* ... He shall be wise and just and free ... because he will be "said" to be so by a free and just and wise city ... The city *isolates* individual needs ... And so it constitutes the production of elementary life: agriculture, arts, crafts ...; it constitutes means of exchange ...; it constitutes the need for *war*; and to defend the justice of those needs with *violence* ... Since this is *necessary* for the continuation of the city, everyone must take their "any" dark and unchanging duty as sufficient life; adapt to being a *material part* of the organism ... Thrown out the door, violence comes in through the window and spreads everywhere ... everyone, at their places, must be taught through violence ... and this is done using the state's weapon: *education* ... The teaching that has a determinate sufficient purpose in life, that aims at forging of every man a certain tool that may be applied for certain uses ... The word for Platonic education in the *Republic* is *mimesis*. ("Appendice II," 144–9)

The state imagined by Plato becomes the abstract expression of *agathon* and the idea of justice, the place in which Good is identified in the categories of the state itself. These, however, are no more than norms abstracted from the relativity of wills in contrast ("the *system* of relativity": *L'anima ignuda*, 60). In his later thought, Plato admits to the possibility of ontological sufficiency in particular and of contingent objectives when these are elevated to the level of social knowledge. He connects the contingency of events with ideas by elevating them to the level of rational knowledge: "Admitting the irrational in life as *sufficient*, Plato no longer looks for *justice* in the elimination of evil from the will of individuals, but rather accepts the *'need to live'* ... On this irrational base ... he founds the rational republic" ("Appendice II," 144).

Naturally, Plato does not call this organization by its true name – "the gang of the evil," an organization of irrational necessities. Instead, "from these single ... *affirmations he abstracts the idea of justice* ... attributing to the state *the figure of justice* ... So that the state ... for him is the *complete fulfillment of good*" ("Appendice II," 153). Alienating himself from himself in the state, the individual reacquires, if only in the form of an abstraction, the appearance of individuality. At this point, in this relationship between single individuals and the state, the violence of the determined wills (*neikos*) loses its violent characteristics by referring to the *knowledge* of the state itself, which is really only the organization of the very same violent determined wills. This relationship of the individual with the social consensus is that "second nature" (rhetoric) to which men will now be forced to conform: "thought, intellect, knowledge, ideas, concepts, categories ..., who can now take them away from men who create their sufficient lives from them, without tearing off their very skin in the process?" ("Appendice II," 155–6).

It is in this reference to social knowledge (to social ideology) that the subject can imagine himself to be a substantial Being in the modes of non-Being, in the categories of relativity, socially expressed as abstractions. Of course, this Being is nothing more than the social affirmation of certain determined ideologies created in the master–slave relationships, a stabilization of the unstable, the illusion of "sufficiency" in the categories of the social being, which are the categories of those subjects who dominate society with property and money. The universality of the state (of its laws, its knowledge, etc.) abstracts the accidentality of the real life of the individual, forming the content of its universality out of the complex of those "accidents," which then are the real content of its universality. Phenomenal reality remains non-being, but the concept of Being surreptitiously changes meaning, becoming the emblem of the categories (rules) expressed by social relationships. In these categories, the same tension to *agathon*, which is one and the same with the sense of "deficiency" of the subject, deteriorates, because *agathon* becomes the "finite power" that the social expresses as adaptation to its forms.

Man socializes himself. He abstracts his individual will in the broader structures of the "connective mode." He adapts by imitating the predominant values (for Michelstaedter, the dominant needs). Thus socialized, men stop relating their needs to the ontological recognition of the "direct mode" and begin echoing them within the values of the social body (the system of relativity); they wear them like a second skin and, forgetting their insufficiency, are able to speak about anything: "*At this point anything is worthy of being said;* every acknowledged relationship is an idea, because good is inherent in everything" ("Appendice II," 155). Every word, at this point, refers to the "categories" the *city* establishes as absolute for its continuation, for its good. The platonic *city* is the place in which the absolute can walk the streets. Michelstaedter's choice of the word "city" is intentional – it was the greatest expression of the reification of social relationships that the rhetoric of his time had to offer; the maximum expression of the social context of his time, the space in which the transformation of the individual will of the subject into a cog in the mechanism – and therefore into a promulgater of the same social knowledge – was most evident. Before this social knowledge, the individual takes on a contemplative function: his task – now identified with social *duty* – is limited to foresight, that is, the attempt to adapt to the functioning of the social mechanism as expressed by the dominant ideologies. Given the historical period in which Michelstaedter was writing (in 1910 the Italian Nationalist Association was founded), it is not surprising that Michelstaedter includes extremely concrete examples, for rhetoric does not exist outside of history; it is a representation of the dominant ideological superstructures of a given period:

> Words and the way in which they are connected: syntax: present the personality of a writer ... A patriotic writer speaks of *goodness*, and will call the war good the idea of nation good, the diplomatic facade good, etc.: his word *goodness* instead of signifying all of the content of *good* does not go beyond the concept of nation. (*Sfugge la vita*, 114–15)

In this way "life has fled the discourse." This discourse no longer expresses, as in Socrates, the affirmation of the insufficiency of he who is, in the correlativity of contrasting wills, a thing among things, that voice whose emergence is so important (it is Michelstaedter's version of Socrates's "know thyself"), because only through its uncovering will the subject be spurred "not to tolerate continuing in the circle of things where he always lacks everything." In "Socrates's voice speaks the insufficiency of every form of power" ("Il prediletto," in *La melodia*, 100–2). The social discourse, on the other hand, will only repeat the reification of the abstract structure ("connective mode") in which the subject wants to remain in order to pretend "sufficiency," to which the subject, through *theory*, wants to relate in order to "be" in it, in order to be "for" it. The unlimited concepts, the unlimited symbolic forms that men produce, will then gradually fall in line with the "finite science of the infinite relations between things" ("Appendice II," in *La persuasione*, 174): with the knowledge that individuals, in order to continue in their "illusion," call absolute. The criterion is consent.

4 The Persuasion–Rhetoric Dialectic: History and Social Being

I. Science, Technology, and the Historical Character of the Second Nature

Aristotle, Michelstaedter said, takes one more step: he puts ideas into the forms of life, giving essence to all that exists: "everything that has a cause for being has in that, for Aristotle, its reason for being" (*Il prediletto punto*, 153).[1]

Everything, driven by its respective need, finds in that need a *telos* that determines the violent action of the will as a just action ("Everything has its cause: everything has its reason: everyone is just": *Il prediletto punto*, 153):

> Everyone is right, no one has a reason ... no one can give "the reason" why he is what he is: since he would not exist as he is if there were no cause or need for it, and he could not exist if he did not exist as he is ... (A reason = right; the "reason" = justice). A reason is any conceptual connection between cause and need, the reason is the concept abstracted from any cause and need. (*Opere*, 740–1)

Aristotle's aim is to create norms for regulating "the plurality of goods as a correlative to mankind's many illusions of happiness" ("Appendice II," 215). The "just" that Aristotle organizes into categories (in taxonomies) is presented as what is given *"from the pre-made theory of the public voice"* ("Appendice II," 218); it is the "they say" that conceals the underlying system of correlativity. With the voice of deficiency silenced, value is affirmed by a thing's mere "being there"; as such, "any contingency becomes worthy of being said and argued and cataloged in a *theory*"

(Fratta, 56). At this point, the task of the subject is solely contemplative. It consists in calculating the occasions that this dogmatized empiricism offers the subject for adapting to it. Responding to sophistic scepticism, Aristotle "sets the relative measurement of the determinations of man as the absolute term of comparison" (*Opere*, 689), claiming that in practice no one has any doubt about what threatens him: "good" becomes for him the most "useful" way of being in life, that is, the affirmation of ever-changing, contingent things as substantial, only because useful. Based on these principles (virtues) made concrete in the "they say" (in the voice of the majority), Aristotle begins preaching Being and gives new meaning to the concept of philosophy:

> Virtue "becomes the most convenient … way of life": therefore, it is something knowable and there is a method for arriving at it … And there is immediately a place for ethics not as a form of philosophy but as a classified science … In Aristotle what has remained of "persuasion" (the only possible philosophy)? Only rhetoric, a catalogue of persuasive things in this or that relationship. (*Opere*, 861–2)

Through theory the subject silences his insufficiency. He places the "norm" not in himself ("direct mode") but in the many theories of life that attach an objective to the sum of objectives; a "catalog of different constituted ends" ("Appendice II," 215), a *rule* that is really only a catalogue of necessities, of needs:

> The social being wants to eat, drink, etc. under the forms of society and his state, which is determined by his necessities in relation to the necessities of the environment …: he is born a social being, and he easily adapts through his atavistic disposition to the forms that society imposes on his egoism … As such, he combats, works, and votes for the nation … – Carried outside of his environment give him other necessities – and his necessities will adapt – they will "acclimatize" (Ibsen). ("Riguardo un punto dato," in *Opere*, 804)[2]

This catalogue (science), which allows Aristotle to define Good as attainable, prepares the ground for the creation of a method aimed at attaining it: knowledge and morality (epistemology and ethics). Yet the elements in the catalogue are still "deficient." They are still comprised of the irrational reality of needs expressed in the correlative flow. A method of achieving power, one that considers the most common beliefs as true and classifies them according to principles (virtues), must be used to arrive at what is most true (useful): "Aristotle ... considers the schemes of causality to be a rational substance" (*Opere*, 861). As La Rocca correctly noted, "his attention to the general becomes subordination to the 'mostly,' ... *Doxa* becomes both the source and the object of knowledge" (101). As such, for Michelstaedter the generalization of these particular *teloi* can never be a form of "convincing" (*convincere*). They can only be a form of "winning" (*vincere*), because it will be a way of guiding the knowledge and actions of others towards the prevailing model, of pushing them to make calculatory adaptations to this model, which is objectified as theory: "If of the first it is impossible to say anything other than that which convinces, of the second ... one can ... speak drawing schemes from the different victories and classifying them" ("Appendice VI," 272).

This gives rise to a system of security that, having its foundations in the insecure place of a rationalized temporality, operates and evolves over time, progressing as knowledge and ethics do through the structures of theorizations whose constant task is to define as true that which is useful, thereby silencing the voice of deficiency. In other words, that which best confirms the ideological level achieved at that time by society: "man finds all he needs in an established form and believes that he knows life when he has learned the norms of this form and obtains without danger what he needs. This form, this straitjacket or rhetorical coat, is woven from all the things of societal life" (*Persuasion*, 138).[3]

Michelstaedter identifies the connection between the development of ideologies (epistemology, ethics, etc.) and the form achieved by the social system, and determines how that system reintegrates (reconciles), epistemologically and socially, the development of those ideological determinations by adapting them to itself. The function of society is to be "the workshop of *absolute values*" (*Persuasion*, 144). Society elaborates objectivity into theories outside the deficient totality the subject represents, and places his values (i.e., his needs) in a system of statistical data, the most common of which (the most useful) will be from time to time labelled the ultimate values of absolute wisdom: "To this mass of true and false truths, *as a pretense*, he must apply the criterion of use ... and at the same time that an argument is favorable to him, it will also be *true* to him" ("Appendice VI," 274–9).

Men are then required to refer to this absolute wisdom – to relate to it as subalterns do to a hegemonic form of knowledge and to force other ideological forms to adapt to it. In our time this hegemonic knowledge is represented by scientific–mathematical knowledge, which has been established as the ultimate result of rationalist systems and their constant restructuring aimed at eliminating any "irrational" content as they move forward towards an increasingly perfected form of objectivity. Science, which for Michelstaedter means "knowledge" as much as it does "science" proper, has inherited the prerogatives of Aristotelianism, or rather, during his time it had become the form of Aristotelianism most adept at creating consensus. Through technology, science attains this hegemonic condition by bringing into play the possibility of practically (usefully) modifying the world, thereby facilitating the satisfaction of human needs and encouraging more and more people to turn to the model of knowledge it offers: "they point the way to the elimination of attrition, so that one *persona* may affirm not to the detriment but to the advantage of another ... Thus do laymen sing the praises of scientists as 'pioneers of civilization' ... by which men, though unable to understand one another, will certainly manage to come to an understanding" (*Persuasion*, 100). We find ourselves in the historical phase in which science, through technology, is able to express itself most effectively (in which it enjoys the highest level of consent). Through technology, science assumes the features of pure rationality as the contingencies (the "accidents") of reality are gradually eliminated, and the relational system gradually conforms to the needs of man:

> They [scientists] can feign the regularity of a correlation disturbed in nature by other elements, *eliminating the contingency and procuring the proximity* so that the relation *occurs* regularly ... They give modern man medicine for his ills and the foresight that, without his power, draws near what he may need, a more secure satisfaction of his needs. This is clear in the machines that transform, bind, and eliminate the contingency from a certain circle of relations ... Scientists can *violate nature* better than others, to the greater comfort of the man wanting to go on. (*Persuasion*, 99–100)

Technology permits the attainment of those things that man retains as useful, and it facilitates the interpretation of the real as a warehouse of usable things. This mathematical spirit – aimed at establishing a nexus from the impressions received – being connected to the new social structure and being therefore the most suitable for the satisfaction of human needs (organic to its time), spreads from the field of science into all the ideological manifestations of life (philosophical knowledge included): "Whereas philosophy has raved through metaphysical exaltation, we have placed it once more on positive ground; and here, maintaining our contact with reality, we have a secure means of conquering truth. In this manner, more or less ... that which gradually supplants the old mother speaks: *modern science*" (*Persuasion*, 86).[4]

When science becomes the hegemonic discipline, all of knowledge (philosophy included) begins to function in a *scientific* manner, and the working principles of science are applied to life itself and to all its manifestations, language included:

> Science, the workshop of *absolute values* ... With the "objectivity" that implies the total renunciation of individuality, it takes the value of the senses or statistical data as ultimate values, and with the seal of absolute wisdom it furnishes ... society with what is useful for its life: machines and theories of all shapes and sizes, out of steel and paper and words. (*Persuasion*, 144–5)

Science reorganizes all of the manifestations of life according to the principle of usefulness that science itself represents, disregarding concerns about the lack of truth. This is even visible in its ability to adapt to the modernist crisis of the concept of truth: "it never arrives at doing anything more than creating empty systems for the forms of life, not an interpretation of life. – It doesn't ever investigate the why and the what for of life" ("La filosofia domanda il valore delle cose," in *La melodia*, 99). As discussed in relation to Ernst Mach, the modernist scientific epistemology views that which science expresses as a result, as nothing more than an "element" at the service of the *economy* of thought. What Mach defines as "elements" are what Nietzsche referred to as the "necessary fictions of life," concepts that serve as fictional models on which reality is erected. This, of course, is a central *topos* of modernist culture – perhaps *the* most important: "The world of representations is a symbol, with the help of which we move ourselves. Science is interested in *making this symbol more and more suitable and useful*; nevertheless it remains a symbol" (Vaihinger, 73). In the same way, "the solution proposed by the pragmatists ... with their clarification about the concept of function, may have inspired Michelstaedter to focus on the logical-epistemological-ideological process responsible for the categorical formalization of human knowledge, ... a theoretical solution, abstracted from knowledge" (Benussi Frandolli, 65). For Michelstaedter, however, this formalization is in no way a "tolerant" and "ironic" convention, because it is not dictated by individual subjectivity, but rather by the social *knowledge* to which the individual (given the insecurity of the "direct mode") is forced to adapt, "binding himself" to his time in history, to the hegemonic knowledge and the power this *knowledge* possesses thanks to its content of "historical truth," that is, social consensus: "the scientist ... [who] is a more domesticated animal than others already has that form of individual negation that with time all men will come to have" (*Sfugge la vita*, 149). As Benussi Frandoli correctly writes, Michelstaedter is in agreement "with Lenin's polemical response to Mach's empiriocriticism, [because] he aims to individuate the organic nexus that exists between the epistemological hypothesis and the social system" (16). In the cynical–sceptical epistemology of figures like Mach and Vaihinger, Michelstaedter, like Lenin, recognizes a reliance on the reified objectivity of the corresponding social model. No form of knowledge can claim to be ideologically neutral. All forms of knowledge come to a position of hegemony through the ideological structure most suitable to the social arrangement of the particular historical moment:

> Science, with its inexhaustible matter and its method made of the proximity of small, finite goals ... with its need of specialization, has taken root in the depth of man's weakness ..., [creating] from the simultaneity or succession of a given series of relations a presumption of causality: a modest hypothesis, which should become theory or law. *Law of what*? Law that in the given coincidence of given relations, the given thing happens at the given point ... But it does not presume to be finite; on the contrary, it professes its infinite way ... What's the use? The premise of the work is dishonest at every point, even if it proceeds along a path professed as infinite ... True, science no longer makes dogmatic affirmations ... But this perpetual confession of insufficiency is nothing but the ultimate artifice for making itself more certain of its future ... It gets rid of its own *persona* in order for the method to remain intact. (*Persuasion*, 96–9)

Michelstaedter is not interested in cynically exploiting the fact that scientific concepts are only centres of relations, but rather in analysing their abstract distribution in society. Within a system in which scientific concepts are hegemonic, the subject must trust in the competence of the specialist and assume the attitude of a "believer" with regard to those concepts. The more specialized the knowledge the more it will require the subject's faith, thus reinforcing the dynamics of adaptation to social knowledge. In this sense, Michelstaedter captures the connection between the depositories of knowledge, the "technicians," the intellectuals who present science as a non-ideological support for progress, and those who direct society in these epistemological forms.

As La Porta rightly notes, Michelstaedter no longer believes that the individual can separate himself from social knowledge, that it is possible for him not to be determined by it.[5] The "element" that is produced by science is a direct abstraction of the social consensus.

For Michelstaedter, the subordination of traditional scientific rationalism to external elements is not the expression of a new anti-dogmatic face of scientific knowledge. Rather, it is the means by which scientific knowledge, "declaring" its transition from classical rationality to instrumental rationality, places itself at the service of the hegemonic ideology. Instrumental rationality no longer needs to assert itself in a dogmatic manner. It needs only to rely on the real needs of the subject (abstracted in social knowledge) and use technology to present its historical form as that which is most suitable for the satisfaction those needs. Science, for Michelstaedter, is not a variant of classical metaphysics. It is the rhetoric of his time, during which the empirical knowledge produced through the specialization of *knowledges* (the mirror of social disaggregation in correlativity) is abstracted from basic needs and catalogued as principles of "good" and "bad," which are in reality "useful" and "harmful." These principles are nothing more than a stabilization of the same correlativity – of the illusions of value expressed in the "direct mode" – into the hegemonic forms of social theory. Michelstaedter's thesis is not simply a rejection of Positivism – Positivism, and Futurism in a different way, merely express the frenetic apex of the matter.[6] Nor it is a rejection of rationality *tout court* in favour of forms of knowledge more directly connected to "life." Rather it is a criticism of the manner in which life, and the irrationality of the needs *this* life expresses, are given shape in abstract forms, mechanizing the subject before them:

> Life is an inadequate thing (an implicit error of logic because it is insofar as it is not). But rational science is twice as inadequate (because as it exists insofar as it is not, it affirms to be insofar as it exists: the error of logic is clear: *cogito ergo sum*). – Every life is a core of relations, its form is no more than this materiality; living [is no more] than affirming these relations before the others ...: affirmation of inadequate individuality. Language as a means ("direct mode") for life is no more than this affirmation ... But

> when man pauses and says "my form is absolute," he begins to draw the lines of these relations presuming a rationality towards a point established as absolute ("collective mode"): "inadequate" affirmation of inadequate individuality. (*Opere*, 730–1)

Modern science, which does not speculate on the reason for life (the wherefore of life), renouncing the idea of truth (of an individual outside the irrational scheme of "needs"), looks at the world from the viewpoint of probability and structures this in regular, quantified elements to be used instrumentally. The manner in which the scientist sees the world is always determined by his need, which gives form to the world (specialization):

> What is the taste of bread? That of the first piece I eat when I am hungry or the one I eat after, when I am full? ... What is the experience of reality? If I am hungry, reality is nothing more to me than an ensemble of more or less edible things. If I am thirsty, reality is more or less liquid, and more or less potable. (*Persuasion*, 88–9)[7]

Yet the scientist calls the result of this *objective*, in that it isolates the empirical data and establishes the givenness of the categories it produces (rationalization). Science divides reality into entities that can be analysed into the abstract categories of single fields of specialization. In doing so, it categorizes the laws of that field as objectivities, but this objectivity is merely the scientist's calculatory adaptation of his own needs in the "direct mode" and the subsequent adaptation of these into the wider social ideologies in the "connective mode":

> "But we do not look at things with the eye of hunger or thirst," the scientists protest. "We look at them *objectively*." "Objectivity" too is a pretty word. To see things as they are, not because one needs them, but in themselves: ... to see objectively either has no sense because it must have a *subject* or it is the extreme consciousness of the man who is *one with things*, *has* all things in himself. (*Persuasion*, 89)

Michelstaedter's critique is not a demystification of the scientific method à la Paul Feyerabend. For him the relationship of the scientist with his *object* cannot produce objectivity because the irrational mechanism of the will/need is still operating within it. For scientists who claim they can attain objectivity, Michelstaedter advises following the experiment conducted by Gilliat, Victor Hugo's hero in *Toilers of the Sea*, who allows himself be drowned by the waters of the high tide as he calmly sits on the rocks of the shore. The only way to attain objectivity is to break the correlative relationships that keep human objectivity chained to the human need that man defines as "consciousness."[8] Tied to these, man does indeed become one with things: by connecting his life to the fictitious "sufficiency" that knowledge expresses in the ideological forms achieved by society – as the adaptation, therefore, of Being to thought – in contrast to the "persuaded" individual who acknowledges in himself the world's insufficiency.

In his criticism of science, Michelstaedter inevitably came to focus his interpretation on the Cartesian *cogito*, exposing it as an intellectual construct through which man "ensures," in an abstract system, his non-being as a down payment on the absolute:

> The "foundation" of the *cogito* (on which we expect to build a "rigorous" philosophy) actually looks like the same process that distracts at the time of succession, where everything oscillates between being and non-being, where nothing is really *present* ... Any intentional conception of truth – in which, that is, truth is reduced to the order of interpretation, to the form of the discourse – is rhetorical ...: the systematic classification of *idiomatic expressions pretends to be* a classification of the *thing itself*. (Cacciari, "Interpretazione di Michelstaedter," 26)[9]

For Michelstaedter, the cognitive moment, being guided by needs in the "direct mode" and by the hegemony of the dominant ideas of society in the "connective mode," can have no supremacy over the ontological moment. The space of the *cogito* communicates not persuasion but rather manifestations of persuasion in the form of their rationalization (i.e., the science of knowledge, the categories of knowledge transmitted by societal consensus): "it gathers and classifies the semblances of individual cases of persuasion ... Rhetoric finds its substance in the conditions of cases of persuasion that have already taken place" ("Appendice IV," 297). Clearly, these cases cannot be interpreted in a subjectivist sense ("direct mode"). They must be considered as a "voluntary" adaptation of the subject to the social ("connective mode"). Therefore, his criticism is not a demystification of science based on sceptical/relativist grounds: the scientific discourse is fictitious precisely *because* it wants to exclude – by not referring to the totality the subject expresses as "deficiency" – the possibility of overcoming the historical horizon of relativism expressed in the correlativity of individual needs. The objectification involved here is not – as it is in Heidegger – a metaphysical objectification of the real, which tends to fix the multiplicity of entities. Rather it is the historical social necessity of organizing – of using – that multiplicity, that is, the plethora of wills in contrast (in which the incipient atomization of society is reflected) that are rearticulated as consensus, as common sense.

This common sense, which must be built on that which is most powerful in society, is conspicuously historical: rhetoric transforms over time because it is continuously reorganizing the materials it has at its disposition. The objectification that takes place is different every time. The supremacy of the rhetoric of science was particular to Michelstaedter's precise historical moment. In a Gramscian sense, these objectifications are concrete historical–cultural sedimentations. As such, they are also able to absorb the philosophical currents of the historical moment – for example, the Kantian and Nietzschean tendencies of Michelstaedter's time. Also, in Michelstaedter, non-value is capable of presenting itself as value when considered in connection with the social structure.[10] It is no longer a question of determining *value* or not, but of rather understanding how these positions (in relation to values) are tied to and determined by the social structure. Michelstaedter is not interested in uprooting the metaphysical and social foundations of society in order to return to the violent correlativity of the *neikos*; he does not sublimate social criticism into a form of philosophy, reifying it as a form of the *condition humaine*. He does not arrive at a critique of the mode of production, but he does identify abstraction historically as an element of a precise (and historical transforming) social assemblage. Michelstaedter moves beyond a simple identification of technology as the primary cause of the social institutionalization of relationships of power, demonstrating how technology follows the dynamics of social relationships as laid out in his interpretation of the master–slave dialectic. In Michelstaedter, technology's hegemony is a reflection of the state that social relationships have assumed.

Establishing connections among science, contingency, and common sense, Michelstaedter characterizes science as an accumulation of likely truths, one that excludes the "deficiency" (cognitive in this case) of the ontological[11] and that replaces it with schemes of abstract "signs," including language:

> Above all, however, by means of the activity of scientists *certain words* infiltrate life as signs of given relations, given words on which men unknowingly prop themselves for their daily needs, and without knowing them they pass them on as they were received. *Technical terms* give men a certain uniformity of language ... The international language *will be the language of technical terms*. (*Persuasion*, 100)

These abstract signs feign more and more perfectly the regularity of the correlative system, orienting more and more intensely the beliefs (based on needs) of men towards the same common purposes. In turn, men acquire the impression that social frictions have declined as they calculatingly adapt to those abstractions in an attempt to satisfy their needs, which increasingly become the needs of all of society (Good and Evil). As always, Michelstaedter is interested in demonstrating how the epistemological revolution that undermined the foundations of the relationship between true and false has led to the superimposition of the two, how the declared fictitiousness of the premises of knowledge and science led to them being absolutized in their adaptation to the dynamics of the social structure:

> This knowledge of the infinite tied and determined materiality in each particular case – rhetoric cannot provide unless it wants to take the endless road of particular cases ... The abstraction of individual relations and their absorption in that regard of so many more possible particular cases belongs to particular sciences ... They have objectives that are as different each time as are the illusions of people ... But the *one* must have *his usefulness* in the fulfilling of the illusions of *the other*, who in trying to attain his *own* illusions *is able himself to be useful to others ... He has what he wants, because he only wants that which is given to him ...*: [he] advises, commands and prevails, but in all of this he *has already obeyed*. ("Appendice VI," 292–5)

"Having already obeyed" means that every single, subjective, individual, and relative position that the crisis of rational/traditional knowledge seems to have finally freed from the absolute ties of metaphysics and ethics, will now simply represent an adaptation of that same position in the pre-existing hegemonic superstructures, those of the "gang of the evil," which the individual will interpret as his own in order to better satisfy his own irrational need. Disaggregation is rearticulated into the abstract forms of its rationalization, and the atomized individual, prey to his own needs in the "direct mode," will situate those needs in the absolutized forms of social knowledge. But these forms are nothing more than the hegemonic state in which the contingent relationships have been situated and catalogued. Michelstaedter does not criticize the system in the name of a relativistic pluralism, because he sees the system as being founded on that pluralism: it is an abstract rearticulation of that same fragmentation. At this point, for each individual "the contingency of his knowledge is the criterion of that form, the criterion of his knowledge is the contingency of that form" ("Appendice II," 205).

The subject who, in an ontological illusion, alienated himself through his possession of the *object* in the "direct mode," now alienates himself by abstracting himself in the public voice, where, better protected from the appearance of individual conflicts, his alienation takes on the appearance of "nature." Of course, the accidentality between individuals, the contrast (*neikos*) between the parts of the system, remains untouched, persisting in its complete irrationality. But owing to the calculatory adaptation required of each individual, the reactions themselves of individuals are objectified before men. They become part of the codes of subsistence of the system itself. Each word, action, theory, prevented from transcending the functioning of the system itself, becomes the repetition of that which the rhetorical system expresses as culture, rights, law, that is, a catalogue of the irrationality of needs in which the desire for "pleasure" on the part of the subject (his will) is subordinated to the voice of the community (knowledge) and models itself on that.

II. Ethics, Practice, and Dialectics

For Michelstaedter, those ethical solutions that were no longer consubstantial with the real life of the subject (with his deficiency) complicitly articulated a branch devoted to praxis in order to provide a theoretical voice for that which expresses its need to adapt to the social structure:

> Aristotle presupposes "value" in all of the forms of life ... and then he fabricates philosophy ... Classic philosophy plainly identified the thinker with the thought, the subject with the object. This was its health ... In this [Aristotle's] way the hierarchy of the cataloged schemes – science – is legitimated. ("Appunti su Aristotele," in *Opere*, 836–42)

But what is theory is not praxis. The instinct for *continuing* is also involved in the idea of "morality," in its attention towards the useful: "morality is pure survival instinct" (*Parmenide ed Eraclito*, 71). Morality is the search for an ethical norm, abstractly (statistically) derived from the plurality of ends; it is a "duty" directed at avoiding any fracture in the ontological illusion, any emerging of pain (of deficiency) – that is, directed at preserving the "second nature" of the society that protects man from that pain. The theory of practice still affirms the sufficiency of any reality. While practice itself is concerned with making men aware of their deficiency, the theory of practice – expressed through *duty* – is no more than a prescription for adapting to the current reality:

> You are all crucified on the timber of your insufficiency ...: it suits you to say you carry the cross like a sacred duty, whereas you are heavy with the inert weight of your necessity ... Duties necessary to obtain your lives in peace. When you conform to the ways of the body, family, city, religion, you say, "I perform my *duties* as a man, son, citizen, Christian," and on these duties you measure your rights. (*Persuasion*, 43–4)

There is no *ought* capable of regulating society, because that *ought* is the expression of an individual will/need that is already socialized as value through the subject's calculatory reaction to what is more true because more useful: "Needs are matched by promises *of reality* as *values* ... As long as one is alive: he desires happiness, postulating a *value* that makes life worth living. He wants the *values of life* to be subordinated to a *greater value*: i.e. the *confirmation of his values*" ("Dialogo della salute," in *Dialogo della salute*, 74–5). Morality (as was true for the intellectuals of *La Voce*) means adapting to the social norms in force (Slataper's labour, Boine's army, etc.), that is, corroborating an already hegemonic *doxa*. When "truth is defined as the common reaction toward reality, based on the common results of senses and morality" (*La melodia*, 153), when the sum of common opinions comes to form the criterion of truth, it is clear that the real criterion is consent. Therefore, the spirit of Michelstaedter's "duty" is not that of German neo-Kantianism (or of its Italian offshoots). The spirit of that duty, for Michelstaedter, converges on the action that is necessary (useful) in relation to the social order that determines the subject himself and from which, if he wants to be "sufficient," the subject cannot break free: "As such they carry out these actions with the illusion of fulfilling a duty, and society requires it of them" (*Opere*, 790). Ethics, then, is no more than a catalogue of ends from which those most common in society in a determined historical moment are chosen in order to best satisfy the will/need of the subject. Ethics ends up legitimizing the status quo. This is why Giovanni Amendola's interpretation of Michelstaedter, though very positive and engaged, ended up missing the mark. Amendola perfectly grasped Michelstaedter's rejection of the "Heraclitean" tendencies in contemporary philosophy: "Carlo Michelstaedter does not belong to the countless legion of those who are whirled around by the storm of life following the mirages of becoming. To live means to stay, to consist" (163). In other words, Amendola understands that Michelstaedter's philosophy is part of a series of attempts to oppose the hegemonic advancement of Nietzschean thought, which, in its understanding of life as an incessant flux that refuses any sort of substantial reconstitution, finds expression in developments such as *Lebensphilosophie,* James's pragmatism, and the conventionalism of Mach and Vaihinger. Nevertheless, in so closely associating Michelstaedter with the neo-Kantian perspective, Amendola loses sight of the fact that for Michelstaedter as well, duty-based ethics is just another light illuminated by the god of *philopsychia*, that is, one of the voices of consensus put in place by the social forum. Neo-Kantianism – of which Amendola and Slataper are the two most important representatives in Italy – while operating within the same, now inescapable, immanentist perspective, continued to maintain – in the words of Weininger – the possibility of a cognitive objectivity of an ideal character related to the revised relationship between *Sein* and *Sollen*.[12] In this framework, the ethical perspective proposes Value in the form of a moral imperative, which – though extraneous to any theoretical certainty – has the capacity to partly restore the fundamental unity of Being and subject, establishing "on unwavering grounds the relationship between life and the value of life" (Giovanni Amendola, 44). Here, the absence of value does not lead, as in the case of the relativist perspective, to the hypostatization of contingency. Rather, this void gives way to an aspiration for value meant to orient the world. The old romantic theme of the journey inward in search of the *authentic* is recycled as the *essence of things*, viewed against the backdrop of the relation between will/duty and form:

> Where there is will there is ethical value; there is good; where there is no ethical value, no good, there is also no will. Will can be neither good or bad, because it is itself the criterion by which good is distinguished from

evil ... Ethical value resides entirely in the volitional principle. (Amendola, "La Volontà è il Bene," in *Etica e biografia*, 9–12)

... moral sense of the unity of the entire universe, of *expression* (form); ... As in the moral field, form is will (Slataper, *Appunti*, 206)

In Michelstaedter, instead, will is always expressed as a form of lacking, which is only corroborated as a "presence" through adaptation to the societal forum. And it is only through this adaptation – through this arrangement in the ideological structures of society – that the will itself (the need of the subject) is transformed into ethics, morality. As Romano Luperini correctly observed, "the absence of a historical alternative and the predominant ideological influence of the bourgeoisie bring about dissent, they forced it to descend into reality and to accept the norms of the system. This new will is experienced as 'morality' par excellence ... Only Michelstaedter is able to escape this fate" (*Gli esordi del novecento*, 65). So it is not surprising that Michelstaedter abandons the eminently ethical and Ibsenian image of the mountain,[13] with its metaphorical significance as an elevated space above the misery of the contingent and the relative, in favour of the desert–biblical hinterland on the way to the promised land, that is a sea devoid of harbour or haven.[14] Furthermore, ethics, within the structures of rhetoric, becomes an instrumental form of morality: a point of social stability, a means by which the subject is convinced he is acting autonomously, though he is really just reiterating the pre-existing social ideologies.

This is also why we cannot associate Michelstaedter's later thought with that of Weininger (as Pirandello and Evola did) and with a tendency towards the tragic, ahistorical myth of a lost authenticity. Opposing time/memory, Weininger was the first to describe the relationship between *finiteness* as the reign of the inauthentic and the need to overcome it in the timeless horizon determined by Value; this also made him one of the first to relate an ethical position to the new cultural horizon generated by the "philosophy of the crisis." Attributing an ethical framework to the tragic task that the subject must carry out in order to *consist* as individuality, as a unity of the self capable of expressing in actions (in the particular) *the peak* – that is, the *duty* equivalent to that acme – Weininger conceived of memory, being the basis of the ability to conceptualize, to give *form*, as the "place that keeps the subject from dispersion" (Manfreda, *Aporie del simbolo*, 33) and that saves him from "time," redeeming what truly has value. Within this framework, all "empirical psychology" – which declares that all our representations, in time, are inauthentic – is rejected in favour of the perspective of a *centre* (the strong identity the subject has conquered), which brings the world its qualitative value and expresses it *significantly*: "The highest expression of all morality is: Be! … A person must act in such way that the *whole* of his individuality lies in each moment" (Weininger, *A Translation*, 42).

Yet in Michelstaedter, the struggle between "time" and "memory" remains entirely internal to societal consensus. In a system in which the relative is constantly elevated through mechanisms of consensus to the sphere of the absolute, this opposition is not characterized by a tension between absolute and relative. Memory, for Michelstaedter, cannot be the space of authenticity, because memory is already contaminated by social knowledge. For Michelstaedter, the way in which the subject constitutes himself as an ontological subject is always a *fiction*. This is not because such an ontology is (as Mach claims) impossible, but because the subject ties himself (in order to *best* satisfy his needs) to the apparent ontology provided by society, by the values, rules, and words of the society in which he finds his presumed "sufficiency."

In Michelstaedter, ethics is the calculatory adaptation of the subject to the dictates of society, to the categorization of the relative into forms of Being. In the final phase of his thought, the "tragic" perspective is no longer determined by an image of lost organicity or by the idea of an ethical overcoming of the intrinsic ambiguity of bourgeois society. If the tragic exists at all in the later writings of Michelstaedter, it is located in the subject's resistance to the hegemonic abstractions of social ideologies: "Life is always this way every time that man lives and wants to live his life, and he does not adapt to the normal forms …: because the individual does not live in these, but rather society itself lives in many individuals" (*Sfugge la vita*, 101).

Before such abstractions, in order to satisfy his need and perceive himself as "sufficient," the individual begins calculating the reactions of the societal system to that same need, and he adapts himself to these, basing his actions, thoughts, and speech on the criterion of "useful." His behaviour becomes contemplative, that is, directed solely at avoiding possible "accidents," possible breaches of the ontological illusion. This is why Michelstaedter assigns so much social importance to insurance policies; they become the protective means for avoiding those accidental elements that a system based on contingency cannot truly eliminate:

"Men created 'Insurance policies' ... and he is weaker now that he no longer needs to overcome any of those dangers" (*Sfugge la vita*, 161).

Like science, morality is the abstract rationalization of the contingent (of needs) as "useful" to mankind; it is the *philopsychia* of the individual augmented by the *philopsychia* of society. Ethics is the duty that becomes the action necessary for respecting the law, for continuing – within the forms of security offered by society – to avoid occasions for pain: "My will, my inclinations, my interest are transmitted to all mankind ... My interest is the highest moral human interest ... The entire and absolute Kant is therefore simply the *philopsychia* of mankind" (*Parmenide ed Eraclito*, 71). It is still a "second nature" (of epistemology as well as of ethics), because what is called Good is still what is convenient for the subject (and for the society to which the subject adapts): "I indicate a good. Socrates makes me agree that good can do no evil – and puts me and my good in a contingency where it is evil. – I no longer care whether it is *good*, but only whether it is *useful* to me" (*La melodia*, 100).

Since the subject is not independent of society he cannot stand before it autonomously; indeed, the more he believes his theorizations to be autonomous the more he is dominated by society, because he looks upon reality as a means for satisfying his need and adapts to its "sufficient" forms. Only by negating himself at every *port*, only in the raw perception of his insufficiency, will he be able to understand how society determines him and *recognize* that "deficiency" as the basis of society's second nature.

This, for Michelstaedter, is the way of the Socratic dialectic. As he did in opposition to relativist and conventionalist epistemologies, Michelstaedter counters ethics through the Socratic way, where value cannot present itself as an abstract concept in the social forms because it must always make reference to the "deficiency" of the individual. Socrates demands a *persuasive* form of value – value that cannot refer to finite contents, that cannot abstract itself from the multiplicity of values in contrast, which are always subject to contingency, even in their social appearance as absolute. Dialectics is the sense of "deficiency," "the necessity to confront life head-on at every point" ("Appendice II," 171), the ability to ask for sufficiency in every instance – not just in particular cases with the pretense of satisfying one's need/will – because every case is in reality constructed on a foundation of contingency into which pain might irrupt at any moment: "this is the driving force that presents Socrates with the presence of *evil* under the appearances of sufficiency ...; in which he comes to demand sufficiency in relation to every case, which they would have if ... they contained value – but demonstrating themselves not to, they show themselves empty of sense" ("Appendice II," 173).

Only by recognizing his insufficiency can man salvage himself before a fictitiously sufficient (reified) reality. The dialectical method does not draw norms (concepts) from the appearance of things; the concept is freed of its finite contents expressed in the modes of relativity (which are the modes of the *neikos*), because the subject does not want to affirm his *persona* before others through the modes allowed by society. As such, he does not consider the material of the world (other subjects included) as a means for attaining self-affirmation and does not replicate the diffusion of the forms of social being:

> That dialectical method is not a heuristic process, in which man behaves toward others as he does toward himself – in which both assume an equal reality, and thus arrive to cancel out single concepts of relativity and affirm the absoluteness of their common faith. Every logic, every topos, every rhetoric teaches the art of appearing triumphant, not the art of persuading others ... This art only belongs to who is able to intuit the content of other's realities and to represent the necessity of an act in corr[elation] to this reality ... The dialectical method involves persuading – the heuristic method does not allow for a response ... The dialectical method involves taking "possession" of the soul of one's interlocutor, the heuristic method only his words ... Thus the art of winning takes the place of the art of convincing. ("La dialettica e l'eristica," in *Il prediletto punto d'appoggio*, 133–4)

The dialectic is the dialogue that exposes insufficient life; it is not the "saying" that "wins" the discussion because it is better suited to the finite contents of the historical moment expressed by society, but rather the "convincing" that exposes the common deficiency. It is not the language intended to cover the abyss of relativity (the communicative agreement), but rather the language that exposes the common deficiency. Rhetoric can only win, not convince, because it must exploit the elements of contingency while simultaneously elevating them to forms of absolute knowledge. Dialectics, when co-opted by rhetoric and focused on the multiplicity of opinions, becomes no more than a logic of *violent* organization (through consensus): "Since *Persuasion* is released and exits from life in this way, in classifications, generalizations, in the method, while maintaining its words and presumptions of the absolute" ("Appendice VI," 271)

In this context, the Platonic distinction between *doxa* and *episteme*, between the realm of opinions and philosophical knowledge, is eliminated. *Episteme*, believing itself to be autonomous, transforms itself according to the common opinions of society, that is, the hegemonic ideologies. The "illusion of persuasion" comes about in the "connective mode," where the hegemonic level of diffusion of the ideas in question is exploited. So it is incorrect for Michelstaedter to hierarchically separate the different manifestations of rhetoric – science, language, ethics, and so on. They are all connected: the predominant position of science – its capacity to connect with the dominant ideas and practices in society – is only relative to the historical moment in which Michelstaedter is writing.

By contrast, the pluralism of opinions does not generate agreement between them. Or when it does, it is only by forcing the weakest to adapt to the dominant opinion of the social sphere. As such, it remains within the logic of force and does not lead – if not in an abstract form – to a uniting of the intentions of the subjects involved. "Winning" is the hegemonic affirmation of determined opinions (common sense) to which the subject is forced to adapt himself; "convincing" is the capacity to demonstrate to others the absence of Being in the reign of the relative. Indeed, for Michelstaedter, isolated persuaded individuals do not exist: an individual is *persuaded* only when he can persuade others: "bring others with him" (*Persuasion*, 43). The persuaded must lead others out of the abstractive logic of the exchange value that determines their relations. The persuaded's function must be maieutic:

> With whomever he speaks and about whatever, it will not be an indifferent encounter for him; but he will feel himself to be an individual in front of an individual and will not believe to be so until he has communicated the individual value of persuasion. The Heuristic "wants to maintain reason" ... The Dialectic wants to persuade. The Heuristic wants it to be impossible for the other to demonstrate that it is possible to act differently than he says ... The Heuristic is the enemy of the interlocutor, he wants to negate him; – The Dialectic loves him as he loves his own life, *he wants to constitute the person.* ("Appendice VI," 280–1)

Rhetoric teaches the art of verbal triumph, but this art, Michelstaedter realizes, is only the technique through which the speaker mimetically adapts – remember Plato's *Republic* – to what the audience is more willing to hear:

> Rhetoric in general has reduced the infinite variety of individuals that a speaker can address to a single scheme for which it has determined the laws of motion, passions, etc. ... When a man wants an act from another, or from a group of other men, for whatever reason – whether for good or evil ends – he will immediately employ the means that the nature of the audience and of its connection with the thing in question [offer him], and completely neglect to examine the real nature of the thing. (*L'anima ignuda*, 38–41)

Michelstaedter had already outlined this principle in 1908 in his term paper for Professor Mazzoni on the topic of *L'orazione "Pro Q. Ligario" tradotta da Brunetto Latini*:

> Oration proceeds according to the quibble, ... it is the science of ordering the representation of the state of things in order to apply to them the terms of a formula that already exists in the code (or in the mentality, the system of interests) to which the orator appeals – ... a consequence that has undisputed value for the subject and that obtains the effect that the orator desires. (*Scritti scolastici*, 190)

This early text already presents – albeit in very idealistic terms – the foundational difference between rhetoric and dialectics: "when the subject has a purely philosophical interest. Then the quibble stops being quibble and becomes dialectical argumentation" (191). While the dialectic seeks to remove the interlocutor from the illusion of Good expressed in the forms of the contingent, the rhetorician (or orator) moulds a mirage of "good" out of the forms of social beliefs, out of the contingent that has been elevated by rhetoric to forms of absolute knowledge. The heuristic individual, by connecting to pre-existing social "forms," seeks to present the other with an absence of alternatives and to negate the other's will if it strays from the modes expressed by social being. That is why, with the progress of the rhetorical system, the speaker's work becomes easier as his intentions and those of his listeners tend to converge. The heuristic individual is a "technician"; he is acquainted with the categorizations of data applied by society, and he knows the "*science of signs*" ("Appendice VI," 288)[15] and can therefore create (operating on contingency) a "theory of expressed beliefs" ("Appendice VI," 297), a classification of what has already happened and will happen again in the same manner. The Heuristic shows others that what is useful to them ("illusion of persuasion") is useful to the whole social body (and vice versa): the rhetorician addresses the interlocutor, presenting him with a classificatory schema for the same subjective illusions that were expressed in the "direct mode," and he exploits the social power of these in order to "win."

The criterion is consent: rhetoric is a technique of violence (and of power) that overcomes disagreements by dissolving them with reference to the apparent logic of "second nature." Defined as truth – a truth that is merely non-being disguised as Being, that is, the appearance of Being – this logic preventively determines the direction of knowledge and action. In Michelstaedter the technique of rhetoric does not cancel out violence through dialogue; it does not promote agreement without suppressing pluralism.[16]

Rhetoric preserves a power situation while simultaneously concealing it by referring to what is already "irrationally" given: "drawing the lines close to the appearance of facts" ("Appendice VI," 288). Since the conditions for the prevalence of one discourse over another always depend on external factors, common sense becomes the point of truth itself. Since the *knowledge* to which the individual is forced to adapt is a reification of current relative opinions, knowledge substantially becomes a legitimization of that which already exists. The subject who expresses his will (determined by need) must situate it within the broader structures of a society in order to ensure its fulfilment. But these structures represent merely an ideological illusion, a second nature (surrogate of totality) that reiterates the fictitious union between the universal and the particular (truth and relativity; instrumental cohesion and atomization) and provides an ideological resting point for bourgeois society.

At this point Michelstaedter takes the only step available to him as a bourgeois thinker who refuses to take part in the mechanism of social violence: he continues to analyse the way in which rhetoric functions, and defines Being as absence. He links it to the "practice" of a subject who refers to himself – beyond any *theorein*, in the continuing praxis of his "deficiency," in the concrete totality expressed by that praxis, in relation to social knowledge – as *deficere* (the impossibility of finding "satisfaction" in the relative):

> The absolute – I've never known it, but I know it in the way the man suffering from insomnia knows sleep, or the man watching the darkness knows light. What I know is that my consciousness, whether corporeal or soulful, is made of deficiency, *that I do not have the Absolute until I am absolute, that I do not have Justice until I am just.* (*Persuasion*, 65–6)

The fear of death is seen as the ultimate element that produces the ideological aberration of rhetoric, and, at the same time, as the final result of rhetoric itself. The unceasing attempts to conceal death by dissimulating the "temporal" element that destroys the presumption of ends and values results in an existence that is dominated by death. For the subject to be released from this commixture of life and death, he must accept (endure) death as the abyss of insufficiency that determines the subject. He must do so in the absence of knowledge (Socrates), in the absence of Being – not through the categorizations of the flow of things that conceal death in the mechanism of *philospychia*:

> Not giving men support against their fear of death but taking this fear away ... this is the activity that eradicates the violence. "That is impossible." Certainly: impossible! For the *possible* is what is given. The possible are the needs, the necessities of continuing, what is within the limited power directed to continuation, in fear of death, what is death in life, the indifferent fog of things that are and are not. The courage of the impossible is the light that cuts the fog. (*Persuasion*, 50)[17]

To accept death is the task of he who is on the way to persuasion; this involves "melancholically" exposing the world and accepting that which expresses the impossibility of continuing to use the things of the world that constitute the ontological illusion. The persuaded accepts his "deficiency" and opposes the objectified structures presented to him by the ideological level that society has historically assumed. Persuasion must always situate itself as a dialectical point with respect to the rhetorical system of its historical moment. Indeed, for Michelstaedter, truth is not something that has been lost. It is the dialectical point that allows the truth about rhetoric to be exposed. And for this reason the way to persuasion allows no pause: "When you ask to 'continue' in peace, you are asking for an illusion" ("Della vita contemplative," in *Opere*, 784). Persuasion negates "time" as it asks for Being, but since it asks for *authentic* Being (not the categorizations of the relative), it knows that it is lacking, and so it continues in time; it continues to oppose – thereby showing the absence of Being – that which has the appearance of Being: "He who truly asks for a value, 'Being,' feels the non-value of the particular and contingent things" ("La rettorica del suicidio," in *Dialogo della salute*, 206)

The totality that the "deficiency" evokes as a union of thought and life is not the regressive dream of an *intact* past truth. It is a consciousness, one that refers in the present (in every present, in the each-time present) to the absence of totality in its denouncement of the each-time "second nature." And that is why man's approach to Justice is said to be asymptotic. It only exists as absence (it cannot be an ethical element), as a struggle in time for its *real* presence: "just as the branch of the hyperbola indefinitely draws nearer to the asymptote so man draws nearer to justice and even if the distance between the hyperbolic curve and the line is small (always smaller), the more the curve must extend in order to touch it so that man's duty remains infinite towards justice" (Di Sorbo, "*La Persuasione e la Rettorica* sul ramo dell'iperbole," in Iermano, 100).

Persuasion does not bring about any form of stabilization, because persuasion is the demand for real stabilization, which drives the persuaded to be continuously in battle. In this way, the image of totality that each time – in history – the subject makes real in his deficiency against the second nature (the dialectic between these two poles is in fact concrete, social, and continuing in time) coordinates the forms of utopia. That is why Christ, for Michelstaedter, saves himself alone. That is why "to follow does not mean *imitating*" (*Persuasion*, 72); persuasion cannot be a method because it itself is in time, although it wants to be the negation of time. Persuasion can be understood (can appear to the subject) only in relation to the forms of "sufficiency" that one sees before oneself: "do not adapt yourself to the sufficiency of what is given to you" (*Persuasion*, 73). And these social forms move through time, because they are not nature, but only the expression of the ideological level historically achieved by society:

> General histories and philosophies of history are the self-praising of mankind as it affirms itself ... not in the sense that man basically never changes and is always in the same position in relation to life – but in the sense that they are always attributed the degree of social individuality that the writer contingently knows because it is his own. (*Sfugge la vita*, 152–3)[18]

Therefore, Christ's ability to perceive "deficiency" expresses the historical form of *his* resistance, of *his* redemption (it shows the fractures of *his* world):

> no one is saved by him unless he follows his own life. But to follow does not mean *imitating*, placing oneself with whatever value one has amid the manners and worlds of the way of persuasion, with the hope of having truth in that ... The path of persuasion ... has no signs or indications that one can communicate, study, repeat. (*Persuasion*, 72–3)

The attitude of the man on the way to persuasion is the same. However, the forms of "sufficiency" he encounters, like the "weapons" he has at his disposal for the fight (vitality, Greece, tragic thought, etc.), will always alter depending on what he encounters – the rhetorical forms of his time – on his way to persuasion.

This is of course a practical problem, something to be confronted in practice: "I know that there is no worse rhetoric than this, the false persuasion of having … encoded images of a life that is impossible to live" (De Monticelli, 99). As Socrates's life demonstrates, the world can only be known through the practice of one's own "deficiency." The separation between Being and thought must lead the persuaded to a level of action capable of revealing the fracture; it must lead him to combat for the attainment of Being. In unmasking the connected mechanism of will and consensus, it must go beyond a mere acknowledgment or existential lament, because even its declaration of pessimism would only end up becoming part of the social structures. Leaving pain intact after contemplating it or criticizing the mechanism without acting to modify it are nothing more than a form of rhetoric. The mechanism can only be exposed through its transformation. This is what makes the road to persuasion a never-ending process of denouncement, as well as the reason why Michelstaedter's thought represents a historical point of passage between an idea of conciliation located in the past and one projected towards the future.

In Michelstaedter's view, if you are unable to live it – if you don't earn it in practice – you haven't understood it: you are only reiterating the dominion of abstraction, of sufficiency over deficiency:

> *The world is not something you say, but something you live.* – But if I am here, and "say" more things than I live, every time in each of these the basic illusion of my being repeats itself …; and as the world is to me, so now any thing upon which I direct my lifeless gaze, that thing will not only be true for me at that point in space and time in whatever way is necessary for my life; but *it will be a world in itself: not something to be lived but something to be said* … there the *theoretical point* is necessary, because there remains in me the deficiency of life and the fiction of the knowing person is necessary to this, and necessary to this person is the sufficiency of knowledge. ("Appendice II," 207–8)

Persuasion is a practical problem: the "pursuit … is not ONE cold analysis but the *life* of this point of contingency towards universality" (*Sfugge la vita*, 119). Persuasion's activity is centred around the real life of the individual into which Rhetoric irrupts. Persuasion is the point at which words turn into deeds[19] and Being coincides with doing (knowledge with action). It is the point at which Being comes to coincide with the actions through which the subject persuades others, revealing their common deficiency and exposing the structures of rationalization that conceal it. Delivering them from the fear of death, from the diminished life of *philopsychia*, he opens up the space for courage: "Who stays with them feels himself strengthened without knowing why: things recover the value and color, and hope and the illusion of an absolute value outside of the perpetual ebb and flow of life returns to him" (*Epistolario*, 409). By communicating the need for persuasion, the only rational end available to individuals, he redeems the violence of the *neikos* by throwing the system of relativity and need into crisis. This does not happen as an attack on "second nature" or the behavioural models of correlative uniformity like language, ethics, and science, but rather through a demonstration of the "deficiency" common to all things, the revelation that Being is estranged from thought.[20] As such, the reconstruction of the single individual – the recovery of the self after having been alienated in the objectification of the social system – becomes the foundation for the reconstruction of the social space. Symbolically, Michelstaedter places the only truly "rational" action under the structures of "giving": "To give everything and ask nothing – that is the way" (letter to Gaetano Chiavacci dated 28 November 1909, in *Epistolario*, 419). "Giving" eliminates violence at the roots because it is opposed to the principle of "exchange" organized around a giving-to-take principle (usefulness), that is, the illusionistic concession by which the other, driven by need, acquires ontological consistency by continuing in the forms of a simulated social stability:

> Giving is not so that the other may keep or be helped to continue ... That would not be you giving, but the other taking and you letting him take. – Giving is so that the other may 'have' ... The will to give is the same as the will to possess ... And the resulting act will not be ... giving another what he believes he is missing, but taking away his fear, giving him courage. (*Opere*, 734)

Giving does not involve an exchange, it is not a giving-to-take mechanism based on need: "*Giving is not for the sake of having given but for giving*" (*Persuasion*, 49). Giving therefore means revealing the deficiency through which man sacrifices the stable forms of his being-in-society:

it is not fictitious reason demanding obedience in the structures of the modes of correlativity expressed in rationalization, but the reference to a totality (because the subject's deficient life is contained in it) that resists rhetoric each-time,

> and through his own firmness makes others firm. – He has nothing to defend from others and nothing to ask of them, because for him there is no future, nothing to *expect* ... The evil of the common deficiency speaks to him with one voice and *he strives to resist it with all his life* and in every point. – He looks death in the face and gives life to the dead bodies around him ... And death, like life, is unarmed before him, who does not ask for life and does not fear death. ("Dialogo della salute," in *Dialogo della salute*, 84–6)

In a sense, then, Chiavacci was right in arguing, contrary to Giovanni Gentile,[21] that persuasion is present in all of Michelstaedter's works – not just as a form of *pars construens*. It is the only possible way to make rhetoric appear historically – in the each-time present – in the consciousness of the individual who is involved in the act of persuasion, who demonstrates the lacking of Being and reintroduces the possibility of redemption by showing the rifts in life:

> He will suffer at one and the same point of his deficiency and theirs: speaking the voice of his own pain, he will speak to them *the distant* voice *of their own pain* ... So he will place near them a *life* by which they will see the weave of what presses and distracts them gradually unravel ... Freed from what they believe indispensable, from cares, from the weight of the myriad little things in which their life always dissipates and around which it always turns. (*Persuasion*, 54)

Michelstaedter's thought is not constructed around a *pars destruens / pars construens* structure, because he does not approach the question as a conflict between absolute and relative, or between authenticity and inauthenticity. Likewise, the analysis of the relativist perspective (what Michelstaedter defined, in the first version of the *Dialogo della salute*, as "modern liberty") serves as a foundation, not as a counterpart, to the rigid and objectifying structures of society. As such, rhetoric can only appear to those who are on the road to persuasion. It can only appear to those who are in pursuit of a form of ontological consistency that, however, is no longer identified with the truth, but rather with opposition itself to the forms of social truth.

So the relationship between Persuasion and Rhetoric is indeed dialectical. It involves an each-time dialectic, one that is activated only by virtue of the very desire to suppress it (Being-as-absence). Without this desire, without the presupposition of a Being that is not given in these social structures, rhetoric would not even appear as such to the eyes of the subject. It would be perfectly concealed. Rhetoric connotes the utopian negation that is expressed in persuasion, just as persuasion reveals the rhetorical system and, in rejecting it, activates the courage to overturn it.

"But men say, 'That's fine, but *in the* meantime, in the meantime you've got to live.' *In the meantime* ... every instant of rest is the way back; no rest for the man who carries a weight upward, for when he puts it down he will have to return and pick it up again where it will have sunk" (*Persuasion*, 41–2).

III. Rhetoric's Peak

There is no stopping: rhetoric changes over time, assigning the criterion of objectivity to the each-time givenness of the hegemonic cultural values. Rhetoric continually constructs Being from the existing relationship between real history and the theoretical production constructed around it: "as it is produced each time from the needs expressed by society in order to protect itself" (Benussi Frandoli, 10). In this way rhetoric adapts to itself (mystifies) the deficient life of the subject, who can no longer express himself in his practice because he can only repeat – in his actions, words, and thought – the current modes of stabilization of the social structures. Only in resisting rhetoric will the individual find it possible to really act for the first time, without repeating the social modes of acting: "Along the usual ways men travel in a circle with no beginning or end ... they are always where they were before, because one place is as good as another in the valley without exit" (*Persuasion*, 43). Rhetoric is the historical form in which the social system expresses itself, in the form of theory and in the State's institutions that mirror that theory. Indeed, the rhetoric that Michelstaedter analyses is the societal organization of *his* time, that is, the ideological organization of his time:

> Always, in every way, the world is shouting at him with its fury and the blows of its infinite wheels: "Find yourself a hub"! And on he goes in his desperate search for this hub ... With no more illusions and no more ideals he all too soon comes to a harsh understanding; the hub you are looking

> for is no more than a sum of contingencies, of necessities outside yourself, where you can swirl away at the required speed, so to engage with the cogs of the wheels next to you in the illusion of being someone and being recognized as such by others. (Michelstaedter, "Quando dorme lo spirito," in *Il prediletto punto*, 124)

The process of rationalization and mechanization that is fulfilled through theory is always a socially real process wherein the protagonists in this "second nature" (the "gang of the evil") mimetically submit others to the same system through the irrational union of universality and contingency:

> But because "knowledge" is needed in this manner, it is also necessary that there be demand ... But the sick are created. When youngsters beat their wings to rise above ordinary life ... this is none other than "*thirst for knowledge*," one says, and with the water of knowledge their flame is extinguished. The certain end, the reason for being, freedom, justice, possession, everything is given them in finite *words* applied to diverse things and then extracted [the Italian word is actually "astratte": "abstracted"] from those things. (*Persuasion*, 69)

The sick are so because "life in every form wants life" (*Persuasion*, 141), and they even want to continue through the *neikos*, as long as it has the appearance of accord. Society presents a criterion for adaptation in the form of theory. From time to time this criterion presents itself in the forms of eternity (of nature), a reified world that grants consistency to the consciousness of the subject under the domination of the relativity of needs. Thus mankind is induced to do without the false, unstable consistency of the "direct mode," provided that this renunciation is expressed for the sake of something greater that can grant them a more perfect illusion:

> The desert becomes a cloister ... the toil of the rites takes on the name of sanctity; the wielding of concepts assumes the name of knowledge; imitative technique assumes the name of art; *any virtuosity assumes the name of a virtue* ... And the brutish, obscure toil *of the minimal life* has the same *name and right to exist* as the postulate *of the maximal life*. (*Persuasion*, 96)

Thus even education takes the form of a social psychology based on the themes of "sufficiency" and "calculation," of ought-to-be and of separation between theory and praxis as a constant form of adaptation to the social good (usefulness):

> The worst violence is exercised on children under the guise of affection and civil education. For with the promise of rewards and the threat of punishment … they adhere to the forms necessary to a polite family, those which, being hostile to their nature, *must* be forced on them by violence or corruption … The great expectation of a value is gradually flattered by means of the fiction of value in the social *persona*, always displayed before him as that which he should cultivate in himself by imitation. "You'll be a good boy like the ones you see there going to school, you'll be like a *grown-up*" … Everyone takes advantage of this temporary *anima*, which dreams of "*when it will be a grown-up*," in order to violate it … From the very first duty allotted to him, all effort tends to render him indifferent to what he does, so that he should perform it according to the rules with complete objectivity. "On one hand duty, on the other pleasure." If you study well, I'll give you a candy. Otherwise I won't let you play" … "You studied – now you can go play!" *And the child grows accustomed to considering study a labor necessary in order to live content, even if, in itself, it is completely unrelated to his life, to candies and playing* and so on. (*Persuasion*, 149–50)

These children will be the future wheels of the mechanism and, with play replaced by profit, will do their "bit of labor" (having found their "hubs"), something that gives them the means to go on living in the forms required by society, reiterating those very forms. They will be the judge who limits himself to mimetically applying the code of laws, the intellectual who mimetically teaches and reproduces the ideological level achieved by society, the executioner who performs his duty, the scientist who produces objectivity: "at the final moment of the free evolution of the system of liberty … the *persona* he dons in the exercise of his office … is his second nature" (*Persuasion*, 107).[22] His social function will become one and the same with the individuality of the subject himself:

> When to candy and playing one substitutes profit, "the possibility of living," that is, "a career" … study or an occupation will conserve the sense of … duty: indifferent, obscure, but necessary in order that one be able to play afterward … His goal is not to see anything but the indifferent unquestioned function that gives him the means to live, to be an unconscious instrument … He will be accustomed from the cradle onward to think that study is one thing and play another. Thus will he be able to

> place himself in a position to solve philosophical problems by manipulating concepts taught by scientific norms according to the norms of science, without ever asking their value: "Theory is one thing, practice another." (*Persuasion*, 150–1)

Michelstaedter relates the culmination of rhetoric with that of Hegel's system, in which negative instances are suppressed in the teleological march towards a conciliation with the State of the absolute *Geist*.[23] At this moment in which the action of rhetoric has been most successful, the subject has fully assimilated the values, the full, irrational transformation of the entity in being:

> He no longer feels the irrationality, the pain of that flux ...: *the stability of the instability*: the door to infinite philosophical rhetoric is open ... every idea has a place in the world of the absolute. The road of abstractions has no limits. ("Appendice II," 155)

Men might even ask themselves philosophical questions about the meaning of life, but they will do so knowing that the serious research pursuit of persuasion is one thing and play is another. Value (stability) will be the convention that societal security offers in exchange for adaptation to its objectivity:

> And when behind those words the smallest needs will impose their exact wills as if they were a tariff, the god's dream will be accomplished: and the science of life will be in the hands of everyone, because everyone will be in the hands of a life reduced to science. ("Appendice VI," 299)

Michelstaedter imagines the possibility of the cyclic institutionalization of this social form, the complete elimination of the antagonistic moment expressed by persuasion. This is the point at which all the relations of correlativity will settle into a repetition of exchange, realizing a mirage of action (also linguistic), which continually and perfectly replicates the structures of society:

> *Language* shall attain the limit of absolute persuasiveness ... It shall arrive at silence when each act has its absolute efficiency. And if one of these poor remnants of humanity should one sunny day sense a spark of life, almost a reminiscence across the ages in his sluggish brain, and tarry in thought over the handle of his machine, and distance himself from labor, his companion

> will have little difficulty in making him see reason: "Come," he'll say. "It's your moral duty!" The other will understand at once, "It is bread," and he will go to his labor with a bowed head ... Before gaining the reign of silence each word shall be ... an absolute appearance, the immediate efficacy of a word that no longer has but the most minimal, obscure instinct of life. All words shall be technical terms when the obscurity is veiled in the same way for everyone, and [because] everyone shall be equally domesticated. Words shall refer to relations in the same determinate manner for all ... One shall say: virtue, morals, duty, religion, people, god, kindness, justice, sentiment, good, evil, useful, useless, and so on, and the given relations of life shall be rigorously understood ... Men shall play one another like as many keyboards. Then will the writer of rhetoric manuals have it easy. For the life of man shall truly have become the divine *mesotis* that from the night of future ages shone forth to Aristotle's societal soul. Men shall speak but ουδεν λεξουσιν [say nothing]. (*Persuasion*, 137–8)[24]

Here no more contradictions are perceived: everything exists, in the full stability of theory, as contradiction called being, like darkness that is called light. And from this point on, the relativist perspectives or the hope of value are forever lost because both, through consent, will have contributed to build the security of the unstable ("the system of relativity"). At this point everything will be subsumed under a form of "value," as both the delight of "flowing" and the hope of consisting will be able to adapt to the modes of rhetoric as they change in time, following the induced oscillations of common sense. Language, the "language of technical terms," will finally have attained the possibility of infinitely reproducing those linguistic structures that reflect the relationships of power in force in society, its social structures. Word will become absolute appearance. Semantic values will tirelessly repeat the modalities of social operations.

Once Michelstaedter realizes that modernity is characterized by a real, not subjective or idealistic use of the powers of abstraction – which are powers very different from those of metaphysics – he is no longer faced with a choice between the way of the universal and the way of the particular – what is henceforth produced will always be a "universal" abstraction of the particular modes that separate men from themselves. Indeed, contrary to the work of Michelstaedter, both the epistemological and ethical approaches had reduced the phenomenon of rhetoric to the abstract picture of the phenomenon itself. While Michelstaedter is certainly far from the epistemological and para-nihilist perspectives of intellectuals such as Prezzolini (persuasion grants no rights to the relative, nor to liberation from the *cages* of Being this would imply), he also does not side with *Vocians* such as Amendola and Slataper: as we have seen, putting morality back into life only means making life the duty *this* life requires. Michelstaedter knows that the crisis is a historical one, and his position allows for historical resistance to the system of abstractions of *his* time, while simultaneously outlining the possibility of an each-time resistance, that is, the possibility of opposing any historical moment that seeks to present itself as nature, the possibility of reactivating history by referring to the lack of Being:

> To those who despair of every fixed point, of every straight path, every destination, for they have seen that the ways of society are twisting and vain, you shall point out the essence of their demands, "the need for a straight path." … You shall draw your sword against the "institutions" that give them their name and sufficiency, you shall destroy the "manger" at which they feed, you shall fight in every way the principle of cowardice … ensconced in society. (*Opere*, 704)[25]

By equating Being with the "deficiency" imposed by society, Michelstaedter effectively demolishes the myth of autonomy of thought, which he connects back to the forms of its social behaviour, the forms to which thought, born out of need, adapts. Therefore, persuasion cannot be a "theory" among others, because it subjects all cultural activity and its actors – once separated from the real life of the subject, from totality – to criticism.

Of course Michelstaedter could not redeem his historical moment all by himself – who would be capable of such a feat? But by exposing its ideologies, he was able to offer awareness to a whole generation: "He who does not live with *persuasion*" – he who fails to oppose the finite forms of abstraction to the totality they are unable to contain, who forsakes and feigns that totality in those same forms by relating his own discourse to them, believing all the while that he is autonomous – well, that man can do many things, but he "*cannot fail to obey, for he has already obeyed*" (*Persuasion*, 35).

Conclusion
The Limits of Bourgeois Thought: *Persuasion and Rhetoric* and *History and Class Consciousness*

Where no gods are, specters rule.

Novalis

The cultural backdrop to Michelstaedter's thought – and herein lies the difficulty of interpreting it – is marked by a dense cross-hatching of overlapping and contrasting tendencies: the new Nietzschean-inspired ideologies that exalted life as a continuous flux, one that negates and annihilates every concretion of itself, found an opposing response in the final offshoots of Romanticism, rehabilitated in the form of "tragic" thought and ethics.

That said, recent critical assessments of Michelstaedter as Protagoraen (and almost deconstructionist) conspicuously miss the mark. Such interpretations misread his correlativity as a world of wills in contrast in which "no one can be right," or they view persuasion as the capacity to destroy every entity that presents itself as Being. But for Michelstaedter, the world of correlativity is not the real world; it is only the phenomenal functioning of the world in the moment in which individuals are blocked in the mechanism of will/need that alienates them from themselves. And persuasion is an attack not on Being, but rather on the organization of the relative carried out by rhetoric.

Other analyses of a Kantian–ethical nature, which focus on the tragic vein in Michelstaedter's work and on his opposition to relativist thought, limit his work to a sort of morally based reactivation of Being expressed as a moment of self-awareness on the part of the subject. Such interpretations overlook that Michelstaedter in his later writings explicitly rejects the ethical perspective (which was only valid for him in 1908) as a form of rhetoric, and that Being in Michelstaedter is a concept that is not unrelated to the forms of rhetoric, but rather exists only in dialectical opposition to those forms. Such a position allowed Michelstaedter to overcome the anti-dialectical opposition between "inauthentic life" and a distant "authentic absolute" (*Zivilisation* and *Kultur*) and to move beyond the new phenomenological perspective that provided the basis for the cultural ascendency of relativist ambiguity, on his way towards a demystificatory attack on ideological structures and abstraction as spaces of control and social exploitation.

Persuasion and Rhetoric is not a response to the crisis of a unitary *Kultur* aimed at reviving that same *Kultur*. *Persuasion and Rhetoric* is not *The Gay Science* or *The Analysis of Sensations*; it is not even *Sex and Character* or *Soul and Form*.

To understand Michelstaedter's work we must jump ahead a few years – beyond the Belle Époque and its cultural binomials still based on the dichotomy of absolute and relative – in order to find a similar analysis of the new epistemology and ethics of his historical moment – in order to find a thinker who understood (albeit from a different starting point) that "the core of existence stands revealed as a social process" (19): György Lukács, in *History and Class Consciousness*.

Persuasion and Rhetoric and *History and Class Consciousness* share many points of contact. The most decisive among these is their common understanding of the concept of abstraction, which is not merely (as it is in Hegel) objectivity as alienation in itself, but rather the alienation of that objectivity – in the forms of historical objectivity – with respect to the subject who produced it. In other words, both understand this objectification as a product of man, as the phenomenal form of a determined complex of social relations in a determined historical period.

For both Michelstaedter and Lukács, in this society man is free only in contradiction with himself; he is free only when he "voluntarily" transfers himself within the universality of reality (society's institutions: what Michelstaedter calls the "security system") and culture (the superstructures) of society – that is, in the semblances of Being. In 1922, Lukács presented the following argument in the opening pages of *History and Class Consciousness*, thereby situating himself in relation to the development of a new scientific method:

> They seek refuge in the methods of natural science, in the way in which science distills "pure" facts and places them in the relevant contexts by means of observation, abstraction ... If such methods seem plausible at first this is because capitalism tends to produce a social structure that in

> great measure encourages such views ... For that very reason we need the dialectical method to puncture the social illusion so produced. (*History and Class Consciousness*, 5)

For both Michelstaedter and Lukács, the process of specialization lies behind the process of abstraction and is reflected in the new Machian-like scientific epistemologies, that is, in the practical use of elements that science itself knows to be in reality non-existent: "Bourgeois thought concerns itself with objects that arise either from the process of studying phenomena in isolation, or from the division of labor and specialization in the different disciplines" (28). Both see abstraction as a form of rationalization of accidental systems (of both men and ideas); in such a society, these systems are inevitably in contrast with one another and must be "reconciled" into a form that allows illusory social agreement to be maintained.

For both thinkers, furthermore, the social system is founded on a surrogate form of totality that is really just an abstraction of reified elements (men and ideas) in an inevitable condition of accidentality: more of "a law of mutually interacting 'coincidences' than one of truly rational organisation" (102). Michelstaedter expresses this concept through the metaphor of the creaking wheels of the mechanism; Lukács does so

> in the incoherence of the system in fact. This incoherence becomes particularly egregious in periods of crisis ... Adventitious connection with each other is suddenly forced into the consciousness of everyone ... yet it can experience a sudden dislocation because the bonds uniting its various elements and partial systems are a chance affair even at their most normal. (101)

For both, this system relies on the necessary reification of human relationships, which they understand as relationships between things. For both, relationships between counterparts are inevitably the result of an objectual relationship – Michelstaedter's criterion of the "useful." The first form of this is in the immediate objectification to which the subject submits his counterparts (in what Michelstaedter refers to as the "direct mode"):

> In capitalist society man's environment, and especially the categories of economics, appear to him immediately and necessarily in forms of objectivity which conceal the fact that they are categories of the *relations of men*

> *with each other*. Instead they appear as things and the relations of things with each other. (14)

The second form involves the abstraction of those same reifications within the conceptual/ideological universe (the sphere of *knowledge*), in a reduplication of reality as second nature: "all human relations … assume increasingly the objective forms of the abstract elements of the conceptual systems of natural science and of the abstract substrata of the laws of nature" (131). Therefore, for both, the subject lives his alienation both in his individual relationships (subject–object) and in his adaptation into the conceptual and concrete forms of the organization and objectivity of society, in a form of objectification that excludes the possibility of real *totality*. And for both, the historical form society has assumed becomes reality *tout court* for the subject.

Finally, and perhaps most surprisingly, for both, society forces the subject to relate to societal objectifications (rationalization) through modes of behaviour centred around the characteristics of "contemplativeness" and "calculation" (they use exactly the same words). Before a system in which the individual perceives himself as incapable of having any influence (contemplativeness), before a system that appears as a form of insurmountable objectivity (second nature), that same individual reacts with mere calculation, that is, by adapting to that which the system offers (in Michelstaedter's "safeguarding from accidents" [*preservarsi dagli accidenti*]: the basis of rhetoric), in doing so preserving the system itself in which the subject alienates himself:

> The more reality and the attitude of the subject … will be transformed into a receptive organ ready to pounce on opportunities created by the system of law, his "activity" will narrow itself down to the adoption of a vantage point from which these laws function in his best interests (and this without any intervention on his part). The attitude of the subject then becomes purely contemplative … His activity is confined to the exploitation of the inexorable fulfilment of certain individual laws for his own (egoistic) interests. But even while "acting" he remains … the object and not the subject of events. (130–5)

For Lukács, as for Michelstaedter, the system sustains itself through the types of behaviours it imposes on its parts – that it imposes on its members, who are rearticulated and polarized in social abstraction and the behavioural model demanded by the system.

Building on this foundation, which we could call macro-speculative (abstraction, alienation, reification, contemplativeness, and calculation), Lukács and Michelstaedter arrive at a critique of the new scientific perspectives and, ultimately, of the philosophical proposals themselves. Both see a connection between scientific method and social orientation, which they recognize as linked by the common characteristic of specialization; both read the new scientific perspective as an attempt to perfect epistemology rather than understand it in relation to social structure:

> The specialisation of skills leads to the destruction of every image of the whole ... We find that science, which is likewise based on specialisation ... [tears] the real world into shreds ... In reply to allegations that "the various factors are not treated as a whole" Marx retorts that this criticism is levelled "as though it were the text-books that impress this separation upon life and not life upon the text-books" ... The more intricate a modern science becomes and the better it understands itself methodologically, the more resolutely it will turn its back on the ontological problems of its own sphere of influence, ... the more it will become a formally closed system of partial laws. (103–4)

The two men's approaches to such an epistemological system, which loses sight of the *whole* and limits itself to the actions of contrasting partial (specialized) systems – in the same way that individuals do in real life – are much the same:

> The unconditional recognition of this problem, the renouncing of attempts to solve it leads directly to the various theories centering on the notion of fiction. It leads to the rejection of every "metaphysics" ... Some schools make this renunciation explicitly (e.g. Mach, Avenarius, Poncaré, Vaihinger, etc). (119–20)

Each of these contrasting systems has its own exclusive value. Every presumption of absoluteness is gone, and their results are equated with "fictions." As a consequence, every attempt to attain a form of overall totality is shown to be impossible even before the attempt is made. Moreover, in this way, the impossibility itself of knowing the system in its totality is given the absolute and unquestionable value of law. In this way, scientific rationalism becomes ideological sentiment, "imitating" a society that – more and more dominated by particular moments of social living – is no longer interested in dominating through a form of thought that expresses itself as totality. Society's inevitable fragmentation is directly expressed in the forms of a second nature, in what Michelstaedter refers to as an "absolutistic" organization of the relative.

Both Michelstaedter and Lukács attack the philosophical perspectives of their time, beginning with a critique of the absolute/relative binomial, that is, of the perceived necessity of including both sides of the binomial in the creation of social being:

> The absolute is nothing but ... the projection into myth of the intellectual failure to understand reality concretely as a historical process ... Every "biological" relativism, etc., that turns its limits into "eternal" limits thereby involuntarily reintroduces the absolute, the "timeless" principle of thought. (18)

Both critique philosophy's relativistic proposals as the cultural expression of an essentially static reality. For Lukács, the philosophical perspective of relativism results in an anthropological and objectifying perspective, where the very theory in which that same anthropological position expresses itself, unable to put itself into a dialectical relationship with historical praxis, ends up seeing itself as immutable – that is, it objectifies itself:

> *History is the history of the unceasing overthrow of the objective forms that shape the life of man* ... For if man is made the measure of all things ... without man himself being measured against this criterion, ... without making man himself dialectical, then man himself is made into an absolute and he simply puts himself in the place of those transcendental forces he was supposed to explain ... At best, then, a dogmatic metaphysics is superseded by an equally dogmatic relativism. This dogmatism arises because the failure to make man dialectical is complemented by an equal failure to make reality dialectical. Hence relativism moves within an essentially static world ... The weakness and the half-heartedness of such "daring thinkers" as Nietzsche or Spengler is that their relativism only abolishes the absolute in appearance. (186–7)

In options like "relativism" Lukács sees a reflection of the culture of the Belle Époque, the image of a continuous conflict, of a continuous contradiction, that – in abstracting itself from the level of historical modification – ends up reconciling itself with the forms of society, that is, as a crystallization of itself, of the conflict it expresses. In 1922, Lukács, as

Michelstaedter had done in 1908, opts for a tragically oriented philosophy aimed at reactivating the *value* of existence:

> So that *here* both *logically and methodologically* Socrates must be in the right as against the sophists, and logic and value theory must be in the right as against pragmatism and relativism. What these relativists are doing is to take the present philosophy of man with its social and historical limits and to allow these to ossify into an "eternal" limit of a biological or pragmatic sort. (188)

Nevertheless "value" only maintains meaning in relation to the problem of relativism. Lukács, by the time he had reached his Marxist phase, had understood that the binomial itself between absolute and relative was an objectified expression of social ideology, existing outside of the possibility of historical modification determined by praxis: "Nor is it a 'duty,' an 'idea' designed to regulate the 'real' process" (22). Lukács, like Michelstaedter, comes to see the ethical perspective as "a purely contemplative way" (38), an abstraction that repeats the structures of the social system/mechanism:

> ... action directed wholly inwards. This is the attempt to change the world at its only remaining free point, namely man himself (ethics). But as the world becomes mechanised its subject, man, necessarily becomes mechanised too and so this ethics likewise remains abstract ... It remains merely normative ... the abstract ethical imperatives of the Kantian school. (38–9)

Like Michelstaedter, Lukács affirms that modern philosophy (Classical Greek philosophy is an exception) operates within the sphere of the "reified structure of the consciousness" (109) on the level of a purely *formal* overcoming of the system in which it operates; as such it ends up mirroring the intellectual production of the system itself, that is, the ideological expression of the same system of alienation: "the resulting ethic becomes *purely formal*" (163). The perspective of an absolute *action,* set outside of its dialectical relationship with the forms of the social (of the inauthenticity of the social), is itself abstracted as an atemporal element. As such it assumes the modalities of the second nature, finding itself impeded from offering a critical perspective on the historical forms assumed by society, which is not itself completely abstract, that is, that would allow it to intervene in order to modify them on the level of praxis. This is also why both Michelstaedter and

Lukács, in contrast to the social criticism of the right-wing intelligentsia (Weininger, Hofmannsthal), level specific criticism at the historically assumed forms of capitalism.

Therefore, only when "theory and practice are united [does] it become possible to change reality and when this happens the absolute and its 'relativistic' counterpart will have played their historical role for the last time" (189). No element (not even "persuasion") is endowed with atemporal meaning: its action is valid in the forms of its historical–dialectical relationship with the social (with rhetoric). A merely ethical response inherently includes its own failure, its complicity. Bourgeois thought is unable to transcend the current mode of operation of a society whose prevailing desire is to avoid any type of transformation on the level of praxis. Bourgeois thought ends up being forced to formalize an idea of stasis:

> On the one hand, we find the utter sterility of an ideology divorced from life, of a more or less conscious attempt at forgery. On the other hand, a cynicism no less terribly jejune lives on in the world-historical irrelevances and nullities of its own existence. (67)

For both Michelstaedter and Lukács this stasis corresponds to the loss of a historical sense of the social forms assumed by society (and of the thought originating from it) – to the formation of a supratemporal image of social phenomena, and the loss of awareness that these phenomena are produced by humanity itself and are not really – as they appear in the second nature with which men calculatingly engage – out of their control: "The view that things as they appear can be accounted for by 'natural laws' of society is … both the highpoint and the 'insuperable barrier' of bourgeois thought" (174). Differently from Michelstaedter, Lukács – following Marx – places this phenomenon at the end of the bourgeoisie's revolutionary moment, at the point at which the bourgeoisie finds itself forced to silence the principle of historical transformation that had led it to overcome feudal society: "The weapons with which the bourgeoisie felled feudalism to the ground are now turned against the bourgeoisie itself" (Marx, *The Eighteenth Brumaire*, 77). Both see the loss of historical awareness as providing the basis for the development of a fictitious *whole* that leads to an incapacity to understand the relationship between real history and theory. Both point to the reification of traditional (humanistic) concepts such as progress, liberty, value, and so on, which come to represent the structure of relations as they are given within the existing system. For both Lukács and Michelstaedter, the subject, through property and money, determines the configuration of the system itself and the members within it – both locate utopia in the capacity to shatter the objectification presented by the system, by relating it to the *wholeness* (the *totality*) that the system cannot possess, rather than opposing it with some form of unreal atemporal value. For Lukács this *whole* is the unity of theory and praxis within the framework of historical development, a point of view that can only be possessed by the proletariat, in whose conditions are reproduced the life conditions of the entire society, beginning with the *objectified* condition of the worker within the process of production, that is, his separation (in the historical moment) from his own labour power. This separation cannot be perceived by the worker as a *deployment* of his own subjectivity. As such, the worker does not recognize anything of his own creation in the objectifying structures of the social situation. Before the objectification of the social system, the worker immediately perceives himself as an object that reifies his own labour power in the structures presented by the current system. As such he recognizes his social existence as antagonistic to the system. The static position, which is contemplative and atemporal, is impossible for him, because he cannot perceive himself as a subject of the social system, of the social being. Social being will begin to appear as an abstraction to him, as a modifiable product of history.

For Michelstaedter this *whole* is connected with a historical form of antagonism; it is historical because the forms that rhetoric assumes as second nature are historical. The antagonism originates in the "pain" (though sometimes it appears as a differentiation of class) that the subject experiences when the unreliable conciliation of social forms is broken apart, revealing what always lay underneath: the absence of a real ontological nexus, an abstraction of the forms of social conflict.

This ontological nexus, which originates in Michelstaedter's inability to apply his social analysis to the mechanisms of production (rather than those of labour) – and therefore to the division of classes – marks a separation between his analysis and that of Lukács. *Persuasion and Rhetoric* does not formulate a comprehensive theory of emancipation because it does not fully and historically grasp the forms of abstraction, alienation, commodification, and exchange, and the nexus of these with the modalities of production, the division of classes, and the exploitation this entails. Therefore, not focusing his analysis on the moment of production, if not in the sense of production of ideas, he does not take into account the genesis of a revolutionary subject in the objectification of the worker (it is worth noting that all of Michelstaedter's intellectual activity takes place at a distance from the industrial centres of his time). As such, though the persuaded has the duty to speak to others, Michelstaedter's vision of praxis remains one of an individualistic nature, able to express itself as a form of resistance, not revolution. And for this same reason Michelstaedter locates the reasons for the subject's adaptation to social being in a psycho-ontological nexus: the fear of death. This is also why Michelstaedter locates the origins of the entire process in the mechanism of the will/need – beginning with the conflictual atomization of the "direct mode" – rather than in the fragmentation of previous modes of production, as Lukács does.

As such, *Persuasion and Rhetoric* is constrained by the limits of bourgeois thought itself, even though it represents one of its most anomalous results, almost the point at which it can no longer continue without rejecting itself, having condemned outright the validity of "autonomous" intellectual activity characterized by its separation from the historical forms of the social structure.

Michelstaedter's thought developed at a moment in which class struggle was at a standstill. A moment in which the socialist-reformist milieux of Italy and Austria, allied with the bourgeois governments, "maintaining the forms, names, schemes of arguments, and all the phraseology of Marx – [have] reduced his negation of bourgeois society to an element of reform *in* bourgeois society" (Michelstaedter, *Persuasion and Rhetoric*, 124–5). Though unable to resolve its own aporias, in its identification of the second nature of the mechanisms of abstraction, Michelstaedter's philosophy represents an invitation to fight (foreseeing some of Gramsci's ideas on the ways in which "consensus" works) for an alternative common sense, identifying the alienated structure of society's mode of operation and undertaking to reveal it. The reconstruction of the consciousness of the individual, beyond his adaptation within the forms of rhetoric, represents the precondition for the reconstruction of society. And in any case: "mankind always sets itself only such tasks as it can solve; ... we will always find that the task itself arises only when the material conditions necessary for its solution already exist or are at least in the process of formation" (Marx, *Capital*, vol. 2, 955).

Mimmo Cangiano – The Hebrew University of Jerusalem

Notes

Introduction

1 Written between 1909 and 1910, *Persuasion and Rhetoric* was published in 1913 (by Formiggini) thanks to the efforts of Vladimiro Arangio-Ruiz, who the year before had printed some of Michelstaedter's poems and his *Dialogo della salute*. In 1922, thanks to the work of Emilio Michelstaedter (Carlo's cousin), *Appendici critiche* and *Il prediletto punto d'appoggio della dialettica socratica* were published by Vallecchi. That same year a new edition of *Persuasion and Rhetoric* was published and the journal *La Ronda* featured some previously unpublished writings. In 1958 Gaetano Chiavacci published *Opere*, which would be expanded over time, thanks especially to the commendable work of Sergio Campailla. During his lifetime Michelstaedter published only three articles: "Reminiscenze del funerale di Carducci," published by his family without his knowledge in *Il Corriere friulano* on 22 February 1907; "'Più che l'amore' di Gabriele D'Annunzio al Teatro di Società," also in *Il Corriere friulano* on 18 September 1908; and "Ancora lo 'Stabat Mater' di Pergolesi," in *Gazzettino popolare* on 29 April 1910.

Chapter 1

1 Cf. Fortunato: *Aporie della decisione*, 187: "Weininger is the hero of the attempted great restoration."
2 Here I use the term "cynical" in relation to the capacity to refer to a multiplicity of theoretical solutions and representations, in thought and in daily life (Pirandello's *forms*), without believing that any of these effectively correspond to a truth.

3 The bourgeois substratum of this reactionary myth was perfectly grasped by Furio Jesi. Cf. *Letteratura e mito*, 24: "The epiphany of the mythos, … to impose the immobile instant, the eternal present of contemplation."

4 Among his contemporaries we can recall Giovanni Papini, who wrote a rather uninteresting essay on Michelstaedter in *Il Resto del Carlino* on 5 November 1910, titled "Un suicidio metafisico." Slataper wrote the article "Scritti di Michelstaedter," in which he speaks explicitly of "moral experience." Prezzolini wrote a small piece in *Rassegna letteraria*. These articles are part of an occasional and sparse collection of writings on Michelstaedter during the period.

5 Cf. Taviani: "Attualità di Michelstaedter," in Merola, ed., *Ricerche sul modern*, 320: "No better way to silence and distance it [persuasion], in perfect harmony with the new-hermeneutic … and/or deconstructionist culture of the last part of the century."

6 Cf. Debenedetti, *Il romanzo italiano*, 171–2: "Michelstaedter marks … with his book, a crisis of the 'person' … which should be considered parallel, in addition to simultaneous, to the crisis of the naturalistic 'character' that Tozzi would exemplify …; in order to locate … the origins we must go back to Pirandello."

7 Cf. Abruzzese, ed., *L'età dell'idealismo*, 180: "Michelstaedter is only one in Italy to anticipate the critique of capitalist society in a manner that will return in Lukács, Benjamin, Adorno."

8 The concept of "modernism" has only recently received attention from Italian scholars. The number of works in English that utilize the concept in reference to Italian culture can be counted on one hand. See Gazzola, *Montale, the Modernist*.

9 Cf. Harrison: "Overcoming Aestheticism," in Somigli and Moroni, eds, *Italian Modernism*, 170: "After all, it was post-Nietzschean philosophy that allowed for this shiftiness emphasizing as it did that being is a play of becoming, where stability of knowledge is a chimera." See also Harrison's fundamental *1910, the Emancipation of Dissonance*.

10 The reference to Heraclitus here is in relation to the Nietzschean philosophical trend at the beginning of the twentieth century that viewed the name Heraclitus as encompassing the image of life as an irreparable contradiction devoid of any possibility of rational and/or dialectical reconciliation. Cf. Givone: "Presentazione," in Laura Sanò, 10: "the 'Heraclitean moment' of philosophy, or rather the recognition that contradiction belongs to reality rather than to thought."

11 Regarding the ideological function of the modernist perspective there is an endless list of publications. For their radically opposed political readings

of those perspectives, see Berman, *All That Is Solid Melts into Air*, and Burrow, *The Crisis of Reason*.

12 Michelstaedter's contemporary, Giuseppe Rensi, writes in *Lineamenti di filosofia scettica*, 373–4: "the inexistence of truth leads to the inexistence of *Being*. *Being*, then, is a word that defines a certain fact, it is an idea or an individual determination, but it has in it nothing of the absolute: it is only that which is susceptible to being perceived … [O]nly Nothingness is the true Being and only in it is the nature of truth permanently and unconditionally realized."

13 The six "Appendici critiche" are a fundamental tool for understanding *Persuasion and Rhetoric*. Unfortunately, these writings have not been translated into English. However, thanks to the work of Sergio Campailla, they have been published in Italian in the volume *La persuasione e la rettorica. Appendici critiche del 1995*. All citations of the "Appendici" that follow here come from this volume.

14 We should specify that this phenomenon cannot be understood without referring to the ongoing conflict between psychology and philosophy, that is, to the inevitable attack on philosophy levelled by Nietzsche when he contends that every standpoint is dictated by the obscure pre-understanding of the world that guides the thinking of every philosopher. It is no coincidence that Mach's background was in psychophysiology. In Italy, the Hegelian Benedetto Croce attacks psychology as a non-philosophy while the neo-Kantian Amendola views psychology as the road to scepticism.

15 Cf. Liliana Albertazzi, Guido Cimino, and Simonetta Gori-Savellini, eds, *Francesco De Sarlo e il laboratorio fiorentino di psicologia*.

16 Salsano, *Michelstaedter tra D'Annunzio*, 75: "suspending existence in a labyrinthine investigation exposed to a hermeneutical infinite, … in a condition launched virtually within certain postmodern spaces of the twentieth century."

17 If Vladimir Bazarov could declare that Mach's perspective represented Marxist epistemology, it is easy to understand the level of cultural hegemony achieved by such a perspective, and also why Lenin wrote about *empiriocriticism*, a philosophy perceived, along the lines of Hume, Berkeley, and Condillac, precisely as relativistic pragmatism. I believe that on this basis we can also understand what Lukács meant when he contended that *History and Class Consciousness* was his attempt to provide Marxism with a theory of knowledge.

18 Cf. Michelstaedter: "Il dialogo della salute" (first draft), in *Dialogo della salute e altri dialoghi*, 92–4: "I would speak to you of God and of real life: I

would support my negative arguments with the deranged hope of eternal happiness for those who have followed the path of health ... – No, I will not speak to you of this, nor do I know how to break the fog with the flash of a miracle – no, God is not with me – he is not with anyone anymore."

19 But as we shall see, Michelstaedter offers some interesting insights in this regard.

20 Cf. Tavano, *Gorizia e il mondo di ieri.*

21 Cf. Altieri, "La famiglia Michelstaedter e l'embraismo goriziano," 39: "Carlo Michelstaedter's father seems ... to be emblematic of the desire to assimilate ... of those families from the Jewish bourgeoisie. Owner of a currency exchange service, an agent with Assicurazioni Generali, he had abandoned the Via Ascoli after his marriage and he had worked to insert himself in the cultural circles of Gorizia ... This implies the abandonment of Jewish traditions, which differed too much from the values of the majority in society, reducing religious observance to a mere exterior act."

22 Cf. Zanello, "Una vita 'non eccezionale,'" 47–90.

23 Cf. Pieri: *La differenza ebraica*, 99: "Michelstaedter maintains that 'consciousness is individual,' while his father, in conformity with the rationalist creed, believes that 'consciousness is generalized,' thus the expression of a socially communal cultural reality."

24 Nordau's *Degeneration* saw five editions in Italy within thirty years of its publication in 1892.

25 Alberto Michelstaedter, *La Menzogna*. Cf. Di Solbrito: "Alberto Michelstaedter"; cf. Cergoly, *Trieste Provincia Imperiale*; cf. Brambilla: "Per Alberto Michelstaedter."

26 And which is existentially reflected in the decision not to move to Vienna to study mathematics but rather to Florence for "an immersion in art and culture."

27 Cf. Michelstaedter, letter to Iolanda De Blasi dated 1–2 May 1907, in *Epistolario*, 206: "Everything appears to me not as crude matter, but as artistic essence, as part of a universal artistic organism."

28 See Cappozzo: "Il percorso universitario."

29 For Professor Pistelli, Michelstaedter had translated the fifth lesson of Tadeusz Zielinski's volume *Our Debt to Antiquity* (Slataper translated the seventh). In the text Michelstaedter found citations, such as "Antiquity should be considered not as a model, but as a seed plot" for modern civilization, that seem to have had a certain influence on his overall development. On this translation, see Gallarotti: "Un manoscritto sconosciuto. Carlo Michelstaedter traduttore di Zielinski," in Campailla, ed., *Dialoghi intorno a Michelstaedter*.

30 On Ibsen's popularity in Gorizia, see Furlan, *Carlo Michelstaedter*. See also Pierangeli: "La via di Ibsen."

31 Michelstaedter would encounter, especially in Ibsen, the fundamental clash between society as a "system of falsehood" and the individual projected towards the principle of authenticity.

32 It is likely that Michelstaedter was introduced to Schopenhauer by his friend Enrico Mreule during the last year of school. Particularly significant is that Michelstaedter wrote to Croce at the end of 1907 offering to do German-to-Italian translations for the publisher Laterza (the Italian translation of *The World as Will and Representation*, prepared by Paolo Savj-Lopez and Giovanni De Lorenzo, would be published between 1914 and 1916). The publication of Nietzsche's third *Untimely Meditation* in 1915 (edited by Arangio-Ruiz), which deals specifically with Schopenhauer, is indicative of the enduring interest in Schopenhauer among the group of Florentine friends.

33 Michelstaedter, letter to his sister Elda dated 8 April 1908, in *Epistolario*, 308: "In those days I read almost all Ibsen. That was a man, by God! He made me think hard, and still does. Apart from Sophocles, he is the artist that has grasped and engrossed me the most."

34 Here Michelstaedter is following a path not unlike Lukács's in *The Metaphysics of Tragedy*: he represents the essentiality of conflict as the sole form of totality, the spirit of tragic conflict as a means of overcoming the adaptation to the ambiguity that characterizes bourgeois life.

35 Cf. Pirandello, *On Humor*, 119–25: "It has often been observed that humoristic works are disorganized, disconnected, interrupted by constant digressions … The disorganization, the digressions … are precisely the necessary and inevitable consequences of the disturbance and disruption which are produced in the organizing movement of the images through the work of the active reflection … We shall see that reflection becomes something resembling a diabolical imp that takes apart the mechanism of each image."

36 Cf. Michelstaedter, *Scritti scolastici*, 66: "The chorus should be considered as one of the elements of action, … not as a spectator."

Chapter 2

1 By this metaphor, already well-known from Schopenhauer (*The World as Will and Representation*, 232), he in pointing to the lack of a stable foundation to existence. But whereas in Schopenhauer this lack is

presented as a noumenal element, in Michelstaedter it remains a phenomenal element.

2 Cf. Harrison, "Carlo Michelstaedter and the Metaphysics of Will," 1020: "By the nineteenth century, the essence of this subject that the Platonic and Christian tradition had considered to be animated by divine *pneuma* is equated with will."

3 Michelstaedter, *Sfugge la vita*, 32: "it is impossible to illustrate an act that is not obedience to the will ... we 'must' live therefore we 'must' follow 'our will.'"

4 Cf. Harrison: "Michelstaedter and Existential Authenticity *Avant la Lettre*."

5 And at this point we are still dealing with a theory of pleasure similar to that of Giacomo Leopardi.

6 Not surprisingly his critiques of D'Annunzio and Wilde had underlined the lack of "unitary vision."

7 Cf. Michelstaedter, "Paolino," in *La melodia*, 156: "when you are a man you will understand this also."

8 At the end of the apologue, Paolino will affirm his desire not to become a man.

9 Highly significant, in this sense, is the fact that Schopenhauer is not included among the great "persuaded men" mentioned at the beginning of *Persuasion and Rhetoric*. Cf. Michelstaedter, 4: "Yet insofar as everything I am saying has been said many times before and with great force, it seems impossible that the world has continued each time such words have rung out. Parmenides, Heraclitus, and Empedocles told it to the Greeks, but Aristotle treated them as untutored naturalists; Socrates said it, but they constructed four systems on him. Ecclesiastes said it, but they dealt with it as a sacred book that could not therefore contradict biblical optimism; Christ said it, but they built the church upon it. Aeschylus and Sophocles and Simonides said it, and Petrarch proclaimed it triumphantly to the Italians, while Leopardi repeated it with pain. But men were pleased by their pretty verses."

10 It is unlikely that Michelstaedter had read Kierkegaard, but he may have been introduced to him indirectly through Ibsen. More generally, however, we can say that the Danish philosopher's speculation on melancholy represents a cornerstone of modernity. The possibility that Michelstaedter was able to read something of his should however be entertained (for example, the chapter from *Aut-aut* that was translated by Knud Ferlow and published in the August 1907 edition of *Leonardo*, when Michelstaedter was already in Florence).

11 This is the same concept that Michelstaedter had tried to express, in January of that same year, with the female protagonist of his story "La leggenda del San Valentin" (27 January 1908). Cf. *La melodia*, 131–3: "Why are you silent Mad[onna], are you sad, what is on your forehead, on your eyes? It is an impenetrable veil of melancholy ... Look at the shining sun, at the lovely fields ..., they seem to want to tell us to live our life without worry ... She could not see the delightful picture that the young man was describing, ... blurry, dark vision mixed with the smallest details of the real things she could see with unspeakable torment, her ears resounding with a sinister rumbling that seemed to come from the bowels of the mountain."

12 Cf. also Michelstaedter, letter to Alberto Michelstaedter dated 31 May 1908, in *Epistolario*, 320–1: "The simple analysis of a translation by Brunetto Latini of Cicero's orations ... The only thing that interested me are the observations that I was able to make about eloquence and 'persuasion' in general." Cf. Michelstaedter, letter to Gaetano Chiavacci dated 1 February 1909, in *Epistolario*, 350: "Through the crack of rhetoric I have contemplated much more interesting things – bitterly interesting."

13 As De Cecco correctly observed (in "Michelstaedter e i presofisti," 68–9), the concept of "persuasion" was probably taken from the fragments of Parmenides's poem *On Nature*, in which an allegory of persuasion appears as a divine figure who is part of Truth's procession.

14 Michelstaedter had read Hegel and also Marx, focusing in particular on the latter's concepts of use-value and exchange-value. Campailla has suggested that his readings of Marx were probably prompted by his relationship with the Russian revolutionary Nadia Baraden. Cf. Campailla, *Il segreto di Nadia B.* Also, it is worth observing that both Löwith (*From Hegel to Nietzsche*) and Kojève (*Introduction to the Reading of Hegel*) identified the seeds of Marx's reflections in that very same Hegelian nexus on which Michelstaedter focused his analysis.

15 Even the analysis of "past labour" follows the Marxian interpretation of the phenomenon that leads to capitalist accumulation.

16 Cf. Michelstaedter, "Dialogo tra l'adolescente e l'uomo," in *Dialogo della salute e altri dialoghi*, 119: "the 'I' that wants pleasure does not always want the same thing, but now one thing and now another ... Then why call it the *I* and not the '*I's*' if every time it is different?"

17 Cf. Michelstaedter: "Dialogo della salute," in *Dialogo della salute e altri dialoghi*, 39: "we are never in possession of our life, we expect it from the future, we look for it in the things we hold dear because they contain for us the future, and in the future we are again empty in every present time,

and turn again avidly to our dear things to satisfy our insatiable hunger and are still wanting of everything."

Chapter 3

1 Malcolm Angelucci recently revisited this argument in "Persuaders and Rhetoricians."
2 Cf. Prezzolini, "Taccuini," in *Faville di un ribelle*, 45: "Calvin's bile and the sexual needs of Luther certainly had an important influence on the Reformation."
3 Cf. Prezzolini, "Vita intima," in *Faville di un ribelle*, 84: "Finding the foundation of the world of the self is the upheaval of modern consciousness."
4 Cf. Garin, *Intellettuali italiani*, 354: "It would be very wrong to isolate the movement of ideas that dominated in Italy between the end of the nineteenth century and the first decades of the twentieth; it would be wrong to consider it no more than a "provincial" episode, comparable to certain aspects of French (Sorel, Bergson) or, perhaps, North American (James) culture; separating, or worse, contrasting it to parallel developments in the philosophy of life, in German historicism ... The critique of science, the distinction ... between life and forms, and so on, are topics of import everywhere."
5 Cf. Bergson, *La filosofia dell'intuizione*, 69: "All this philosophy starting with Plato up to Plotinus is the development of a principle that we shall express as follows: 'There is more in immobility than there is in mobility' ... [T]he opposite is true."
6 Cf. Prezzolini, "Il linguaggio come causa d'errore," in *Studi e capricci*, 91: "Bergson ... discovered the semi-conscious falsifications which the needs of active social life produced in the problem of knowledge."
7 On Michelstaedter's poems, see Cappozzo, "Il percorso poetico," 33–47.
8 Cf. Camerino, "La 'Rettorica' di Michelstaedter," 67 "only in the twentieth century do we see, from various points, a rupture of the epistemological space that guaranteed the articulation of discourse as a reproduction of senses and the manifestation of truth, as a logical-rational organization (univocal) of semantically hypostatized perceived and intellectual content."
9 Of course, it is important to note that Hofmannsthal's perspective contains none of the Heraclitean joy of Mach's conventionalism. With regard to the linguistic crisis, Hofmannsthal will instead move towards an attempt at an ethical (and then political) reactivation of language, joining the

progressive move "to the right" characteristic of the neo-Kantianism tragic perspectives. A similar response to the epistemological (and therefore social) crisis expressed by the Nietzschean perspective will be proposed in Italy by Giovanni Boine. Boine tends to underscore a link between nation-state and Catholicism in which the latter becomes, on the one hand, the cornerstone of a communitarian principle of aggregation (the Catholic soul of Italy), and, on the other, an ethical–social–political perspective aimed at restoring the values that have been shattered by modernity. On a linguistic level, the equivalent is purism. For Boine, linguistic purism involves expressing words as the echo of the foundation by which it is determined and substantiated.

10 Cf. Musil, *Diaries*, 78: "today responsibility's center of gravity is not in people but in circumstances. Have we not noticed that experiences have made themselves independent of people? … A world of qualities without a man has arisen, of experiences without the person who experiences them."

11 Cf. Michelstaedter: *Persuasion and Rhetoric*, 103–5.

12 In illustrating the ability to resist this atrophy, Michelstaedter underscores class difference. Cf. *Opere*, 749: "With regard to security against the cold compare the woodcutter who does not suffer working in the cold and the bourgeois who warms himself with the firewood he buys."

13 Cf. Michelstaedter, *Sfugge la vita*, 160: "as he with his work does not work for himself but sees to the interests of so[ciety] …, and living in its forms he enjoys a level of security to which in his cowardice he would otherwise have no right."

14 The reference to "mobile [movable] property" is of course another reference to Marx. In Marx "movable property" refers to the hegemony of the economy of profit over that of income; that is, the new economy that finds its representation in money and commodities.

15 Fratta, *Il dovere dell'essere*, 115: "the greater the insurances that come from society, the weaker his personal resources in the face of contingency and the more his life depends on the social forms to which he has adapted."

16 Meaning that the exchange of *goods* (including words and thoughts) is increasingly mediated by the abstraction constituted by money. Michelstaedter may have arrived at that perspective through Simmel's *Philosophy of Money*. While his critique of capitalist society from a cultural perspective seems to share a lot with Simmel's, in Michelstaedter the phenomenon of reification is not presented as "eternalized," but rather as historically determined by its intertwinement with the dynamics of societal consensus. This divide may lie in their different conceptions of individual *Erlebnis*: Simmel continues to postulate a space of freedom for

the subject while for Michelstaedter such space is completely colonized by social ideologies.

17 For Michelstaedter, in contrast to Marx, money is clearly not the alienated essence of labour; it is just one of the vehicles of social abstraction.

18 Michelstaedter carried out his studies on the work of F.G.A. Mullacj, *Fragmenta philosophorum graecorum.*

19 Cf. Michelstaedter, *Persuasion and Rhetoric*, 32–3: "men live in order to live, in order *not to* die. Their persuasion is *the fear of* death ... *They are already dead in [the] present.* All that they do and say with fixed persuasion, a clear purpose, and evident reason is nothing but fear of death ... Every present in their lives contains death ... What is given them is nothing but fear of death, and this, as sufficient life, they wish to rescue from what was also given them then: the certainty of dying ... For a future that cannot help but repeat the present (for as long as it will repeat it), they pollute *the present*, which is in their hands ... *He who fears death is already dead.*"

20 Cf. Michelstaedter, *Persuasion and Rhetoric*, 81: "one of the most daring and least reverent, having observed that while speaking the teacher kept his eyes always fixed on the distant earth."

21 Cf. Michelstaedter, *Persuasion and Rhetoric*, 84n: "the last dialogues and especially the *Parmenides* are pervaded with an Aristotelian spirit and seem like a prelude to the Categories and the *Metaphysics* of Aristotle. Of the Platonic they have no more than clichés ... The dissolving of the world of ideas in the infinite weave of forms."

22 As already noted, for Michelstaedter fog is a metaphor for "correlativity."

23 Michelstaedter composed this text during the last days of his life.

24 Cf. Michelstaedter, "Appendice II," in *La persuasione e la rettorica*, 190: "If the sophists were petty thieves ... Plato ... is a gentleman thief, who has his own method for stealing, not this or that, as those others did, telling everyone: 'I am a thief'; but with method and earnestness, *in order to steal everything*, and telling people: 'I am the one who saves you from robbers once and for all' ... Indeed, by legitimating the trade-offs of human weakness, he takes ... from men any possibility of feeling insufficient in it, any need to free themselves from it."

25 Cf. Nietzsche, *The Birth of Tragedy*, 100–1. Cf. De Leo, *Una convergenza armonica*, 32: "the re-evaluation of the figure of Socrates in the work of the Gorizian, while among Nietzschean intellectuals he was accused of having corrupted and dissolved the tension between the Apollonian moment and the Dionysian moment."

26 Cf. Michelstaedter, "Appendice II," in *La persuasione e la rettorica*, 172: "the value of the *Socratic way* ... in that point *imagining it done and considering*

it, it has already stopped. And since the Socratic way unlike others rejects any stopping and it always declares itself not finished, stopping to seek satisfaction means *abandoning it forever.*"

Chapter 4

1 Cf. Michelstaedter: letter to Enrico Mreule dated 14 April 1909, in *Epistolario*, 363: "Aristotle is a wretch. I'll say nothing more [altro dirti non so]." Note well that in "mistreating" Aristotle, Michelstaedter makes an allusion to Leopardi, another of the "great persuaded": "I'll say nothing more" inevitably recalls "altro dirti non vo" from *Sabato del villaggio*. Michelstaedter views Leopardi as a philosopher (in clear contrast to Croce's vision) and sees the intellectual's ability to oppose the societal consensus in which he is immersed. As Campailla has noted, he was also critical of the particular type of pleasure that Leopardi derived from discovering the truth, however horrible that truth might be. For Michelstaedter, Leopardi's "truth, once known, has its sad delights" from *Ode al Conte Carlo Pepoli*, risks transforming itself into a type of sublime, though no less complicit, form of *philopsychia*.

2 Note here that Michelstaedter shifts Ibsen from a horizon that is no longer ethical, but rather critical of the entire social sphere.

3 In this sense Michelstaedter also perfectly grasps the distinction that bourgeois culture makes between the "healthy" and the "sick," in a way that is not so dissimilar to that of Italo Svevo: fundamentally, the "healthy" are those who have been absorbed by the social system. Cf. Michelstaedter, *Persuasion*, 145–6n: "The phrase 'He's mad' is the most common form of vengeance taken by the deluded man against someone whose actions disturb his illusion and force him – terrifying thing – into bewilderment (which proves his own insufficiency) … But the service of consecrating a phrase of frightened mediocrity, 'That man is mad,' by means of absolute scientific authority, which translates it into a dogma, 'When "objective" experience is insufficient to "make sense" of an individual, that individual is crazy' – this service could not be rendered to society by any other than the most enslaved to it, namely, the modern man of science."

4 Pragmatism, with its insistence on the *useful*, is the most blatant example.

5 Cf. La Porta: "Il romanzo mancato di Michelstaedter," 77.

6 As such Max Horkheimer, in his *Eclipse of Reason*, places Positivism and Pragmatism on the same level, as cultural expressions of that eclipse. Cf. Horkheimer, *The Eclipse of Reason*, 15: "at a certain point thought became unable to conceive objectivity or started to deny it."

7 Cf. Brianese, *L'arco e il destino*, 99: "also within the presumed objective sphere of science, need is the lens through which my eyes look upon reality."

8 David Micheletti (in "Michelstaedter e la cultura francese," 156) correctly noted how Michelstaedter adapted the myth of Gilliatt eliminating the woman who Gilliatt (in Hugo's novel) is watching move away from him. Indeed, this detail would have repositioned the situation within the realm of correlativity.

9 Cf. Micheletti: "Michelstaedter e la cultura francese," 152: "For Michelstaedter, Descartes is a modern Artistotle."

10 For Michelstaedter, in fact, the nihilism perspective is characterized by the same calculatory–contemplative attitude towards social knowledge.

11 Cf. Michelstaedter, *Persuasion and Rhetoric*, 70–1: "If hunger remains unsatisfied, if time removes every good from every present, if pain continues, mute, ungraspable, if the darkness outside presses ever more – what does it matter? We *are reflecting*: we are in the freedom of thought when we apply its forms of things: *cogitamus ergo sumus* … Oh the vanity, fenced in by dense oak! But *cogito* does not mean 'I know'; *cogito* means I seek to know: that is, I lack knowledge: *I do not know.*"

12 Cf. Slataper, in *Appunti* 78: "Kant gave to man what man gave to God … What our life is missing is the conclusion: the gesture that gives value." Cf. Amendola, *Etica e biografia*, 41: "the Kantian God lives in the conscience of man under the form of ethical law."

13 What Scipio Slataper writes of the Ibsenian model is indicative. Cf. Slapater, *Ibsen*, 91–2: "For Brand … action is will … *Brand* is the poem of the *Critique of Practical Reason* … because after Kant, the moral truth that every man finds in himself is Kantian … Every man who is not content with being also moral, but wants all his life, all of life, to become ethical reality, ethical fact." At this point, Michelstaedter has distanced the Ibsenian model from Kantian ethics in order to make *him* into a heroic critic of social ideologies.

14 Cf. Michelstaedter: "Alla sorella Paula" (2 August 1910), in *Poesie*, 72: "Let me go, Paula, into the night / to create a light from myself, / let me go beyond the desert, to the sea."

15 Cf. Michelstaedter, "Appendice VI," in *La persuasione e la rettorica*, 288: "Rhetoric is also *psychology*, Rhetoric understands passions and characters."

16 Cf. Brianese: "La consistenza del relativo," 27: "At first sight, what is more 'civil' than a practice like rhetoric that proposes to incite adhesion and consensus through argumentation, without making use of violence, in

order to heal the inevitable disagreements that are formed between human beings? ... They hide behind the mask of 'civilization' and pacification – the logic of the will of power."

17 The hypostasization of death (the overcoming of the fear of death) as the limit for the recognition of the real may have come to Michelstaedter from the fourth book of Schopenhauer's *The World as Will and Representation*. This theme, however, is common in the anti-relativist (and anti-nihilist) culture of the beginning of the twentieth century: Lukács's essay at the end of *Soul and Form: The Metaphysics of Tragedy* is perhaps one of the clearest examples of this. On this cf. Fortini: "Lukács giovane," in *Verifica dei poteri*.

18 Michelstaedter is not critiquing history. Rather, he is critiquing a mechanism for doing history that re-presents the same features of the epistemological and ethical mechanisms: presenting the majority view of society as your own.

19 Cf. Michelstaedter, letter to Enrico Mreule dated 29 June 1910, in *Epistolario*, 442: "How *your words have turned into action*! instead, I still feed on words and I'm ashamed of it."

20 Cf. Michelstaedter, *Persuasion and Rhetoric*, 74: "What is certain is that at the point where one *turns to look at one's profile in the shadow, one destroys it*. Thus, by turning toward *knowing*, which is the *persona*, the actual consciousness of the honest will of persuasion, man destroys it forever."

21 Gentile wrote a review of the new edition of the book (1922) for *La Critica* 20, no. 4, 332–6, in which he says he finds interesting the parts dealing with "rhetoric" but finds unconvincing, on the philosophical level, the parts dealing with "persuasion." Cf. Russo, "Gaetano Chiavacci interprete di Michelstaedter." Licia Semeraro, in *Lo svuotamento del futuro*, 18, correctly notes: "According to Chiavacci, the absolute in Michelstaedter is the infinite need to impede man from fully satisfying his needs in the succession of determinations."

22 Cf. Michelstaedter, *Persuasion and Rhetoric*, 150–1. Cf. Franchi, "Attualità di Michelstaedter," in Michelstaedter, *Il prediletto punto d'appoggio*, 49: "A hint of the of final stage is already there, the Eichmann-like bureaucrat."

23 Cf. Rizzo: "Carlo Michelstaedter lettore di Hegel." Cf. Negri, *Il lavoro e la città*, 14: "He is able to envision the Austrian 'world of security' as the Hegelian world of 'object spirit.'" Michelstaedter does not reject dialectical thought, but rather the synthesis that leads to Hegel's teleology. As such, Michelstaedter follows the Marxian critique of Hegel. Using Karl Korsch's analysis of Hegel, we can say that Michelstaedter interprets Hegel's final triumphalism as a forced superimposition of real history (in this case the Prussian state) and the theoretical production that grows out of it.

24 This should have explained why persuasion cannot be identified with silence, as well as with "duty": silence is the accomplishment of rhetoric as a language that is forever reproducing the same reifications. Silence is the final expression of rhetoric: perfect agreement.

25 Perhaps that is why, as Garin observed, the writings of Michelstaedter arrive to us in every dramatic moment in the history of Italy. Cf. Bassi: "Eugenio Garin interprete di Michelstaedter," 148–9: "His philosophy ... could not be more different than those who understand philosophy and knowledge as the pursuit of transparency. Michelstaedter's philosophical perspective did not privilege so much the cognitive aspect, often subject to mystification, as it did the realm of the real."

Bibliography

Abruzzese, Alberto, ed. *L'età dell'idealismo e l'Italia giolittiana. Storia e antologia della letteratura italiana.* Firenze: La Nuova Italia, 1973.

Adamson, Walter. *Avant-Garde Florence: From Modernism to Fascism.* Cambridge, MA: Harvard University Press, 1993.

Adorno, Theodor W. *Negative Dialectics.* Trans. E.B. Ashton. New York: Continuum, 1983.

Albertazzi, Liliana, Guido Cimino, and Simonetta Gori-Savellini, eds. *Francesco De Sarlo e il laboratorio fiorentino di psicologia.* Bari: Laterza, 1999.

Altieri, Orietta. "La famiglia Michelstaedter e l'ebraismo goriziano." In Campailla, ed., *Dialoghi intorno a Michelstaedter*, 35–41.

Amendola, Giovanni. *Etica e biografia.* Milano: Ricciardi, 1953.

Amendola, Khün Eva. *Vita con Giovanni Amendola.* Firenze: Parenti, 1960.

Angelucci, Malcolm. "Persuaders and Rhetoricians: Michelstaedter, Prezzolini, and the Problem of Language in Early Twentieth Century Florence." *Italica* 89.3 (2012): 338–56.

– *Words against Words: On the Rhetoric of Carlo Michelstaedter.* Leicester: Troubador, 2011.

Aristotle. *Metaphysics.* Trans. David Bostock. Oxford: Clarendon Press, 1994.

Asor Rosa, Alberto. ed. *Genus italicum: saggi sulla identità letteraria italiana nel corso del tempo.* Torino: Einaudi, 1997.

– *Letteratura italiana / Il Novecento. L'età della crisi.* Torino: Einaudi, 1995.

– "Ritratto dell'intellettuale da giovane." Giuseppe Prezzolini, ed. *L'arte di persuadere*, 11–31. Napoli: Liguori, 1991.

Astori, Bruno. *Gorizia; nella vita, nella storia, nella sua italianità.* Milano: Treves, 1916.

Bahr, Hermann. *Expressionism.* London: F. Anderson, 1925.

Barthes, Roland. *La retorica antica.* Milano: Bompiani, 1972.

Bassi, Simonetta. "Eugenio Garin interprete di Michelstaedter." In Fabrizio Meroi, ed. *L'inquietudine e l'ideale*, 141–54. Pisa: Edizioni ETS, 2010.

Bazlen, Roberto. *Il capitano di lungo corso*. Milano: Adelphi, 1973.

Benussi Frandoli, Cristina. *Negazione e integrazione nella dialettica di Carlo Michelstaedter*. Roma: Edizioni dell'Ateneo & Bizzarri, 1980.

Bergson, Henri. *La filosofia dell'intuizione*. Ed. and trans. Giovanni Papini. Lanciano: Carabba, 1910.

Berman, Marshall. *All That Is Solid Melts into Air: The Experience of Modernity*. New York: Simon and Schuster, 1982.

Bini, Daniela. *Carlo Michelstaedter and the Failure of Language*. Gainesville: University Press of Florida, 1992.

Boine, Giovanni. *Il peccato; Plausi e botte; Frantumi; Altri scritti*. Ed. Davide Puccini. Milano: Garzanti, 1983.

Brambilla, Alberto. "Per Alberto Michelstaedter." *Studi Goriziani* 89 (luglio–dicembre 1997): 106–7.

Brianese, Giorgio. *L'arco e il destino: interpretazione di Michelstaedter*. Abano Terme: Francisci, 1985.

– "La consistenza del relativo. Michelstaedter e Aristotele." In Campailla, ed., *La via della persuasione*, 17–29.

– "Michelstaedter e la retorica." In Campailla, ed., *Dialoghi intorno a Michelstaedter*, 121–35.

Burrow, J.W. *The Crisis of Reason: European Thought, 1848–1914*. New Haven: Yale University Press, 2000.

Cacciari, Massimo. "Interpretazione Di Michelstaedter." *Rivista di Estetica* 26.22 (1986): 21–36.

– *Posthumous People: Vienna at the Turning Point*. Stanford: Stanford University Press, 1996.

Calabrò, Daniela, and Rosella Faraone, eds. *Carlo Michelstaedter e il Novecento filosofico italiano*. Firenze: Le Lettere, 2013.

Camerino, Giuseppe Antonio. *La persuasione e i simboli: Michelstaedter e Slataper*. Milano: IPL, 1993.

– "La 'Rettorica' di Michelstaedter e la 'Sprachkritik' viennese." *Rivista d'Europa* 18 (1984): 57–63.

Campailla, Sergio, ed. *Un'altra società: Carlo Michelstaedter e la cultura contemporanea*. Venezia: Marsilio, 2012.

–, ed. *Carlo Michelstaedter: far di se stesso fiamma*. Venezia: Marsilio, 2010.

–, ed. *Dialoghi intorno a Michelstaedter*. Roma: Istituto poligrafico e zecca dello Stato, 1987.

– *Scrittori giuliani*. Bologna: Pàtron, 1980.

– *Il segreto di Nadia B.: la musa di Michelstaedter tra scandalo e tragedia*. Venezia: Marsilio, 2010.
–, ed. *La via della persuasione: Carlo Michelstaedter un secolo dopo*. Venezia: Marsilio, 2012.
Cappozzo, Valerio. "Il percorso poetico di Carlo Michelstaedter con due poesie inedite del 1903." In Yvonne Hütter, ed. *Carlo Michelstaedter: kunst, poesie, philosophie*, 33–47. Tübingen: Narr Verlag, 2014.
– "Il percorso universitario di Carlo Michelstaedter dall'archivio dell'Istituto di Studi Superiori." In Campailla, ed., *Un'altra società*, 20–31.
–, ed. *Storia e storiografia di Carlo Michelstaedter*. Oxford: Romance Monographs, University of Mississipi, 2017.
Cergoly, Carolus. *Trieste Provincia Imperiale*. Milano: Bompiani, 1983.
Ceronetti, Guido. "Michelstaedter e l'Ecclesiaste." In *Qohélet: colui che prende la parola*, 73–6. Milano: Adelphi, 2001.
Cerruti, Marco. *Carlo Michelstaedter*. Milano: Mursia, 1987.
– *Notizie di utopia*. Padova: Liviana Editrice, 1985.
Colli, Giorgio. *La nascita della filosofia*. Milano: Adelphi, 2007.
D'Annunzio, Gabriele. *Più che l'amore*. Milano: Treves, 1907.
Debenedetti, Giacomo. *Il romanzo del Novecento*. Milano: Garzanti, 1971.
– *Saggi critici. Prima serie*. Milano: Il Saggiatore di A. Mondadori, 1969.
De Cecco, Daniela. "Michelstaedter e i presofisti." In Campailla, ed., *La via della persuasione*, 66–75.
De Leo, Daniela. *Una convergenza armonica: Beethoven nei manoscritti di Michelstaedter e Merleau-Ponty*. Milano: Mimesis, 2011.
– *Michelstaedter filosofo del "frammento": con appunti di filosofia di Carlo Michelstaedter*. Lecce: Milella, 2004.
– *Mistero e persuasione in Carlo Michelstaedter: passando da Parmenide ed Eraclito*. Lecce: Milella, 2003.
De Monticelli, Roberta. *Il richiamo della persuasione: lettere a Carlo Michelstaedter*. Genova: Marietti, 1988.
De Sarlo, Francesco. *Il concetto dell'anima nella psicologia contemporanea prolusione letta nell'Istituto di studi superiori di Firenze*. Firenze: Ducci, 1900.
Di Nunzio, Novella. "Debenedetti lettore di Michelstaedter." In Sandro Gentili, ed. *Carlo Michelstaedter. Un intellettuale di confine*, 77–94. Perugia: Morlacchi, 2012.
Di Solbrito, Augusto Riccio. "Alberto Michelstaedter." *Studi Goriziani* 7 (1929): 125–7.
Di Sorbo, Domenica. "*La Persuasione e la Rettorica* sul ramo dell'iperbole." In Iermano, ed., *Sotto il segno di Michelstaedter*, 89–103.

Eagleton, Terry. *Culture and the Death of God*. New Haven: Yale University Press, 2014.

Evola, Giulio Cesare Andrea. *Teoria dell'Individuo assoluto*. Torino: Fratelli Bocca, 1927.

Fortini, Franco. *Verifica dei poteri: scritti di critica e di istituzioni letterarie*. Milano: Il Saggiatore, 1965.

Fortunato, Marco. *Aporie della decisione: separatezza del soggetto e saggismo filosofico da Weininger e Michelstaedter ad Adorno*. Milano: Guerini Scientifica, 1996.

Franchi, Gianandrea, ed. "Attualità di Michelstaedter." In Carlo Michelstaedter, *Il prediletto punto d'appoggio della dialettica socratica e altri scritti*, 7–60.

Fratta, Francesco. *Il dovere dell'essere: critica della metafisica e istanza etica in Carlo Michelstaedter*. Milano: UNICOPLI, 1986.

Furlan, Laura. *Carlo Michelstaedter: l'essere straniero di un intellettuale moderno*. Trieste: LINT, 1999.

Garin, Eugenio. *Intellettuali Italiani Del XX Secolo*. Roma: Editori riuniti, 1987.

Gazzola, Giuseppe. *Montale, the Modernist*. Firenze: L.S. Olschki, 2016.

Gentile, Giovanni. "Recensione a Carlo Michelstaedter – La persuasione e la rettorica." *La Critica* 20.4 (1922): 332–6.

Gramsci, Antonio. *Quaderni del carcere*. Ed. Valentino Gerratana. Torino: Einaudi, 1975.

Harrison, Thomas. *1910, the Emancipation of Dissonance*. Berkeley: University of California Press, 1996.

– "Carlo Michelstaedter and the Metaphysics of Will." *MLN* 106.5 (1991): 1012–29.

– "Overcoming Aestheticism." In Luca Somigli and Mario Moroni, eds. *Italian Modernism: Italian Culture between Decadentism and Avant-Garde*, 167–90. Toronto: University of Toronto Press, 2004.

– "Michelstaedter and Existential Authenticity *Avant la Lettre*." In Valerio Capozzo, ed. *Storia e storiografia di Carlo Michelstaedter*, 25–46. Oxford, MI: University of Mississippi, 2017.

Hofmannsthal, Hugo von. *The Lord Chandos Letter and Other Writings*. Trans. Joel Rotenberg. New York: New York Review Books, 2005.

Horkheimer, Max. *The Eclipse of Reason*. London and New York: Continuum, 2004.

Hugo, Victor. *Toilers of the Sea*. Trans. W. Moy Thomas. New York: Dutton, 1961.

Ibsen, Henrik. *The Pillars of Society*. Trans. Michael Meyer. Garden City: Doubleday, 1961.

Iermano, Toni, ed. *Sotto il segno di Michelstaedter: il valore di una identità.* Cosenza: Periferia, 1994.

Intermite, Vincenzo. *Carlo Michelstaedter: società rettorica e coscienza persuasa.* Firenze: Atheneum, 2008.

James, William. *Pragmatism.* Cambridge, MA: Harvard University Press, 1975.

– *The Principles of Psychology.* Chicago: Encyclopaedia Britannica, 1955.

Jesi, Furio. *Letteratura e mito.* Torino: Einaudi, 1968.

Kojève, Alexander. *Introduction to the Reading of Hegel: Lectures of the Phenomenology of Spirit.* Trans. James H. Nichols. New York: Basic Books, 1969.

La Porta, Filippo. "Il romanzo mancato di Michelstaedter." In Campailla, ed., *Un'altra società,* 76–80.

La Rocca, Claudio. *Nichilismo e retorica: il pensiero di Carlo Michelstaedter.* Pisa: ETS, 1983.

Lenin, Vladimir Ilich. *Materialism and Empiriocriticism.* Peking: Foreign Languages Press, 1972.

Levi, Adolfo. *L'indeterminismo nella filosofia francese contemporanea: la filosofia della contingenza.* Firenze: B. Seeber, 1904.

Löwith, Karl. *From Hegel to Nietzsche: The Revolution in Nineteenth-Century Thought.* Trans. David. E. Green. New York: Holt, Rinehart and Winston, 1964.

Lukács, György. "Aesthetic Culture." In Arpad Kadarkay, ed. *The Lukács Reader,* 146–59. Cambridge, MA: Blackwell, 1995.

– *History and Class Consciousness: Studies in Marxist Dialectics.* Trans. Rodne Livingstone. Cambridge, MA: MIT Press, 1971.

– *The Metaphysics of Tragedy.* In *Soul and Form,* 175–98.

– "The Parting of the Ways." In Arpad Kadarkay, ed. *The Lukács Reader,* 167–73. Cambridge, MA: Blackwell, 1995.

– *Soul and Form.* Trans. Anna Bostock. Cambridge, MA: MIT Press, 1974.

Luperini, Romano. *Gli esordi del Novecento e l'esperienza della Voce.* Roma and Bari: Laterza, 1990.

Mach, Ernst. *The Analysis of Sensations.* Trans. C.M. Williams. London: Routeldge, 1996.

– *Knowledge and Error: Sketches on the Psychology of Enquiry.* Trans. Erwin Hiebert. Dordrecht: Reidel, 1976.

Magris, Claudio. *Un altro mare.* Milano: Garzanti, 1991.

– *L'anello di Clarisse: grande stile e nichilismo nella letteratura moderna.* Torino: Einaudi, 1984.

Manfreda, Luigi Antonio. *Aporie del simbolo: saggio su Otto Weininger.* Napoli: Liguori, 1995.

– "Note sull'idea di linguaggio nella *Persuasione.*" In Sorrentino and Michelis, eds, *E sotto avverso ciel*, 223–8.

Marin, Biagio. *Gorizia: la città mutilata*. Gorizia: Comune di Gorizia, 1956.

Marx, Karl. *Capital*. Trans. Samuel Moore and Edward Aveling. Chicago: Encyclopaedia Britannica, 1955.

– *The Eighteenth Brumaire of Louis Bonaparte*. New York: International Publishers, 1972.

Meroi, Fabrizio. *Persuasione ed esistenza: filosofia e vita in Carlo Michelstaedter*. Roma: Edizioni di storia e letteratura, 2011.

Merola, Nicola, ed. *Ricerche sul moderno: terza serie*. Soveria Mannelli (Catanzaro): Rubbettino, 2005.

Micheletti, David. "Michelstaedter e la cultura francese." In Silvio Cumpeta and Angela Michelis, eds. *Eredità di Carlo Michelstaedter*, 150–65. Udine: Forum, 2002.

– "Il razionalismo delle menti ebraiche." In Sorrentino and Michelis, eds, *E sotto avverso ciel luce più chiara*, 39–61.

Michelis, Angela. *Carlo Michelstaedter: il coraggio dell'impossibile*. Roma: Città nuova, 1997.

Michelstaedter, Alberto. *La Menzogna*. Conferenza tenuta al Gabinetto di Minerva di Trieste la sera del 13 aprile 1894. Udine: Tipografia Del Bianco, 1895.

Michelstaedter, Carlo. *L'anima ignuda nell'isola dei beati: scritti su Platone*. Ed. David Micheletti. Reggio Emilia: Diabasis, 2005.

– *Il dialogo della salute e altri dialoghi*. Ed. Sergio Campailla. Milano: Adelphi, 1988.

– *Dialogo della salute e altri scritti sul senso dell'esistenza*. Ed. Giorgio Brianese. Milano: Mimesis, 2009.

– *Epistolario*. Ed. Sergio Campailla. Milano: Adelphi, 1983.

– *La melodia del giovane divino: pensieri, racconti, critiche*. Ed. Sergio Campailla. Milano: Adelphi, 2010.

– *Opere*. Ed. Gaerano Chiavacci. Firenze: Sansoni, 1958.

– *Parmenide ed Eraclito, Empedocle: appunti di filosofia*. Ed. Alfonso Cariolato and Enrico Fongaro. Milano: SE, 2003.

– *La persuasione e la rettorica; Appendici critiche del 1905*. Ed. Sergio Campailla. Milano: Adelphi, 1995.

– *Persuasion and Rhetoric*. Trans. Russell Scott Valentino, Cinzia Sartini Blum, and David J. Depew. New Haven: Yale University Press, 2004.

– *Poesie*. Ed. Sergio Campailla. Milano: Adelphi, 1987.

– *Il prediletto punto d'appoggio della dialettica socratica e altri scritti*. Ed. Gianandrea Franchi. Milano: Mimesis, 2000.

– *Scritti scolastici*. Ed. Sergio Campailla. Gorizia: Istituto per gli Incontri Culturali Mitteleuropei, 1976.
– *Sfugge la vita: taccuini e appunti*. Ed. Angela Michelis. Torino: Aragno, 2004.
Mullacj, F.G.A. *Fragmenta philosophorum graecorum*. Paris: Scientia, 1860–81.
Musil, Robert. *The Confusions of Young Törless*. Trans. Shaun Whiteside. New York: Penguin Books, 2001.
– *Diaries, 1899–1941*. Trans. P. Payne. New York: Basic Books, 1998.
– *The Man without Qualities*. Trans. Sophie Wilkins. New York: Vintage, 1995.
Muzzioli, Francesco. *Michelstaedter*. Lecce: Milella, 1987.
Negri, Antimo. *Il lavoro e la città: un saggio su Carlo Michelstaedter*. Roma: Edizioni lavoro, 1996.
Nietzsche, Friedrich Wilhelm. *Beyond Good and Evil: Prelude to a Philosophy of the Future*. Trans. R.J. Hollingdale. London and New York: Penguin Books, 1990.
– *The Birth of Tragedy*. Trans. Douglas Smith. Oxford: Oxford University Press, 2000.
– *The Gay Science: With a Prelude in German Rhymes and an Appendix of Songs*. Ed. Bernard Williams. Trans. Josefine Nauckhoff and Adrian Del Caro. Cambridge: Cambridge University Press, 2001.
– *Human, All Too Human I*. Trans. Gary J. Handwerk. Stanford: Stanford University Press, 1997.
– *Human, All Too Human II and Unpublished Fragments from the Period of Human, All Too Human II (Spring 1878–Fall 1879)*. Trans. Gary J. Handwerk. Stanford: Stanford University Press, 2013.
– *On the Genealogy of Morality*. Trans. Carol Diethe. New York: Cambridge University Press, 1994.
– *Untimely Meditations*. Trans. R.J. Hollingdale. Cambrdige: Cambridge University Press, 1997.
– *Thus Spoke Zarathustra: A Book for All and None*. Ed. Robert B. Pippin. Trans. Adrian Del Caro. Cambridge: Cambrige University Press, 2006.
– *Twilight of the Idols, Or, How to Philosophize with a Hammer*. Trans. Duncan Large. New York: Oxford University Press, 1998.
Nordau, Max. *Degeneration*. New York: H. Fertgi, 1968.
Papini, Giovanni. *Il Crepuscolo Dei Filosofi*. Firenze: Vallecchi, 1927.
Peluso, Rosalia. *L'identico e i molteplici: meditazioni michelstaedteriane*. Napoli: Loffredo, 2011.
– "La repubblica teoretica. La variante michelstaedteriana dell'antiplatonismo contemporaneo." In Campailla, ed., *Un'altra società*: 106–126.
Perli, Antonello. *Oltre il deserto: poetica e teoretica di Michelstaedter*. Ravenna: G. Pozzi, 2009.

Pierangeli, Fabio. "La via di Ibsen." In Campailla, ed., *La via della persuasione*, 97–110.

Pieri, Piero. *La differenza ebraica: ebraismo e grecità in Michelstaedter*. Bologna: Cappelli, 1984.

– *Michelstaedter nel '900: forme del tragico contemporaneo*. Massa: Transeuropa, 2010.

– *Il pensiero della poesia: Carlo Michelstaedter e il romanticismo della tragedia*. Bologna: Nautilus, 2001.

– "Per una dialettica storica del silenzio. La 'vergogna' del filosofo e l'autoinganno dello scrittore." In Silvio Cumpeta and Angela Michelis, eds. *Eredità di Carlo Michelstaedter*, 150–65. Udine: Forum, 2002.

– *La scienza del tragico: saggio su Carlo Michelstaedter*. Bologna: Cappelli, 1989.

Pirandello, Luigi. *On Humor*. Ed. Antonio Illiano and Daniel P. Testa. Chapel Hill: University of North Carolina Press, 1974.

– *L'umorismo e altri saggi*. Ed. Enrico Ghidetti. Firenze: Giunti, 1994.

Plato. *The Collected Dialogues*. Trans. Lane Cooper and others. New York: Pantheon Books, 1961.

Prezzolini, Giuseppe. *L'arte di persuadere*. Napoli: Liguori, 1991.

– *Il Cattolicismo rosso. Studio sul presente movimento di riforma nel Cattolicesimo*. Napoli: Ricciardi, 1908.

– *Faville di un ribelle*. Ed. Raffaelle Castagnola. Roma: Salerno Editrice, 2008.

– *L'italiano inutile*. Firenze: Vallecchi, 1964.

– *Studi e capricci*. Ed. Fabio Finotti. Abano Terme: Piovan, 1992.

Rensi, Giuseppe. *Lineamenti di filosofia scettica*. Bologna: Zanichelli, 1919.

Rizzo, Francesca. "Carlo Michelstaedter lettore di Hegel." *Filosofia e società* 5–6.4 (1976): 65–102.

Russo, Antonio. "Gaetano Chiavacci interprete di Michelstaedter." In Campailla, ed., *La via della persuasione*, 111–31.

Salinari, Carlo. *Miti e coscienza del decadentismo italiano*. Milano: Feltrinelli, 1960.

Salsano, Roberto. *Michelstaedter tra D'Annunzio, Pirandello e il mondo della vita*. Roma: Bulzoni, 2012.

Sanò, Laura. *Leggere* La persuasione e la rettorica *di Michelstaedter*. Como: Ibis, 2011.

Schopenhauer, Arthur. *The World as Will and Representation*. Trans. E.F.J. Payne. New York: Dover, 1966.

Semeraro, Licia. *Lo svuotamento del futuro: note su Michelstaedter*. Lecce: Edizioni Milella, 1986.

Sessa, Giovanni. *Oltre la persuasione: saggio su Carlo Michelstaedter*. Roma: Settimo sigillo, 2008.

Simmel, Georg. *The Philosophy of Money*. Ed. David Frisby. Trans. Tom Bottomore and David Frisby. London: Routledge & Kegan Paul, [1900]1978.

Slataper, Scipio. *Appunti e note di diario*. Milano: Mondadori, 1953.

– *Ibsen*. Firenze: G.C. Sansoni, 1944.

– *Scritti letterari e critici*. Ed. Giani Stuparich. Verona: A. Mondadori, 1956.

– *Scritti politici*. Ed. Giani Stuparich. Milano: A. Mondadori, 1954.

– *Scritti politici, 1914–15*. Ed. Giorgio Baroni. Trieste: Italo Svevo, 1977.

Soffici, Ardengo. *Opere*. Firenze: Vallecchi, 1959–68.

Sorrentino, Sergio, and Angela Michelis, eds. *E sotto avverso ciel luce più chiara. Carlo Michelstaedter tra nichilismo, Ebraismo e Cristianesimo*. Troina: Città aperta edizioni, 2009.

Spampinato, Graziella. "Sogno della lingua universale e critica della storia in Michelstaedter." In Sorrentino and Michelis, eds, *E sotto avverso ciel luce più chiara*, 243–60.

Stirner, Max. *The Ego and Its Own*. Ed. and trans. David Leopold. Cambridge: Cambridge University Press, 1995.

Storace, Erasmo Silvio, ed. *Carlo Michelstaedter: l'essere come azione*. Milano: Albo versorio, 2007.

Stuart Hughes, Henry. *Consciousness and Society: The Reorientation of European Social Thought*. New York: Kompf, 1958.

Stuparich, Carlo. *Cose e ombre di uno*. Ed. Giani Stuparich. Caltanissetta-Roma: S. Sciascia, 1968.

Szondi, Peter. *An Essay on the Tragic*. Stanford: Stanford University Press, 2002.

– *Theory of the Modern Drama: A Critical Edition*. Minneapolis: University of Minnesota Press, 1987.

Tavano, Sergio. *Gorizia e il mondo di ieri*. Udine: Arti grafiche friulane, 1991.

Taviani, Giovanna. "Attualità di Michelstaedter." In Merola, ed., *Ricerche sul moderno*, 317–21.

– *Michelstaedter*. Palermo: Palumbo, 2002.

Vaihinger, Hans. *The Philosophy of "As if": A System of the Theoretical, Practical, and Religious Fictions of Mankind*. Trans. C.K. Ogden. New York: Barnes and Noble, 1968.

Weil, Simone. *Oppression and Liberty*. Trans. Arthur Wills and John Petrie. Amherst: University of Massachusetts Press, 1958.

Weininger, Otto. *Sex and Character. E Carattere*. Trans. Ladislaus Löb. Bloomington: Indiana University Press, 2005.

– *A Translation of Weininger's Über Die Letzten Dinge, 1904–1907, On Last Things*. Trans. Steven Burns. Lewiston: E. Mellen Press, 2001.

Wittgenstein, Ludwig. *Tractaus logico-philosophicus*. Trans. D.F. Pears and B.F. McGuinness. New York: Humanities Books, 1961.

Zanello, Gabriele. "Una vita 'non eccezionale.'" L'ironia e la rettorica di Alberto Michelstaedter." In Valerio Capozzo, ed. *Storia e storiografia di Carlo Michelstaedter*, 47–90. Oxford, MI: University of Mississippi, 2017.

Zielinski, Tadeusz. *L'antico e noi. Otto lezioni in difesa degli studi classici.* Napoli: La scuola di Pitagora, 2013.

Index

www.ingramcontent.com/pod-product-compliance
Lightning Source LLC
LaVergne TN
LVHW040149080826
844660LV00014B/894/J
9781487504649